The Future City on the Inland Sea

The Future City on the Inland Sea

A History of Imaginative Geographies of Lake Superior

Eric D. Olmanson

Ohio University Press
Athens

Ohio University Press, Athens, Ohio 45701
www.ohio.edu/oupress

Printed in the United States of America

Ohio University Press books are printed on acid-free paper ∞ ™

14 13 12 11 10 09 08 07 5 4 3 2 1

Library of Congress Cataloging-in-Publication Data

Olmanson, Eric D.

The future city on the inland sea : a history of imaginative geographies of Lake Superior / Eric D. Olmanson.

p. cm.

Includes bibliographical references and index.

ISBN-13: 978-0-8214-1707-2 (cloth : alk. paper)

ISBN-10: 0-8214-1707-X (cloth : alk. paper)

1. Superior, Lake, Region—History, Local. 2. Wisconsin—History, Local. 3. Superior, Lake, Region—Geography. 4. Landscape—Superior, Lake, Region—History. 5. Superior, Lake, Region—Description and travel. 6. Chequamegon Bay (Wis.)—History. 7. Frontier and pioneer life—Superior, Lake, Region. 8. Land settlement—Superior, Lake, Region—History. 9. Regional planning—Superior, Lake, Region—History. 10. City planning—Superior, Lake, Region—History. I. Title.

F587.S9O44 2007

977.4'9—dc22

2006026806

To Don and Barb,

voyageurs extraordinaires

Contents

Illustrations

Acknowledgments

THIS BOOK began as a dissertation in geography at the University of Wisconsin–Madison. I was fortunate to have a committee made up of scholars who are as congenial as they are brilliant. Each, in his own way, was an important mentor to me. The idea for the project initially took shape when I heard Bill Cronon's lectures entitled "A Place for Stories" and "Kennecott Journey." Both essays were intended as statements on how to do environmental history but inspired me to think about different ways to approach historical geography. I had the good fortune to take the first seminar Bill taught at Madison and to begin working with him that semester. Bob Ostergren has been a reliable source of levelheaded advice whenever I have needed it, and I learned much from him when I completed my master's thesis under his guidance. Tom Vale encouraged me and provided an inspiring model of how one can turn passionate interests into brilliant scholarship. Jim Leary offered keen insights every time I talked with him about my project, and his written comments on the first draft of this work were much appreciated. Most of all, I am grateful to Yi-Fu Tuan, whose accessibility has always astounded me. Some of the best ideas in this book were percolated over long talks at the Sunroom Cafe or in Yi-Fu's office. Since the moment I met him, he has treated me as a colleague. He is a great teacher, mentor, and friend whose office door is still always open. It is impossible for me to imagine Science Hall without him.

Neil Whitehead encouraged me and gave me useful advice at an early stage of my research. Gerry Kearns was kind enough to comment on an early version of chapter 5 and encouraged me to think about publishing it. Patrick McGreevy's detailed comments on a paper I presented at the 1999 annual meeting of the Association of American Geographers helped me to better conceptualize chapter 4. John Hudson, Michael Conzen, John Borchert, and

Fred Lukerman have also provided valuable comments on AAG papers that are now a part of this book. More recently, I have benefitted from conversations with Larry Nesper.

I owe a special debt to John W. Jenkins and E. David Cronon. If they had not offered me a project assistantship with the University History Project, finishing graduate school would have been a more difficult undertaking. John is a sterling example of an independent scholar, and I have learned a great deal working with him. Along with archivist Bernie Schermetzler and oral historian Barry Teicher, he provided timely encouragement and more than a little prodding.

Special thanks go to the knowledgeable and friendly staff of the University of Wisconsin–Madison Geography Library, the Map and Air Photo Library, and the Wisconsin Historical Society Library and Archives, especially Miriam Kerndt (now retired), Tom Tews, Laura Hemming, Harry Miller, Andy Kraushaar, Richard Pifer, and Lisa Hinzman. In addition, I encountered many helpful people on trips to my study area. Early on, I visited every local historical society from Superior to Hurley, including the Ashland County Museum, where the staff dug out copies of *Ashland Press* yearbooks not available at the Press Office in Ashland or on microfilm at the State Historical Society in Madison; the Madeline Island Museum; the Area Research Center, then at Northland College; the Bayfield Heritage Society Museum; the Northern Wisconsin Research Center, then in Ashland; and the archives at the Apostle Islands National Lakeshore Headquarters in Bayfield, where park historian David Snyder and park ecologist Robert Brander dropped what they were doing and patiently answered my questions when I stopped by unannounced. Stephen Dunker, owner of the "What Goes 'Round" bookstore was kind enough to let me stay at his place near Cornucopia after I helped him move some boxes to his newer location in Bayfield. Stephen knows a lot about local history and has been part of it since 1967, when he decided to go back to the land near Corny. Everywhere, museum staff, park personnel, business owners, bartenders, and people on the street were friendly and helpful.

I thank the Great Lakes American Studies Association and Ohio University Press for selecting my manuscript for publication. In particular, I appreciate Gillian Berchowitz's encouragement, the anonymous outside reader's comments, and the hard work of Nancy Basmajian, the copy editor Joan Sherman, and other staff who turned my manuscript into a book.

I benefited beyond measure from warm friendships and wide-ranging conversations with graduate student colleagues. Those who commented on early drafts of this work (or responded to my descriptions of what I was working on) include Tim Bawden, Duane Griffin, Christina Dando, Steve Hoelscher, Mary Braun, Kimberley Little, Sue Haswell, Patrick Mayotte, Joe Cullon, Lynn Heasely, Steve Silvern, Paul Adams, Hannah Nyala, Drew Ross, Valentin Bogorov, Jennifer Grek, Jeff Zimmerman, and Kimberly Coulter. Matthew Liesch, who is currently doing interesting work on the Gogebic range, has also taken time to comment on my work. The members of the Wednesday morning breakfast seminars, chaired by Bill Cronon, offered constructive critiques of presentations of some of the material in this book. My brother, Thor Olmanson, also provided useful insights from an archeological perspective.

I am grateful to Alex Turner, Tom Simmons, Robert Sommerfeld, Mike Barrett, Pam Barrett, Dan Sebald, Robbie Webber, Mike Rewey, Pam Rewey, John Rider, Terri Felton, Bob Schneiker, Linda Cykana, Anné Knezevic, Clarke Brownell, and Juan Carlos Draye for bike rides, canoe trips, barbeques, and Friday nights at the Memorial Union terrace.

Special thanks to my sons, Garth and Karl, and to Andrea Baker (who also read and commented on most of this book), Andrico, and Hypatia. Finally, I dedicate this book to my parents, M. Donald Olmanson, M.D., and Barbara Olmanson, who raised their children to love books, travel, hard work, and a good story. They will always be an inspiration to me.

The Future City on the Inland Sea

Prologue

LAKE SUPERIOR AS THE "EVIL ONE'S EMPIRE"

In early August 1665, Jesuit missionary Claude Allouez left Trois-Rivières, located midway between Montreal and Quebec on the St. Lawrence River, with six Frenchmen and four hundred Indians.[1] He had prepared long and hard for this moment. His first attempt to leave Trois-Rivières had been thwarted when the canoes he hoped to travel with departed without him, forcing him to wait for the next season. Fortunately, Allouez was well trained to be patient and to endure whatever hardships the land held for him. His first challenge was simply to reach his destination because on more than one occasion the Indians abandoned him en route. Once he arrived, his toughest task would be to convince the Indians that holy baptism would not cause their children to die. Allouez thought this widespread belief was mere superstition and surely evidence of the work of the devil, but such notions were based on empirical evidence: often, the missionaries were the first Europeans to come in contact with indigenous groups, and the first to introduce them to European diseases.[2]

Allouez's destination was Chequamegon Bay on the south shore of Lake Superior, where he would establish a mission among the Indians. He chose the site because some eight hundred Indians of various bands who sought refuge from the Iroquois Wars had formed a village there. In his journal, published in *Jesuit Relations*, Allouez repeatedly described the region as the empire of the "Evil One."[3] He saw death all around him, and his primary goal was to save as many souls as he could. From Allouez's perspective, the "Devil offered all conceivable opposition" to his journey. Meanwhile, the Indians with whom he caught a ride were suspicious of the "black robes," as they called the priests, and were not eager to let Allouez accompany them on their trip. Early on, one of the Indians brusquely warned him that if he came along they would abandon him "on some desert Island."[4] Later, when the Frenchmen's canoe in which the Jesuit had been traveling was damaged, the party was forced to split up, and a crew of Hurons reluctantly agreed to take Allouez. Coming as he did from a society where a priest enjoyed many privileges, especially among the peasant classes, it took Allouez a painfully long time to realize that his fellow travelers expected him to carry his own belongings. The first time he was abandoned, the Frenchmen rescued him in the broken canoe they had towed along. Although they managed to catch up to the Indians, it was clear that the Frenchmen and the Jesuit could not keep up with the Indians on their own. The Indians did not mind taking the Frenchmen on board, but none wanted to be burdened with Allouez, who did not know how to paddle and seemed too weak to carry a load on his shoulders.

Abandoned yet again, the priest went into the forest and thanked God for making him "so acutely sensible of [his] slight worth." He also "confessed before his divine Majesty that [he] was only a useless burden on the earth." But when he returned to the water's edge, he discovered that one of the "savages" had returned for him. As he boarded the canoe, his savior put a paddle in his hand and indicated that he was expected to use it. At that point, Allouez "willingly took the paddle and, offering up to God this labor in atonement for [his] sins, . . . imagined [himself] a malefactor sentenced to the Galleys." Eventually, the Jesuit found he had the strength to paddle all day and into the night. Yet he still was the butt of the Indians' jokes. They repeatedly took his fine wide-brimmed hat and stole his blankets while he slept. He did his best on the portages but often collapsed under the weight of his load, which prompted the Indians to roar with laughter and loudly suggest that perhaps they should find a child to carry the load for him.[5]

On their way to a rendezvous point on Lake Huron, Allouez and the others encountered a group of Indians who had been badly wounded in an explosion which resulted when a spark hit a powder keg. They took the injured with them and arrived at their encampment on August 24. There, the Indian healers went to great lengths to help the wounded men. Offended by what he perceived as superstitious idolatry, Allouez decided he had to accost the "chief Jugglers" (conjurers), and in the end, he convinced a dying man to forgo the Jugglers' help so that he could save the man's soul before he died. Allouez feared that this small victory over "the Evil One in the heart of his empire" would bring the devil's wrath, so he prayed to God that the Evil One's vengeance would fall only on him; "my prayer was not in vain," he wrote, "we lost only our canoe, which that wretch broke into pieces."[6] Allouez explained even minor incidents as the direct interventions of God or the devil and saw himself as a selfless crusader in the devil's realm, struggling against great odds to save the inhabitants—or rather, to save their souls. He seemed especially eager to save those on the verge of death. A more secular-minded modern might think that Allouez was the superstitious one, but the Jesuit had complete faith in his worldview and considered it utterly superior to that of the region's residents. At least at first, it never occurred to Allouez that there was anything worthwhile the Indians could teach him—he was there to teach them. But he did eventually learn quite a bit from them, even if his chief motive was to figure out how better to save their souls.[7]

By early September 1665 Allouez and his party reached the "Sault" (as the settlement at Sault Ste. Marie was often called, from a seventeenth-century French term for "rapids"). On setting up their camp on an island, the Indians expected to catch fish immediately, but according to the priest, "God chose to punish their presumption" until the next day. As they embarked upon Lac Supérieur (as the French called it), Allouez declared that it henceforth would bear the name of his colleague Father Tracy, "in recognition of indebtedness to him on the part of the people of those regions." At least one map did identify Lake Superior as Lac Tracy, but the name did not stick. Allouez noted the clarity of the water and compared the Great Lake to the sea. He observed that the Indians revered the lake like a deity, offering it sacrifices to appease its power, and also in thanks for the abundant fish it provided them. He noted findings of pure copper, which was valued by the Indians. Allouez described Lake Superior as a "resort" for the people of several nations that came to the lake from all directions to trade and to fish—or so they thought. In actuality, according to the Jesuit, "God's purpose was to facilitate the proclaiming of the Gospel to wandering and vagrant tribes" by concentrating them on Lake Superior.[8]

Allouez did not mention whether he carried a paper map with him, but he did possess a fairly accurate mental map of the lakes. He described Lake Superior, for instance, as being formed nearly like "a bow, the southern shore being much curved, and the Northern nearly straight" (although he seems to have mixed up the north and south shores, he got the shape right).[9] Indeed, he has been credited with helping to make the first accurate map of Lake Superior, which was published in *Jesuit Relations* in 1672 and was not surpassed until Henry Bayfield's surveys of the 1820s (fig. 0.1).

Allouez spent the month of September traveling the south shore of Lake Superior, saving souls when he could and almost hoping his new converts would pass quickly into heaven before they could revert. He was with the Frenchmen for this part of his journey and took the opportunity to say the Holy Mass for them. Until he arrived at Chequamegon (he called it Chagoüamigong) Bay, he seemed to care little about the landscape he traversed. But when he arrived at his destination on October 1, 1665, he became more descriptive, and gradually provided the most detailed early picture of the place and its inhabitants. In addition to descriptions of the residents' "false gods and some superstitious customs," he wrote:

> It is a beautiful Bay, at the head of which is situated the great Village of the Savages, who there cultivate fields of Indian corn and lead a settled life. They number eight hundred men bearing arms, but are gathered together from seven different nations, living in peace, mingled one with another.[10]

In the long run, the impact of Allouez and other Jesuits on the Lake Superior Indians was probably slight, but the Jesuits' exploits, recorded in their journals, added to the knowledge as well as the mythology of the place. Chequamegon Bay continued to provide refuge to Indians and travelers, and it would one day attract surveyors, speculators, and Euro-American settlers. Allouez a

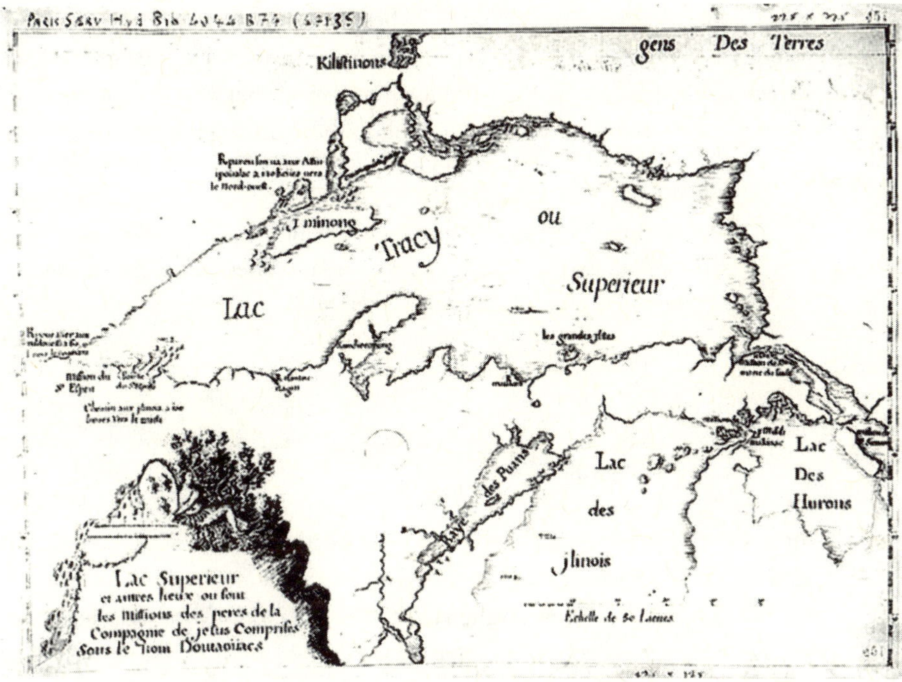

FIGURE 0.1 "Lac Superieur," by the Jesuits Claude Dablon and Claude Allouez, 1672. Courtesy of the National Archives of Canada (NMC006407). (Available at http://www.collectionscanada.ca/explorers/h24-150.17-e.html.)

selfless and pious priest enduring great danger and severe hardships to save souls contributed a key popular image of the Lake Superior country. The Frenchmen (who played a secondary role in Allouez's narrative) would have a more lasting impact on the region.

Between the lines of Allouez's narrative account of his 1665–67 journey into the Lake Superior country was a story of the culture clashes that were endemic to the place and would continue for the better part of two more centuries. The upper Great Lakes watershed (known then as the *pays d'en haut*, or "upper country"), including Lake Superior, was part of New France until 1763, when it became part of Britain; in 1783, with the Treaty of Paris, the southern part of the Great Lakes officially became part of the United States territory. From the seventeenth century until well into the nineteenth century, the fur trade dominated the region. The best analysis of the region during this period is by historian Richard White, who used the term "middle ground" to characterize the place and the complex interactions between various groups of Europeans and Indians which took place there during the centuries when no group was hegemonic. As White put it:

> On the middle ground diverse peoples adjust their differences through what amounts to a process of creative, and often expedient, misunderstandings. People try to persuade others who are different from themselves by appealing to what they perceive to be the values and practices of those others. They often misinterpret and distort both the values and practices of those they deal with, but from these misunderstandings arise new meanings and through them new practices—the shared meanings and practices of the middle ground.[11]

Allouez's own account of his journey is a good example of these cultural misunderstandings because, although well educated for his time, he brought with him a rigid worldview so alien to this land that on several occasions, according to his own account, it almost led to his demise. He was obsessed with saving the souls of people he perceived as "savages," but for their part the Indians perceived him as an eccentric fool or, worse, as a nefarious sorcerer. The priest's sense of superiority contrasted strikingly with his self-professed helplessness in the Great Lakes country.

In the 1660s, Montreal, just upriver from Trois-Rivières, was the main center of the fur trade. Indian middlemen brought furs to the traders there, who exported them to Europe. The Frenchmen who traveled with Allouez must have been *coureurs des bois,* literally "runners of the woods," who were the precursors of the French Canadian *voyageurs.* The coureurs des bois were independent traders who bypassed the Indian middlemen and ventured into the pays d'en haut to trade directly with native trappers. Just a decade before Allouez's journey, a coureur des bois by the name of Médard Chouart, Sieur des Groseilliers, had been one of the first Europeans to see Lake Superior (Allouez may have known Groseilliers, and almost certainly knew of him). A few years later, in 1659, Groseilliers returned to the region with Pierre Esprit Radisson and discovered the fur-rich region around Hudson's Bay. But when Radisson and Groseilliers returned with thousands of furs, the

French authorities fined them and confiscated their furs. When New France did not support the men's efforts to start a trading company, Radisson and Groseilliers turned to England and became instrumental in establishing the Hudson's Bay Company in 1670. Sixteen years after Allouez's journey, in 1681, the French authorities limited the numbers of coureurs des bois by requiring them to have a permit (or *congé*) or to work for a trader who held one. This created a second generation of coureurs des bois known as voyageurs, literally "travelers." Unlike the coureurs des bois, the voyageurs were not independent—they were *engagés,* employees of the fur traders. They paddled the canoes through the lakes and rivers and carried thc packs over the portages. Many of the coureurs des bois were educated Frenchmen, while most voyageurs were descended from French peasants.

The relationship of the coureurs des bois and the voyageurs with the peoples and landscapes of the middle ground contrasted sharply with that of the Jesuit. Most of the voyageurs were part Indian, or métis. They inhabited a realm between the European and Indian worlds. Indeed, the worldview of the average French peasant may have been closer to the Indians' than to the priest's. According to historian Eugene Weber, before France was tied together by a railway system Frenchmen as prominent as Honoré de Balzac compared French peasants to "the Redskins of Fenimore Cooper."[12] Like many people in the world today, these peasants retained much of a pre-Christian cosmology while outwardly adopting Catholicism, and they knew how to appease the priests. The voyageur hedged his bets, often wearing an Indian medicine bag on his belt and a Christian cross around his neck. When French peasants migrated to North America for employment in the fur trade, they adapted quickly. In part because they did not feel so superior to the indigenous peoples, they did not hesitate to learn what they could from the inhabitants of the land. The Hudson's Bay Company frowned on intermarriage between Europeans and the Indian peoples with whom they traded, but the earlier French traders, the North West Company (formed in Montreal around 1779 to challenge the Hudson's Bay Company), and the American Fur Company (1808) had a more tolerant view. Theirs was also a pragmatic policy because intermarriage of voyageurs and traders with Native American women forged family ties that often reinforced trading networks. Until the mid-nineteenth century, voyageurs held a prestige beyond their employment status due to the position they occupied between the two cultures and their special knowledge of the land. To this day, especially in Canada, the voyageurs possess a mythical status comparable to that of the American cowboy, and their descendants continue to be an important part of the cultural fabric on both sides of the border.[13]

Introduction

IMAGINATIVE GEOGRAPHIES

LIKE THE Dust Bowl area of the Great Plains states, the northwoods region below the Great Lakes, from Lake Huron to northwestern Minnesota, was the site of one of the great environmental miscalculations in U.S. history.[1] Beginning in the eastern part of the region in the early nineteenth century and generally migrating westward until the early twentieth century, lumber companies cut vast tracts of timber, and when the most valuable trees had been removed from a given area, they moved on to untouched forests. Once the biggest logs had been removed, the lumber companies picked up and left the Great Lakes states to harvest other forests, such as those of the Pacific Northwest. For years thereafter, the cutover region was plagued by intense forest fires and often-disastrous attempts to farm the land.

Nowhere was there more official encouragement to settle the cutover lands than in Wisconsin: the state's immigration office made a concerted attempt to lure settlers from as far away as Europe; the University of Wisconsin published booster materials and provided technical support to farmers (devising, for example, elaborate schemes for stump removal); railroads published immigrant guides and other booster literature; and local newspapers editorialized on how the region would equal or even surpass the southern parts of the state in agricultural productivity. This vision of the region and its future was persuasively summed up by William Henry, dean of the University of Wisconsin's College of Agriculture, in the introduction to his *Northern Wisconsin: A Handbook for the Homeseeker,* a publication that had been mandated by the state legislature to promote agriculture in the area. In his introduction, Henry confidently predicted: "With farms supplanting the forest, northern Wisconsin will not revert to a wilderness with the passing of the lumber industry, but will be occupied by a thrifty class of farmers whose well directed, intelligent efforts bring substantial, satisfactory returns from fields, flocks and herds."[2] Beginning in the mid-nineteenth century and continuing well into the twentieth, agricultural boosters stubbornly ignored the realities of climate, soil, and topography, which doomed most attempts to create productive farms. The failures, compounded by low agricultural prices in the 1920s and the Great Depression of the 1930s, finally led policymakers to reverse course and to implement pioneering forestry legislation and rural zoning policies that relocated many settlers and resulted in extensive reforestation.

The story of this process is well documented, and the literature on the subject is extensive. The classic works are Vernon Carstensen's *Farms or Forests* (1958) and Arlan Helgeson's *Farms in the Cutover* (1962).[3] Recently, historian Robert Gough challenged the accepted view and presented an alternative interpretation of the history of the region. He asserted that Carstensen, Helgeson, and others shared the perspective of state officials and planners. Gough took a different approach. By looking at the same region from the perspective of the farmers themselves, he argued that many farmers actually did succeed, even as others were thwarted by a fickle government that first supported them and then worked against them by zoning them off the land and encouraging reforestation projects.[4] Gough made an important contribution to our understanding of the cutover region, yet the hard fact remained that the environment—with average growing seasons in some counties of less than three months and with a danger of frost in every month—was simply not suited to the type of agriculture that had proven so successful in southern Wisconsin. Furthermore, with increasing numbers of tourists, hunters, and other outdoor enthusiasts flocking to the region, restoring the "wilderness" offered alternative economic opportunities that were better adapted to the environmental conditions found there.[5]

Gough's alternative history raises an important issue. As William Cronon demonstrated with his analysis of Donald Worster's declensionist history of the Great Plains and Paul Bonnifield's progressive history of the same region, different points of view can lead even rigorous historians to different conclusions.[6] Even composing a simple chronology of events involves decisions about what to include and what to leave out. Choices made about the beginning and ending of the story and the geographical scale to be used also involve judgments that can affect outcomes. Cronon concluded that the way to escape the relativistic problem inherent in storytelling was for scholars to strive to tell the most plausible stories they could. Carstensen and Gough both told plausible stories. Though Gough seemed to contradict Carstensen, they both spoke about important parts of the large and complicated historical and geographical reality of the Wisconsin northwoods. The viewpoint of the farmers was as valid as the viewpoint of state officials and planners, but the latter was arguably more important to understanding the larger political and economic structure within which the farmers operated.

Like Carstensen's and Gough's studies, this book is about northern Wisconsin, but it focuses on the Chequamegon Bay region, located at the western end of the south shore of Lake Superior and roughly bounded by the Apostle Islands to the north, Bayfield Peninsula to the west, the Gogebic iron range to the south, and the Montreal River to the east. In the 1820s, the Chequamegon Bay area was perceived as one of many stopping points between Sault Ste. Marie and Fond du Lac, but by the 1840s and 1850s, geologists saw it as a region to explore, analyze, measure, and map out, and by the 1870s, boosters saw the place as a wilderness paradise on the verge of becoming a great metropolis with a productive agricultural hinterland. But after the iron boom of the 1880s, the communities around Chequamegon Bay began to slowly adjust to a more modest and more realistic regional identity.

Instead of taking the perspective of distant planners and politicians or of individual farmers, I will examine the region from the viewpoint of early travelers, geological surveyors, and boosters in an attempt to explain how the image of the region was formed during the nineteenth century. I employ a narrative-descriptive approach, most eloquently advocated by geographer Yi-Fu Tuan, to show how language played a crucial role in place creation in the vicinity of Chequamegon Bay.[7] Tuan has argued that geographers have not focused enough on the role of words in the making of place: "A curious gap in the extensive and growing literature on place is the attempt to address directly the role of human speech in the creation of place: curious because, obviously, without speech—without the use and exchange of words and the ideas they convey—there cannot be, in the first instance, any *human* action or force directed toward preconceived goals." Tuan urged geographers to fill this gap and to consider "speech and the written word . . . integral to the construction of place, and therefore integral to the geographer's understanding of place."[8] Not long after Tuan's essay appeared, geographer Michael Williams stated that "good environmental history and good historical geography could well be regarded as a series of place stories," and he agreed with historian William Cronon that scholars should tell not only stories but also "stories about stories."[9] Analyzing the words and viewpoints of geologists who traveled through the bay region and of boosters who settled there reveals how larger cultural movements influenced environmental perception. The descriptions of the region by early geologists were steeped in romantic imagery, and even the later geological reports utilized romantic aesthetic conventions; boosters then drew on the aesthetics as well as the data in geological reports to bolster their arguments for development.

Although this book builds on the works of scholars in many fields, place, region, and environmental perception have long been core foci of geographical research. The leitmotif of this book is succinctly captured by the historical geographer Ralph Hall Brown in the first chapter of his 1948 classic, *Historical Geography of the United States:* "Men at all times have been influenced quite as much by beliefs as by facts."[10] And to paraphrase Brown, there is no better illustration of this truth than the initial settlement and boosterism of the Chequamegon Bay region. Geologists and boosters played key roles in shaping how people perceived this place. Environmental cognition—how people perceive a place, and what people believe about a place—influences their behavior within the physical and social environment, thereby affecting the development and even the creation of place.[11]

Place is a complex word, applied to units of space of varying and sometimes overlapping dimensions that have meanings that shift over time and may differ radically between individuals and groups at any given moment.[12] Geographers naturally have a proprietary interest in place, just as psychologists do for the term *cognition*, and they have arguably produced the best work on the subject. Despite the fact that some excellent and often better-known work on the topic has been done outside the field of geography, the concept of place has always been central to the discipline. It is related to the concepts of region and area and can be used interchangeably, but the word *place* itself generally implies a more intimate unit of space and is tied to two other and equally complex terms: *milieu* and *landscape*.

By the end of the nineteenth century, German geographers had begun to define geography as landscape science, or *Landschaftsgeographie*. In his influential 1925 essay, "The Morphology of Landscape," geographer Carl Sauer introduced the concept to American geographers as an alternative to environmental determinism in order to refocus attention on human impact on the environment rather than the reverse.[13] With an increasing emphasis on cultural history, this line of thought became known as the Berkeley school. Like *place* and *milieu*, the word *landscape* implies an accessible and intimate portion of the earth. Thus, we have the definition derived from landscape painting, meaning "a portion of the earth's surface that can be comprehended at a glance." J. B. Jackson, who is credited with founding the field of landscape studies, usefully expanded the artist's definition, noting that a landscape is "a composition of man-made or man-modified spaces to serve as infrastructure or background for our collective existence."[14] Jackson dramatically entered the American landscape scene in 1951 with the first issue of the influential journal *Landscape*. He encouraged a wide range of contributions to his journal but was especially successful in enticing an eclectic group of academic geographers not only to submit articles but also to let their hair down and write for a larger audience.[15] Ever since, landscape has been an acceptable focal point for qualitative geographical research. More recently, scholars have applied techniques borrowed from literary criticism to read landscape like a text and discern power relations and ideology in the landscape.[16]

Recent historiography identifies three broad themes in environmental history: ecology, cognition, and production. Worster has argued for focusing on modes of production—or agroecology—and especially on how the rise of a capitalist mode of production has massively reorganized and simplified natural systems.[17] Craig Colten and Lary Dilsaver have identified three organizing themes in the lineages of environmental inquiry in historical geography: cultural landscapes, environmental understanding and evaluation, and resource use and management.[18] Colten and Dilsaver do not argue for one theme over another but rather plead for historical geographers to refocus their attention on environmental themes. William Cronon has argued that the main challenge for environmental historians is to integrate ecology, cognition, and production in their studies.[19] He has cited Arthur McEvoy's *The Fisherman's Problem* as one of the few studies that have done so.[20] McEvoy developed a cognitive theory of nature and culture that he used as his model to interpret changes in resource laws and the California fisheries.[21] The laws resulted from a changing understanding of the environment—organized behavior that altered the environment, to which people adapted again. As Ralph Brown observed, people are influenced quite as much by what they *believe* to be true as by what *is* true. And decisions are often based as much on misunderstanding as on understanding; people misunderstand each other, and they also misunderstand the land. Their responses lead to unexpected changes in their social and physical environments.

Putting the dynamics of people-land and people-people interactions into spatial and temporal context can help explain why humans behaved as they did in a given environment in the past. During the nineteenth century, the Chequamegon Bay region on Wisconsin's Lake Superior coast was the scene of dramatic cultural, economic, and environmental changes. The changes were complex and can be attributed to Euramerican immigration, industrialization, capitalism, globalism, and an emerging mass culture. But the best way to understand the changes that created the place known as Chequamegon Bay is by analyzing the written documents about and of the place, which not only reflected shifting visions of the region but also were intimately tied to the larger processes named earlier. These documents include maps, expedition narratives, geological surveys, railroad pamphlets, local and distant newspapers, periodicals, and advertisements.

There are two main parts to this book. The first part (chapters 1, 2, and 3) is about reconnaissance and geological surveys. Here, the scale is larger and encompasses the entire south shore of Lake Superior. These chapters are more about moving through space than about being in place. Chapters 1 and 2 analyze the texts written by Henry Rowe Schoolcraft and Thomas L.

McKenney on the journey from Niagara Falls to the western end of Lake Superior in 1820 and 1826, respectively. Chapter 1 describes the logistics of the journey as well as the political economy of the Lake Superior country. Chapter 2 shows how both men, Schoolcraft the mineralogist and McKenney the Indian agent, were deeply influenced by romantic poets, painters, and novelists: romanticism shaped the way they saw the land and its inhabitants. Chapter 3 explores the social, economic, political, and environmental implications of the first rigorous geological and ordinance surveys of the south shore of Lake Superior, set in the context of mid-nineteenth-century science. David Dale Owen, son of the utopian industrialist Robert Owen, orchestrated a geological survey of most of Wisconsin, Iowa, and Minnesota and parts of Nebraska Territory during the late 1840s that was so impressive that it served as a model for future surveys. Charles Whittlesey, of Cleveland, Ohio, surveyed the northern Wisconsin sections of Owen's survey. Whittlesey was probably the best field surveyor of his day, and history would prove him to be one of the most brilliant scientists as well. His surveys would shape the way settlers and speculators saw the land and would have a lasting impact on the economic development of the region.

The focus of the second part of this volume (chapters 4, 5, and 6) is on place. Chapter 4 shows that by the time the first towns were platted in the 1850s, two paradoxical images of the region had emerged. One envisioned a port city that would surpass Chicago in population and industry; the other promoted the region as an escape from places such as Chicago. Geological surveys had mapped out the resources to actualize the first vision, but conventions for depicting geological features used in the surveys (and arguably influenced by artists and poets such as Lord Byron) were copied in pamphlets designed to bring tourists to the area. Chapter 5 begins by showing the crucial role played by local newspapers in place making, and then, drawing on the work of William Cronon, Richard Slotkin, Richard White, and others, it identifies three popular narrative models that recurred in the local newspapers from the 1870s to the 1890s. The first was the booster's "future city" model, the second was the (very Turnerian) "independence on the land" model, and the third was the "Wild West" or "cosmopolitan frontier" model. Having a grasp of these three models is crucial to understanding the self-image of the Wisconsin north coast towns during the period. Chapter 6 contrasts the bucolic vision in artist Henry Wellge's bird's-eye views of the towns of Bayfield, Washburn, Ashland, and Hurley with widely published depictions of Ashland and Hurley as "hellholes"—centers of extreme violence and vice. Finally, the epilogue analyzes the First Annual Apostle Islands Indian Pageant, held in 1926, and explores what the event said about the revisioned landscapes of Lake Superior.

This book might be characterized as a regional geography, but it does not start with a region. Instead, it begins with something less defined: space or territory sought by explorers under government, commercial, or scientific sponsorship. It documents what might be called cognitive imperialism—how new visions of the place absorbed old visions and became hegemonic and how grandiose visions later crashed against environmental limitations. Interrogating the texts of Schoolcraft and McKenney in the 1820s, the geological surveys of Owen and Whittlesey in the 1840s and 1850s, and the articles and publications of newspaper editors and other boosters in the late nineteenth and early twentieth centuries, this work shows how what was seen as mere space became filled first with romantic images, then with scientific images, and finally with images based on the desire to entice people to settle and begin economic development in the region. It was only in the later stages of the image-making process that all the images, past and present, began to cohere to produce what might be called, for the first time, a region. Throughout this volume, I have tried to meld the geographies of physical nature with the geographies of human ideals and thereby demonstrate how thoroughly and paradoxically those two realms are entangled with one another.

Poets, Bedrock, and Chains

PART ONE

Survey: To look at from, or as from, a height or commanding position; to take a broad, general, or comprehensive view of; to view or examine in its whole extent.

—*Oxford English Dictionary*

Reconnaisance

1

BY THE 1820s, industrialization, urbanization, and a growing number of people with the time, money, and inclination to travel had transformed the Great Lakes region. The completion of the Erie Canal in 1825 made virtually every point on the chain of lakes accessible by ship from the major eastern population centers. Only Lake Superior, at the top of the chain, lay beyond easy reach. Because of the geographical barrier represented by the rapids below the outlet of the lake at Sault Ste. Marie, the largest vessels that could navigate up the fastwater gateway to Lake Superior were birchbark canoes and twelve-oared barges. Although larger vessels could be and were built on the upper lake before the locks opened in 1855 (or were hauled overland), there was little incentive to do so, since the boats were essentially confined to the one lake. Because of its isolation, the Lake Superior region had changed little in the 160 years since the Jesuit Claude Allouez had traveled to Chequamegon Bay. Even the priests had all but given up on the area.

The War of 1812 marked a turning point for the region because in its aftermath, the south shore and the west end of Lake Superior became part of the aggressively expanding United States. Although the middle ground was giving way to a new political economy, it would take a few more decades before Lake Superior was fully opened up to the rest of the country. First, sovereignty had to be exerted over the widely dispersed inhabitants of the region, and the land had to be made safe for Euramerican settlement. Most important of all, the region had to be brought within the realm of the nation's mental map: the place had to be experienced, described, and popularized. Only then would there be enough governmental support for the systematic surveys, conducted to identify resources and delineate property boundaries, that would lay the groundwork for rapid development.

Two works are key to understanding this pivotal moment in the history of the region: Henry Rowe Schoolcraft's account of the Lake Superior portion of the 1820 Cass Expedition and Thomas L. McKenney's account of a similar journey through Lake Superior (in an expedition that also included Lewis Cass and Schoolcraft) in 1826. Schoolcraft's *Narrative Journal of Travels: Through Northwestern Regions of the United States Extending from Detroit through the Great Chain of American Lakes to the Sources of the Mississippi River in the Year 1820*, published in 1821, was widely read.[1] McKenney's *Sketches of a Tour to the Lakes, of the Character and Customs of the Chippeway Indians, and of Incidents Connected with the Treaty of Fond du Lac* reached a smaller audience.[2] Together, these two texts provide a snapshot view of the south shore of Lake Superior at a crucial moment in the region's history. Through Schoolcraft's and McKenney's narratives, one can get a sense of how each man experienced the land—slowly and intimately, while hugging the shoreline in a birchbark canoe.

Schoolcraft's Travels, 1820

In 1819, Schoolcraft published the first scientific account of the lead mines in Missouri, and he made a point of sending copies to influential people.[3] His publication caught the attention of the secretary of war, John C. Calhoun, who offered the twenty-seven-year-old Schoolcraft a position as the "miner-

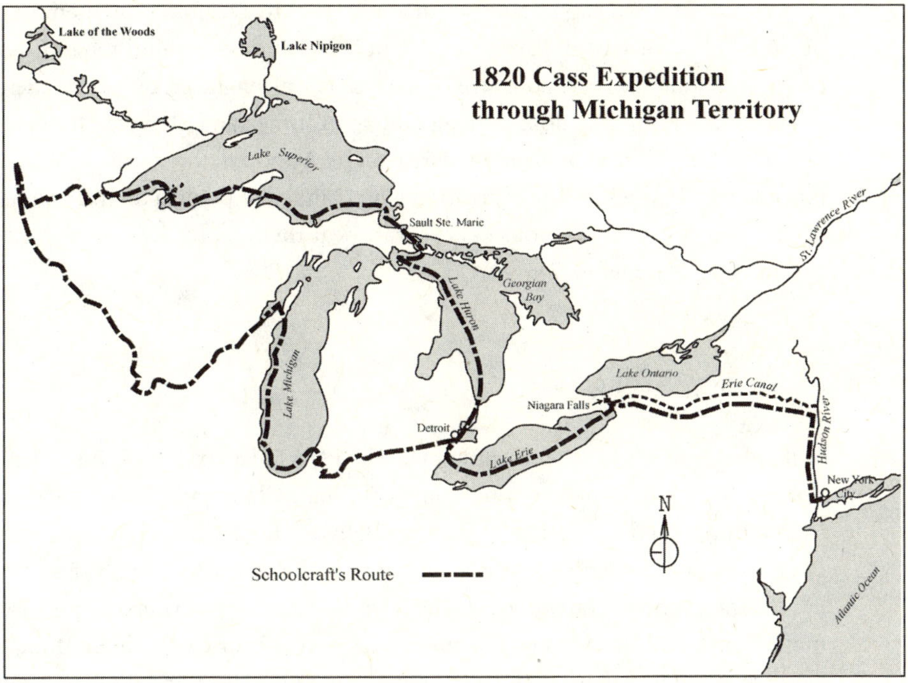

FIGURE 1.1 Schoolcraft's route on the 1820 Cass Expedition. Map by author.

alogist" of the 1820 expedition, which was led by territorial governor Lewis Cass (fig. 1.1).[4] The main purposes of the expedition were political: to establish sovereignty over the indigenous peoples, to identify potential sites for forts, and to test local attitudes toward the United States (the Chippewa in the region had sided with the British in the War of 1812). A secondary aim of the expedition was scientific: to conduct a reconnaissance geological and natural history survey of the region and, if possible, discover the source of the Mississippi River.[5]

The south shore of Lake Superior was only one segment of a larger tour through what was then known as the Northwest. The expedition officially began in Detroit and passed through Lake Huron and Lake Superior, up the St. Louis River, deep into what would become Minnesota in search of the source of the Mississippi River, and back via Prairie du Chien, Dubuque,

Green Bay, and Chicago before returning safely to Detroit. The members of the expedition accomplished this feat in only 123 days. In addition to Cass and Schoolcraft, the party consisted of a physician, an engineer, two secretaries, a topographer, about a dozen voyageurs, ten Ottawa and Shawnee Indians, seven U.S. soldiers, an interpreter, and a guide. Although there was an official journalist and others on the expedition who planned to publish their accounts of the journey, the ambitious Schoolcraft beat them all to the presses with his *Narrative Journal of Travels.*[6]

McKenney's Tour, 1826

McKenney's 1826 tour was a follow-up to the 1825 Treaty of Prairie du Chien, through which seasoned commissioners William Clark and Lewis Cass had settled long-standing territorial disputes between the Sioux, Chippewa, and other northwestern tribes; the agreement would, not coincidentally, also facilitate the eventual transfer of the land to the federal government. Because many Chippewa bands had not been present at the Prairie du Chien signing, a clause stipulated that all of the Chippewa would gather on Lake Superior to affirm the treaty and to acknowledge the authority of the U.S. government. Soon after the treaty was signed, McKenney wrote a congratulatory letter to Cass and invited him to Washington to discuss McKenney's ideas for a proposed Indian bureau. Cass spent a month in Washington with McKenney, and eventually, the latter decided that he would like to accompany Cass to the Fond du Lac treaty site to visit his Indian charges, assess their situation, and write an account of the journey to help convince Congress of the need for a bureau of Indian affairs. He also hoped that his book would enhance his reputation and increase his chances of being appointed to head the new department if it was created. With Cass's encouragement, Secretary of War James Barbour appointed McKenney along with Cass as commissioners of the treaty.[7]

The organizers of the 1826 trip believed it was crucial to impress on the Indians of the region the strength of the United States. The 1820 trip had consisted of about forty men in canoes, but the 1826 party included more than one hundred men, among them a company of soldiers from Fort Brady at the Sault and four musicians. Most members of the party traveled in three twelve-oared barges, and four additional barges carried provisions and gifts. McKenney chose to travel in Schoolcraft's canoe. The barges made slow progress, but the voyageur-powered canoes were free to dart ahead and explore at will. The treaty site, at Fond du Lac near an American Fur Company (AFC) outpost, was beyond the extreme western end of Lake Superior, about 24 miles up the St. Louis River.

Schoolcraft was expected to handle the complex logistics for the 1826 trip, but McKenney approached the journey as a much-needed vacation. Although he was paid by the day as well as by the mile, McKenney's services would only be needed at Fond du Lac. For the rest of the trip, he was free to view the sites at his leisure and record his thoughts on what he saw.

Two Men and Their Missions

Schoolcraft and McKenney were similar in many ways. Both men came from middle-class business backgrounds, experienced economic difficulties, were ambitious and calculating, and sought to improve their personal situations by creating careers for themselves with the federal government. In addition, their careers were intertwined. Directly and indirectly, these men would have a lasting impact on the Lake Superior country. Schoolcraft would serve as the Indian agent for the entire region from 1822 until 1841 and would become the most prolific collector of Chippewa stories in that era. McKenney was the chief administrator of Indian affairs from 1816 to 1830, when he was dismissed by Andrew Jackson. Like Schoolcraft, he worked hard to preserve something of American Indian culture. His main legacy was a gallery of portraits of great chiefs that he had commissioned by artists including George Cooke, Charles Bird King, and James Otto Lewis. McKenney was also the principal architect of the Indian removal policy, which forced Indians to move west of the Mississippi. He was convinced that this forced migration would be for the Indians' own good. Regardless of the intent, however, the policy would prove disastrous for the Lake Superior Chippewa, even though their removal from Wisconsin in the 1850s would only be temporary.[8]

Historians have emphasized the importance of imagination in the development of the Great Plains, an area that had to overcome being labeled the Great American Desert. But they have not given an equal weight to the role played by imagination in the development of the upper Great Lakes region, which is odd because an initially negative image was at least as big an obstacle for the Lake Superior south shore hinterlands as it was for Kansas. The area was scouted in 1786 by James Monroe, who declared that much of it was "miserably poor" and predicted that it would never have enough inhabitants to become a state.[9] In October 1817, Edward Tiffin led a reconnaissance survey of Michigan Territory and concluded that "the land was not worth the expense of surveying it."[10] Before the boosterish Governor Cass had convinced him otherwise, the prominent geographer Jedidiah Morse considered the lands of the upper lakes region to be poor and barren; some maps even labeled lower Michigan as "interminable swamp."[11] Also, public fears of hostile Indians had to be overcome, for stories of atrocities during the Iroquois Wars had been well publicized.

The 1820 and 1826 expeditions helped to change the image of the Lake Superior country in two ways. First, as official government missions, they exerted and reinforced U.S. sovereignty through treaties established with the indigenous populations and symbolic displays of military force. Second, Schoolcraft's and McKenney's books about the expeditions contributed to the public's knowledge of the place and its inhabitants. Actually, neither of these men did much to refute popular notions that the place was inhospitable to "civilized" occupance, and this, perhaps as effectively as the rapids on the St. Mary's River, helped to delay the assimilation of the region into the growing urban industrial complex.

As chroniclers of the regions they traveled through, both Schoolcraft and McKenney brought heavy intellectual and cultural baggage with them. The ways in which they perceived the land and its inhabitants were influenced not only by what they expected to see but also by how they understood they were expected to see certain aspects of the environment, such as the scenery. A close reading of their texts suggests multiple influences on their thinking. For example, Schoolcraft had been raised hearing tales from his father and other relatives of atrocities committed by Indians during the Iroquois Wars, which may have predisposed him to see Indians as so-called savages. McKenney, by contrast, was an avid reader of James Fenimore Cooper's novels, and he related scenes from *The Last of the Mohicans* (1826) and *The Pioneers*

(1821) to his field observations of Indians and the land. Cooper's novels surely influenced McKenney's more romantic notions of American Indians, as well as his conviction that they were defiled by contact with whites and therefore needed to be protected.

As influential as his writings were, Henry Rowe Schoolcraft made his most lasting contribution to the imagery of the Lake Superior country indirectly, through his impact on Henry Wadsworth Longfellow: Longfellow's popular poem *The Song of Hiawatha* (1855) was drawn largely from stories collected and published by Schoolcraft.[12] What James Fenimore Cooper had done for the imagery of eastern forests with his Leatherstocking novels, Longfellow would do for the Lake Superior region with *Hiawatha*, attaching romantic visions of moccasins treading along forested paths, birchbark canoes, deep waters, and mighty fish.[13] And it was the Cass Expedition of 1820 that sparked Schoolcraft's interest in the lore of Lake Superior Indians.[14]

Schoolcraft and McKenney were both fascinated with Indian stories. Schoolcraft believed those stories were the key to unlock the Indian mind, which was one reason he collected their stories. To Schoolcraft, McKenney, and their contemporaries, Indian stories seemed exotic, but they also made Indians seem more civilized, in the way that European folk tales made peasants seem more civilized. It was not uncommon for writers of the period to express astonishment at finding empirical evidence that Indians had feelings and that they appreciated beauty—even art. It was widely thought that Indians were by nature poverty-stricken in terms of culture as well as economy. Euramerican writers praised Indian stories, but at the same time, those stories seemed to be evidence of the Indians' superstitious and irrational belief system. Ironically, the self-described rational men Schoolcraft and McKenney were both influenced by their own cultural stories. Popular fiction colored their lived experience.

In addition to the publications of authorities such as leading geologists and the geographer Jedidiah Morse, three classes of stories, each representing a different belief system, affected the ways in which both Schoolcraft and McKenney saw the region they traversed. First, each man was influenced by his religious upbringing. The more sentimental of the two, McKenney had been raised a Quaker, which certainly shaped his more benevolent attitudes toward the Indians. Another influence stemmed from their educational backgrounds.

Throughout the nineteenth century, even scientists were not considered educated without a thorough grounding in the classics. Knowledge of the Greek myths provided an alternative lens through which to view the world, and both Schoolcraft's and McKenney's texts contain references to ancient mythology. Finally and most significantly, the work of the romantic poets, painters, and novelists had a distinct impact on both men.

McKenney especially kept up with the latest popular literature and seems to have been deeply influenced by it. His book is full of lines from romantic poems. Early in the book, in pages written while he was traveling through the Erie Canal, McKenney invoked Cooper's just published novel, *The Last of the Mohicans*, and reflected on the extinction of the Mohawks in that region. At Sault Ste. Marie, he was given a *Wa-ba-jick*, or white fisher skin. When Charlotte Johnston, daughter of fur trader John Johnston, informed him that it represented her grandfather, whose name was White Fisher, McKenney asked if that was also the totem of his band. According to McKenney, she replied that it was not and that his band's totem had been the reindeer:

> This totem among the Indians, appears to me to be something like the binding obligations of brotherhood that unite the masons—though, perhaps, it may exceed even these in its practical influences. You have so fine an illustration of its power and sacredness in the last of the Mohicans, that I have not the heart to do more than to refer to the scene in which Cooper has introduced it, and leave you to imagine how deep was the wisdom that devised, and how binding and humane the policy that confirmed its sacredness, *among the Indians.*[15]

Yet another example occurred on McKenney's return trip. While sitting around a smoky dinner fire, reading Cooper's *The Pioneers*, McKenney declared how "true" it was and how well Cooper captured what he was experiencing.

The two documents, Schoolcraft's *Narrative Journal of Travels* and McKenney's *Sketches of a Tour to the Lakes*, are alike in format, purpose, and style. Indeed, McKenney probably sought to duplicate the success of Schoolcraft's book. Both men dedicated their books to the secretaries of war serving at the time of their expeditions—Schoolcraft to Calhoun and McKenney to Barbour. And both books are structured as day-by-day accounts of the trips. Schoolcraft wrote his book as a daily journal directed at no one in particular, whereas McKenney composed his book as a series of intimate letters to Secretary Barbour. The original editions of both texts were supplemented by numerous illustrations. In addition to recording empirical observations of temperature, weather, geology, vegetation, Indians, voyageurs, and traders, the authors also recorded their thoughts and impressions as they moved through the landscape. To the extent that they were candid, their narratives reveal how they perceived the environment and the people in it.

The two men intended their books for similar audiences as well. Both sought to impress a secretary of war and other influential people who might assist their careers. Further, they wanted to reach a scholarly audience to burnish their academic credentials. Finally, they also wrote for a mass audience, hoping to acquire fame as well as fortune. Of the two books, Schoolcraft's was the most successful and probably had the most lasting influence on popular impressions of the area he wrote about. McKenney's book created an initial stir and increased interest in the area and its inhabitants but was soon largely forgotten.[16] Several years later, Margaret Fuller (1810–50), a journalist and literary critic, said that "McKenney's Tour to the Lakes is the dullest of books, yet faithful and quiet, and gives some facts not to be met with elsewhere."[17] Nevertheless, McKenney's account is a valuable supplement to Schoolcraft's because the author was more introspective and revealed more of his subjective thought process. Furthermore, he provided important details that Schoolcraft's account neglected. For example, Schoolcraft let the reader assume that he paddled along with the voyageurs, but McKenney not only gave the precise dimensions of the canoe he traveled in (34 feet long, 4 feet wide, and 2.5 feet deep at center) but also noted that it was equipped with an awning for the passengers. Schoolcraft and McKenney were not obliged to paddle, and because the canoes were loaded and unloaded in the water, they got in and out of the canoes on the backs of the voyageurs to avoid getting wet.[18] Figure 1.2, from Schoolcraft's *Narrative Journal,* shows Indian manufactures, including a canoe. In design, the vessel would be similar to the ones used on both expeditions, sans the canopy.[19]

Members of the 1820 Cass Expedition traveled comparatively light. Like Allouez a century and a half before, the entire party went by birchbark canoe. The group left Detroit in three large canoes, probably the *canot du maître,* or "Montreal" canoes, that were then commonly used on the Great Lakes. These

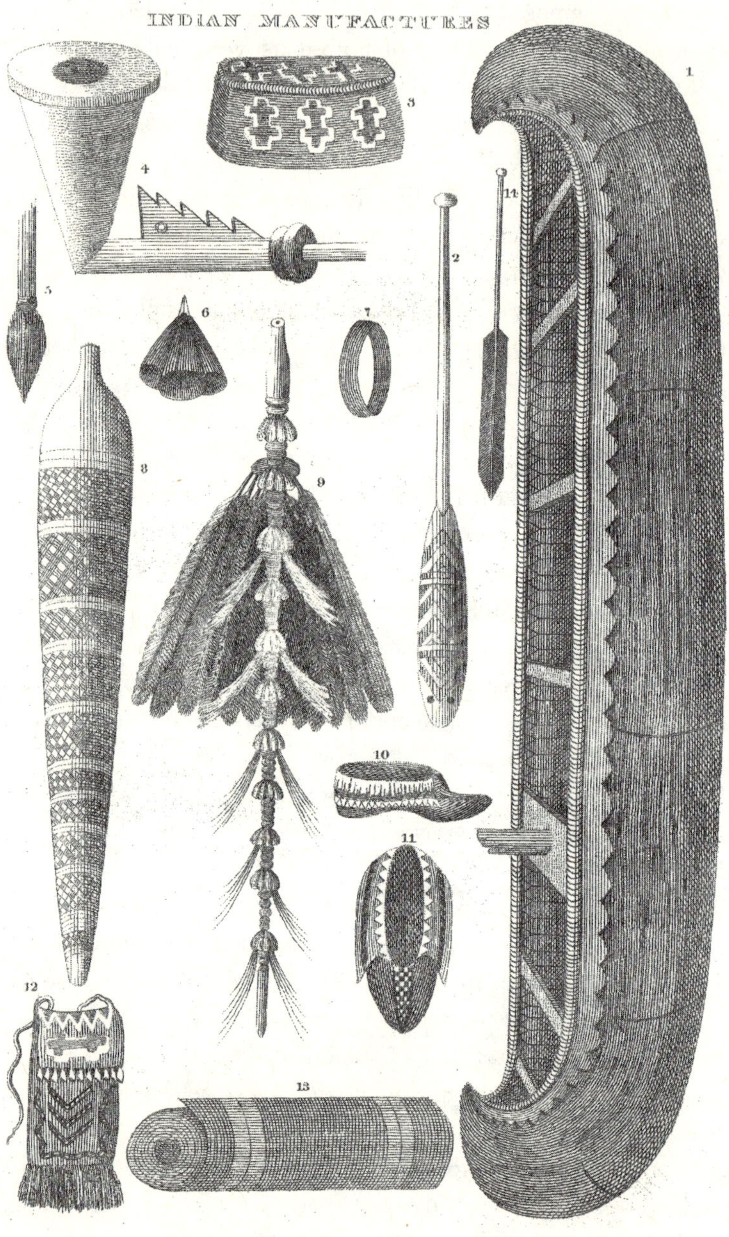

FIGURE I.2 "Indian Manufactures," from Schoolcraft, *Narrative Journal* (1821). Collection of the author.

were the largest of the birchbark canoes and ranged anywhere from 30 to 40 feet in length. They were built and repaired entirely from the forest—the rind of the yellow birch was stretched over a frame of white cedar, stitched together with *wattape* (a fiber from the root of a conifer), and sealed with pine gum. They weighed less than 300 pounds and could carry up to 5 tons of cargo and crew.[20] The advantages of canoes were multiple. They could transport a significant load yet were light enough to be carried over portages. They could be repaired en route, with materials close at hand in the forest. They could be navigated through rapids and across rough open waters by skilled canoeists. And when the weather became too rough and travel too dangerous, they could simply be pulled out of the water.

It took fourteen days for the 1820 Cass party to reach Mackinac (then known as Michilimackinac) Island from Detroit. They used this leg of the journey to test their canoes and gear. Otherwise, they could have made the journey in a fraction of the time by catching a ride on a steamboat because by 1819, a boat was making regular trips all the way from Buffalo, New York, to Mackinac in just twelve days.[21] In his narrative, Schoolcraft complained that the scenery up to Mackinac was "monotonous" and "less interesting in the main, than was expected."[22] A few scenes did attract his admiration, but that was entirely due to "the mildness and beauty of their outlines, and the pleasing effect of water; and not from any features of boldness or sublimity" (79). However, Mackinac Island did impress him and would, he wrote, "even present attractions to the eye of the solitary traveler [such as himself two years before] among the romantic and sublime scenes of the wilderness of Arkansas" (78). By 1820, Mackinac was already within the growing realm of tourist destinations. Schoolcraft gave a detailed description of three natural features that he said were "generally visited by strangers"—Giant's Arch, Natural Pyramid, and Skull Rock (81–82). The names suggest how much this area just below the Lake Superior country was part of the Euramerican mental landscape. They also attest to the growing popularity in that era of scenes that were immense, ancient, or dangerous.

Mackinac Island was poised strategically between Lakes Huron and Michigan and just below the route to Lake Superior through the St. Mary's River. For members of the Cass Expedition, this was the time and the place to regroup and assess their equipment. They realized that their canoes were inadequate and thus acquired additional canoes. They repacked their food (which included corn, flour, and bacon) in 10-gallon kegs in order to better protect it from moisture and to facilitate loading and unloading.

Six years later, McKenney and Cass made the trip from Detroit to the top of Lake Huron on a schooner. On July 2, 1826, they bypassed Mackinac because of poor weather and dropped anchor near Detour Village. There, they witnessed a scene that surely contributed to McKenney's growing conviction that Indians needed to be protected from the influence of Euramericans. A nearby island was, he reported, "filled with Indians—drunk, noisy, and naked!" who had just exchanged their annual presents from the British traders on Drummond Island for whiskey "and were now enjoying the luxury of being drunk and naked."[23] Later, after being shown around by the officers of the military post at Drummond's Island and invited to tea, they overheard a group of Ottawa singing a hymn. McKenney wrote that the Ottawa of L'Arbre Croche (20 miles west of Mackinac) "[are the] most improved Indians in those regions, and upwards of fifty years ago supplied Michilimackinac with corn, and other articles of subsistence. They are the best dressed Indians I have met with; and are so superior in cleanliness, and comforts, and conduct, to the Chippeways, as to be known from them by their gait and exterior" (167). As if to accentuate the contrast between the civilized Ottawa and the "savage" Chippewa, McKenney described stopping on the island on the way back to the schooner to "see how drunken Indians looked by torch light." He compared the scene to "that of hell of which we read, where the wicked are said to gnash their teeth, and from whence the smoke of their torment ascends!" and he blamed the evil on whiskey (169). This Dantean image stayed with McKenney as he observed the Chippewa on the south shore of Lake Superior. It seemed to be his default expectation: he expressed surprise only when they did not fit that mold.

Gateway to Lake Superior: Sault Ste. Marie, 1820

Lake Superior was just as remote from the rest of the country politically as it was geographically. Most of the residents identified more with Canada than with the United States. Indeed, many of them had sided with the British during the War of 1812. The Indians at Sault Ste. Marie were expected to be particularly hostile to Americans, so when the Cass party left Mackinac for the

Sault on June 13, 1820, they were joined by twenty-two U.S. soldiers in a twelve-oared barge in case there was trouble. They arrived at Sault Ste. Marie one day later, just in time to pitch their tents before dark. Schoolcraft described the village there as having the appearance of "an ancient settlement fallen to decay."[24] To him, the demolished fort and the still-standing stone chimneys of former houses attested to the "barbarous policy of war" (94).

As he walked about the next day, Schoolcraft observed the strategic location of the Sault: he reported, "[The] Sault de Ste. Marie, is the largest of three rapids which impede the navigation of the river St. Mary between Lake Superior and Lake Huron, and puts a final stop to the ship navigation of the northern lakes" (94). All of the fur trade of the Northwest passed through the Sault, which was also "the grand thoroughfare of Indian communications for the upper countries, as far as the arctic circle" (96). In addition, the abundance of easily caught whitefish at the foot of the rapids attracted Indians from all over the Lake Superior region, especially in the summer when hunting was slow. Schoolcraft concluded that "no place could, therefore, be better adapted to acquire influence over the savage tribes, to monopolize their commerce, and to guard the frontier settlements against their incursions" than a fort at Sault Ste. Marie.[25] Indeed, one of the primary objectives of the expedition was to identify an appropriate site for such a fort.

Toward this end, a council of the Chippewa chiefs was summoned to the governor's marquee on June 16, 1820, so that Cass could explain the federal government's position. U.S. title to the Sault was based on a savings clause inserted by General Anthony Wayne into the Treaty of Greenville, which guaranteed the United States the right to place forts wherever they had formerly been granted to the British or the French in Indian Territory.[26] Governor Cass had been directed by the president to claim the right to establish a U.S. military reservation based on the concession made earlier to the French at the Sault. The assembled Indians listened politely to Cass but made it known that they were against a U.S. presence at the Sault. One chief was so strongly opposed to the Americans that he expressed his disapproval by hoisting a British flag in his encampment as soon as the council was over. Governor Cass brought the situation to a head by ordering that the rest of the Indians' party be put under arms while he and his interpreter went to the encampment and took down the British flag, and he threatened severe consequences should it be raised again. The tense standoff was defused when a group of older chiefs proposed a compromise. By evening, a treaty had been signed, ceding a 4-square-mile tract of land centering on the Sault to the U.S. government but reserving fishing and camping rights for the Chippewa.[27]

At the Sault, the Cass party stayed with the family of fur trader John Johnston, Schoolcraft's future in-laws. Johnston was born in 1762 and emigrated from Ireland to North America in 1790. Through an old family friend, he obtained work in the fur trade on Mackinac Island. He soon found himself managing the trading post at La Pointe, on Chequamegon Bay. He survived a difficult winter, overcame severe obstacles to doing business, and by spring was conducting a profitable trade at La Pointe. Johnston gained the trust of Waub Ojeeg, a well-known and influential chief of the La Pointe band of Chippewa. He had cemented his relationship with the Indians by marrying the chief's youngest daughter, Ozha-guscoday-way-quay, whom he renamed Sarah.[28]

Johnston's story illuminates how the far-flung outposts and villages on Lake Superior were connected by social relations. Intermarriage between Indian women and fur traders and voyageurs was a well-established practice in the middle ground. Richard White has proposed that this may have been one reason why available data suggest male Indians in the Great Lakes region outnumbered females. By the late eighteenth century, only the Chippewa had more women than men, which allowed them to remain a strong and sustainable presence in the area even as other tribes disappeared.[29] In any case, by virtue of location, family relations, and political connections, John Johnston was the most influential trader on Lake Superior by 1820. He based his operations strategically at Sault Ste. Marie and maintained a key position—geographically as well as culturally—between the Chippewa and various government entities. He had a brief setback during the War of 1812 when U.S. troops pillaged his property, but he recovered, and despite his continued affinity with the British, he established good relations with the United States. Indeed, by some accounts, it was Johnston's wife and children who, in his absence, played a pivotal role in averting violence in the flag incident at the Sault. Johnson was rewarded by being granted land near the Sault by the U.S. government.[30]

While at the Sault, Schoolcraft observed several barges and canoes, laden with furs, descending the rapids. He was impressed with the voyageurs' skill.

Earlier in his journal, he had expressed surprise at the degree of environmental knowledge the fur traders must have possessed to site their posts so well, with the Sault being a prime example. The Lake Superior country was the last holdout in the United States of the middle ground, and the residents still ruled the land in practice, if not by international law. But members of the Cass expeditions were more concerned with the future of the region, which could include Indians and fur traders only marginally. Imbued with a sense of cultural and economic superiority, they read the landscape not only through their own personal and cultural lenses but also with an aim toward paving the way for a new inhabitance of the land, choosing what to value and devalue as they went.

Sault Ste. Marie, 1826

By the time McKenney arrived at the Sault in 1826, the United States had established Fort Brady and Schoolcraft had married John Johnston's eldest daughter, Jane, and had been living at the Sault for four years as the territory's Indian agent. According to McKenney, in addition to the 200 soldiers stationed at the fort, the village had a population of 152 (47 men, 30 women, and 75 children). He counted fifty-seven buildings, including several warehouses, three retail stores, a bakery, a cooperage, a tailor shop, and a blacksmith. Most of the smaller houses were inhabited by voyageurs and their families.[31]

McKenney expressed surprise at the productivity of the place:

> I see a much more abundant show of vegetables than I expected, from accounts which I had read of the total barrenness of this place. It is poor enough, however; and the seasons and location are all unfriendly to great productiveness, but the specimens of the military gardens, and those also of Mr. Johnson [*sic*], demonstrate that man can accomplish much, even over the most forbidding state of things, and in the very face of nature, who frowns, as she certainly does here, upon all such efforts.[32]

He also noted the abundance of whitefish, which supported the resident population in addition to a large Indian presence in the summer. Another staple was maple sugar.

On Lake Superior—"Beyond the limits of civilization"

To early nineteenth-century travelers, the Sault represented the last outpost of civilization. To enter on Lake Superior was to pass through a gateway into the unknown. Schoolcraft's narrative suggests that he felt disturbed as he passed for the first time between the two high promontories that marked the beginning of Lake Superior—Point Iroquois to the south and Grande Cape to the north. He said that the scene appeared "at some remote period of the creation, to have been rent asunder, by one of those unaccountable convulsions which have produced so much confusion upon the surface of the earth."[33] The landscape enhanced the perception of passing into a different realm, beyond the familiar and safe, and across a political and economic divide. This land was still ruled by traders, voyageurs, Indians, and Nature. The 1820 expedition's topographer, Charles Trowbridge, wrote of the passage into the Lake Superior country:

> We prepared to take a serious departure (for we had hardly considered it so as yet,) from civilized beings. The natural reflection that it would be the melancholy lot of some of us never to return, here strongly suggested itself to our minds, and our spirits were enlivened only by the animated boat songs of our canadians.[34]

The party was dependent on information obtained from traders, voyageurs, and Indians as well as the accounts of previous travelers. Everything seemed different on Lake Superior: the people were more alien, the biting insects more fierce, and the weather more intense and unpredictable.

By 1826, little had changed. McKenney described his destination at the head of Lake Superior as "six hundred miles beyond the limits of civilization . . . where we shall be alone among the mountains, and forests, and lakes" (175). On June 10, 1826, about to embark on the lake the next morning, he wrote to the secretary of war:

> I have a world before me, but perhaps a barren and unfruitful one, and in all things, except those which relate to nature; and I expect to find her asleep; and in the same slumber in which she has reposed since the creation. I may, perhaps, find some traces of her beauty, or deformity, (the latter made so, however, since she first came from the hand of her creator,) and these I will endeavor to sketch, and reserve for you.[35]

FIGURE 1.3 "Chippeway Indian Lodge," from McKenney, *Sketches of a Tour to the Lakes* (1827). Courtesy of the Wisconsin Historical Society (WHi-36629).

These two sentences speak volumes regarding McKenney's attitude toward the place he was about to enter. First, he engendered this world: it was female. Although he suspected that he would find her "barren" and "unfruitful," he acknowledged that might not be her true nature. The world before him was "asleep"—"reposed" and waiting, perhaps to be made fruitful and productive? As if the secretary of war were a potential suitor, McKenney described the land's natural beauties for him and promised to "reserve" them for him, while also assessing how badly she had been "deformed." But who had deformed her and how? It was as if the Lake Superior country were a sleeping beauty, guarded by crude dwarfs and awaiting her prince.[36]

Although the quotation implies a sense of anticipation and that McKenney expected to see natural beauty, it also reveals that he did not hold a high opinion of the inhabitants of the region. What influenced his preconceptions? He had never visited the region, so he must have formed his impressions from what he had heard and read. One likely source was the geographies of Jedidiah Morse, whom McKenney cited as an authority on the region. In terms of numbers, Indians dominated the Lake Superior country well into the nineteenth century. Second in importance were the métis voyageurs, followed by other laborers, traders, and a military presence that fluctuated in nationality as well as numbers. Long before the 1820s, the upper lakes region had developed a reputation as being socially and economically backward. Morse's 1810 *American Gazetteer* explained the causes by pointing to Detroit, which began as a French military post:

> These soldiers came out from France without women. Their connexion with the savage females, and their not having any legal title to their lands, naturally led them to a savage course of life, and while English settlements of the same date have become populous, and opulent, enlightened by science, and elevated by religion, these people are sunk in anarchy, ignorance and poverty.[37]

By 1819, Morse's opinion had changed little. Regarding the (non-Indian) people of what was then Michigan Territory, he had this to say:

> The greater part of the inhabitants of this territory till lately, were Catholics, descendants of French traders and were sunk in a state of deplorable ignorance and wickedness. Lately the state of religion and morals has been rising. A flourishing Presbyterian church and society has been established in the city of Detroit, to which the ordinances of the gospel are regularly administered, the benefit of which is already visible in the existence of a Bible, a moral, and humane society.[38]

Morse went on to claim that "the first immigrants had all the common characteristics of new settlers. The descendants of the original French settlers employed in the fur trade, were in a degraded and miserable state, occasioned by the nature of their employment, and association with Indians" (633). He expressed, even as he shaped, commonly held attitudes of the time, based more on ethnic and religious prejudice than on actual empirical observation and data.

Navigation and Orientation in the Lake Superior Country

Although the Lake Superior environment inspired romantic musings, it also imposed a hard materiality on the intellectual voyageurs. Wind, water, rocks, cold, and heat posed real dangers and numerous challenges. On Lake Superior, the topography and prevailing winds seemed to conspire to impede westward travel along the south shore, while facilitating eastward travel. The most prominent physical barrier was the Keweenaw Peninsula, near the center of the shoreline. But weather was the most constant obstacle. All Lake Superior travel journals, especially those of the canoe era, contained frequent references to the weather. The second day on Lake Superior, Charles Trowbridge wrote that while he and his group were on the lake, a "violent wind arose," forcing them to land quickly. Later, he noted that the party "experienced one of those dreadful mists so common on this Lake: it is dangerous to travel in them for the prominent objects are scarcely distinguishable at a short distance, and unless the guides are competent we are every moment running the risk of losing our canoes."[39] After ten days on Lake Superior, Schoolcraft wrote:

> During this time, we have had rain, with violent wind, three days,—clear, with moderate wind, five days,—and variable, (calm, misty, cloudy, windy,) three days. The highest degree of heat during the same period, has been 83°, and the mean temperature, from sun rise to sun set, 66°. The transitions of temperature have often been sudden, and the heat, during the middle of the day, (from eleven to four) generally severe, and sometimes almost insupportable. Dense fogs have prevailed during the morning, and in one or two instances, mists have been observed during the day. Gusts of wind, arising with a momentary warning, have often driven us hastily ashore; and the whole route may be characterized as stormy, and yet we are told this is one of the most favorable months for performing the journey. In the autumn it is seldom attempted. The winds, which generally prevail from the northwest, expose the southern shore to the fury of continental storms.[40]

Travelers in birchbark canoes were at the mercy of the weather.

Because of the northwesterly winds that prevailed in the region, it was generally believed that the northern British shore was safer to follow than the southern American shore. Just twenty-six years before the Cass Expedition, Morse's *American Geography* (1794), the standard reference of the time, claimed that there was only one river tributary to the south shore of Lake Superior. From a map that accompanied the text, it is clear that Morse was referring to the Ontonagon River. Although he did not name the river, the words *Copper Mines* were written across the base of it. This map also confused what we now call Bayfield Peninsula with the much larger Keweenaw Peninsula and showed the former as being slightly larger than the latter. Even more striking was the large—and imaginary—island far offshore between the two points.[41] Morse's later *American Universal Geography* (1819) was more accurate.[42] Fortunately, members of the Cass Expedition had other sources to draw on. In addition to the reports of previous travelers, which were often erroneous, they relied most heavily on information received from traders and voyageurs and sometimes the local Chippewa.

Schoolcraft provided lists of points and distances between points for the entire journey. Those for the south shore of Lake Superior were compiled from estimates provided by traders and voyageurs and were translated from French leagues to English miles. Actually, before being given to Schoolcraft, the distances must already have been translated into leagues, for the voyageurs typically measured distance on the water by "pipes," or the number of times they would stop and rest long enough to have a smoke (a pipe was roughly equivalent to 4 miles). Stretches between landing points were called *traverses,* and long ones were to be dreaded.[43] On land, the portages were divided into *posés,* or the number of rests, generally about half a mile apart. In a land where travel was marked by paddling long distances and carrying loads over portages, it is no wonder that a common way of measuring distance and time reflected the human body and its endurance in the environment.

Schoolcraft's list of points along the south shore provides clues about the way in which early travelers oriented themselves and what features of the environment were important to them. Between Sault Ste. Marie, near the eastern outlet, and the American Fur Company establishment on the St. Louis River inlet to Lake Superior, Schoolcraft listed a total of forty-eight points together with the distances between them.[44] The official distance between Sault Ste. Marie and Duluth is 394 statute miles; therefore, the average distance between the forty-eight points listed by Schoolcraft was 8.2 miles.[45] However, it is important to bear in mind that his data sources probably varied in accuracy and that Schoolcraft himself was prone to making errors.[46] These factors may help to explain why the sum of Schoolcraft's distances between Sault Ste. Marie and the mouth of the St. Louis River (near current-day Duluth) was 504 miles. Another reason for the discrepancy is that unlike today's ships, which would probably take a more direct route, the fragile and low-riding birchbark canoes of Schoolcraft's era were more likely to hug the irregular shoreline. Therefore, his figures may be a more accurate estimate of mileage by canoe. Furthermore, reference to recent and historical maps shows that the points mentioned are indeed there, just as Schoolcraft described them, and roughly where they should be.

Using Schoolcraft's figures, the average distance between the forty-eight points from the extreme east end to the far west end of Lake Superior is about 11 miles. Unlike the high and rocky north shore of Lake Superior, the south shore is comparatively low and sandy. On either shore, the primary concern for those traveling by birchbark canoe was accessibility to emergency pullout points, where, on very short notice, one could go ashore and haul the canoe out of the water if the weather suddenly changed. It was also important to have regular breaks because paddling all day was exhausting work. Finally, being able to reference several places was vital to navigation. Each place had a meaning associated with it and a name. As Grace Lee Nute has pointed out, this was just one of the important services provided by the voyageurs because place-names facilitate bearings.[47] Often, the voyageurs simply adopted or translated names used by the native inhabitants, and many of the place-names were later anglicized. The result is a mixture of Chippewa, French, and English place-names throughout the upper Great Lakes region. Of 43 names of rivers, points, islands, or distinctive landforms, 21 (or 48 percent) are English, 17 (40 percent) are French, and 5 (12 percent) are Native American. Of the total of 48 south shore places listed by Schoolcraft between the Sault and the AFC post on either end of Lake Superior, 32 (67 percent) were rivers; 7 (15 percent) were points; 3 (6 percent) were fur trade posts; 2 (4 percent) were islands; 2 others were distinctive landscape features; 1 (2 percent) was an Indian village; and 1 was portage. This listing probably reflected the relative importance of places to travelers in terms of potential refuge from rough waters, orientation, and trade.

By 1820, every major landmark on the south shore of Lake Superior had been named. Nevertheless, Schoolcraft recounted at least two instances when members of the Cass Expedition attached names to points in the landscape. Just past "La Pointe La Grande Sable," which is Au Sable Point on current maps, the party camped near a creek. In honor of a severe storm that raged the night they spent there, they called the stream Hurricane Creek. The name apparently stuck, and on a 1968 U.S. Geological Survey (USGS) map, it is called Hurricane River. On June 22, 1820, Schoolcraft himself named Granite Point, about 8 miles northwest of Marquette, Michigan. Current USGS maps retain the name. Schoolcraft also attempted to rename the Apostle Islands the Federation Islands, giving individual islands the names of states. He published a map showing the new designations, but these names never caught on.

Although Schoolcraft and McKenney often described the Lake Superior country as wilderness, the entire shoreline was an intensively humanized landscape. Everywhere they went ashore, they saw traces of human occupance. Since the first French traders began penetrating the region in the early seventeenth century, a complex economy had developed between the region's Chippewa and a succession of distant powers—first the French, then the British, and finally the Americans. By the time France's dominance of the fur trade ended with the surrender of Montreal to the British in 1760, all tribes had essentially abandoned their woodland material culture and become dependent on European tools and weapons and fond of European luxury items, including ornaments and liquor. When the British took over the European end of the trade, the Lake Superior Chippewa controlled the highly productive territory between Keweenaw Peninsula and the upper Mississippi Valley. It was for control of this region that the Chippewa often fought the Sioux, whom they had displaced.[48]

French economic dominance of the fur trade ended in 1760, but the British quickly learned that it was prudent to live up to the expectations established by the French, and so, in modified form, the French-Chippewa mores and customs continued. After a bloody adjustment period, peace was restored to the Northwest in 1764, and the region's fur trade entered its most prosperous period. British traders and voyageurs flocked to the region. After agreements had been made with various tribes, fleets of the standard 35-foot canoes resumed traveling Lake Superior, each powered by a dozen hardy voyageurs capable of carrying 4 tons of crew, merchandise, and provisions in and furs out.[49]

By the 1820s, the population of the Lake Superior region continued to be widely dispersed but was not insignificant. In terms of sheer numbers, the region was dominated initially by the Chippewa and later by French and métis peasant laborers. Then there were a few traders who tied the Indians and métis inhabitants to a larger economy; various military personnel who came and went (first French and British and later American); and finally, after 1822, one or more Indian agents.

Political Economy

According to Morse, the manufactures in Michigan Territory in 1810 were 37,000 pounds of soap, 19,400 gallons of whiskey, 1,000 gallons of brandy, 1,500 barrels of cider, 6,500 pounds of candles, 2,720 sides of leather, 2,405 yards of woolen cloth, 1,195 yards of flax stuffs, 600 hats, 60 saddles, and 20 yards of hemp. He estimated the total value of the manufactures at $50,000.[50] Presumably, these products were made in Detroit, not in Sault Ste. Marie or the other widely scattered population centers of the region, and many of them, especially those of a liquid form, likely flowed into the economy of the Lake Superior country. Morse's geography did not list the fur pelts that came out of the region.

In the 1820s, both Schoolcraft and McKenney mentioned passing brigades of canoes and barges that were heavily laden with furs and heading toward Sault Ste. Marie. For instance, in mid-June 1820, Schoolcraft observed five heavily loaded barges of AFC furs making the annual return trip from Fond du Lac, at the western head of the lake, to Mackinac, at the top of Lake Huron.[51] Perhaps because of the remote origin of the furs, they were considered a raw material, but there was actually much manufacture involved in their production. After the furbearing animals had been captured, they had to be skinned, salted, graded, and packed into the 90-pound bales that were standard for the trade. No matter how difficult the portage, voyageurs were expected to carry at least two of these packs at a time.

The Chippewa were a vital part of the local economy. The Indians not only supplied the furs that enriched the traders but also produced vital foodstuffs, such as dried fish and maple sugar. They manufactured the canoes, from smaller family models to the 40-foot Mack Trucks of the fur trade. The French peasant stock and the métis formed the main labor pool for transporting the goods produced by the Indians. The voyageurs transported commodities and people over water, whereas the packers transported goods over long and difficult portages.

Before Whitefish Point at the mouth of the Shelldrake River, the 1820 party encountered a group of Indians drying whitefish. They traded tobacco for the dried fish.[52] Schoolcraft predicted that the abundance of whitefish would "hereafter render them an important article in the commerce of the upper lakes" (96). Beyond Whitefish Point, he recorded a sparse pine-spruce-birch-aspen forest, which suggested to him the "sterility of the soil" (104).

The party frequently encountered apparently well-fed Indians camped near rivers with fish weirs. On the Montreal River, the expedition secretary, James Doty, noted the weir constructed by the Indians to take sturgeon and whitefish. While there, he claimed that "almost unlimited numbers of pigeons came flying over the banks into the gulf, from thence they ascended opposite. They flew so low that thirty or forty were killed by our men with clubs & sticks thrown into the flocks as they passed."[53] In terms of biotic resources, the Lake Superior country seemed promising. Yet Schoolcraft and McKenney saw the American shore of Lake Superior as a barren land and its inhabitants as paupers. Neither man envisioned more than modest development, except perhaps of copper mining. Commercial agriculture, significant settlement, and the development of cities did not seem to be realistic possibilities there. Besides fish and copper, the most salable resource was scenery.

In the 1820s, the south shore of the Lake Superior country was undergoing profound political and economic changes. The economy of several generations of the region's Indians had been dependent on trade, with the French, then the British, and later the American traders. The decline of the fur trade economy coincided with Washington's political desire to formalize control of the region. The timing was good for the Americans and bad for the Indians. Wittingly or unwittingly, Henry Schoolcraft and Thomas McKenney were significant agents of this transformation.

Through the Poets' Eyes

2

By the 1820s, one commodity that was highly valued in the United States as well as in Europe was scenery. Those who traveled and wrote about what they saw seemed to consider themselves connoisseurs of landscapes, and Schoolcraft and McKenney were no exceptions. Quite in tune with their times, both men frequently made aesthetic pronouncements on the landscapes they traveled through.

Tourism had become well established in Europe by the end of the eighteenth century, and many travelers sought to experience the *sublime*.[1] In Britain, the most important statement of the concept was Edmund Burke's *Philosophical Enquiry into the Origin of Our Ideas of the Sublime and Beautiful.* Burke wrote that "whatever is fitted in any sort to excite the ideas of pain, and danger, that is to say, whatever is in any sort terrible, or is analogous to terror, is a source of the *sublime*; that is, it is productive of the strongest emotion which the mind is capable of feeling. . . . When danger or pain press too nearly, they are incapable of giving any delight, and are simply terrible; but at certain distances, and with certain modifications, they may be, and they are delightful, as we every day experience."[2] Scores of poets, landscape painters, and novelists explored and celebrated sublimity in their work.[3]

Why did people become obsessed with experiencing the sublime? In the beginning, the search for sublimity was closely tied to religious experience and an attempt to get closer to God, but over time, it increasingly involved growing closer to nature.[4] The pursuit of the sublime became a socially acceptable way to escape, to transcend the self, and to leave the mundane behind, if only for the moment. Whatever drove them, many educated Europeans and Americans traveled in search of sublime scenery.

European painters and poets often put ancient ruins into their compositions because ruins were thought to enhance the experience of the sublime. Obviously, this presented a problem for North American seekers of the sublime. The solution was twofold. First, American painters, writers, and poets emphasized dramatic natural phenomena and features that were bigger, wilder, more difficult to reach, or more pristine than Old World scenery. Second, they *imagined* ruins in natural features. The paradigmatic example of the former was Niagara Falls, which had become "*the* American icon of the sublime" by the early nineteenth century.[5] As Patrick McGreevy has pointed out, the site, because of its remoteness, had an image of mythic proportions by the time the Erie Canal made it more accessible in the 1820s; it was considered a unique feature that was unparalleled in the Old World.[6] Even though few people had actually seen Niagara Falls until the nineteenth century, it was widely known. Possibly in an unconscious attempt to make it conform to archetypal ideals of waterfalls, early descriptions of the place were highly distorted and tended to exaggerate the height and underestimate the width of the falls. By 1820, accurate descriptions were available, but myths still prevailed.

Conveniently, both Schoolcraft, beginning in New York, and McKenney, from Washington, D.C., visited the falls on their way to Lake Superior, so comparisons can be made between their descriptions of Niagara and scenes on the south shore of Lake Superior. The timing of their visits—in 1820 and 1826—is significant because it was during these few years that Niagara Falls was brought within the reach of ordinary Americans. Indeed, from the 1820s until the Civil War, it was the prime tourist destination for a growing middle class. According to Elizabeth McKinsey, Niagara was transformed "from a national icon, remote and imaginistic, . . . into a fashionable resort, accessible by easy transportation."[7] Schoolcraft was one of the last to visit the falls while the site was still relatively inaccessible, whereas McKenney was one of the first visitors to take advantage of the recently completed Erie Canal. By the 1820s, however, Niagara Falls was no longer a remote object of imaginative geography, so new icons of American sublimity and beauty were needed. And it seems that in their narratives, both Schoolcraft and McKenney consciously sought to offer potential candidates, as well as descriptions of a new region for imaginative geographies, far beyond the reach of most travelers. McKenney had little more authority than the average travel writer, but Schoolcraft was a published geologist and thus had ideal credentials as a mythmaker.

According to Mircea Eliade, "Myth tells how, through the deeds of Supernatural Beings, a reality came into existence, be it the whole of reality, the Cosmos, or only a fragment of reality."[8] And as John Sears pointed out, "By the nineteenth century science had begun to assume some of the function of myth, and before the publication of Charles Darwin's *Origin of Species* (1859), the science which functioned most successfully in this way was geology. . . . Geology furnished nature with a history. It suggested the world was far more ancient than people had formerly thought and that prodigious geological forces had transformed it in startling ways over time."[9] The evidence of these forces on the face of the earth often resulted in the most sublime scenery. Sears made a strong argument that geologists played a vital role in the creation of what he called "sacred places"—American tourist shrines. Geologists also contributed to the experience of the sublime by discovering the awesome and cataclysmic forces that shaped the landscape, initially by finding evidence of a great deluge and later by recognizing evidence of glaciation.

Niagara Falls, 1820

Schoolcraft's *Narrative Journal* began with a "preliminary tour" from New York City to Detroit, where he was to meet the rest of the Cass party. Along the way, he experienced Niagara Falls for the first time. He arrived on May 1, 1820, and spent two days at the location. The first section of the Erie Canal had just opened up; the entire project would be completed within five years. In his 1821 book, Schoolcraft claimed that Niagara Falls had already been "the free and fashionable resort of all sections of the Union" for thirty-six years. It had also become the most important symbol of the sublime in the United States,[10] and according to Sears, it was the premiere American tourist destination of the nineteenth century. Many saw their trip there as a pilgrimage that would bring them closer to God. Sears argued that the origin for this notion was in Edmund Burke's 1757 treatise: "By providing a paradigm for the emotional experience that grand objects were supposed to evoke, Burke's work served, in effect, as the first guidebook to the Falls. The early travel accounts and guidebooks are full of Burkean rhetoric about the astonishing height, enormous volume, stupendous force, and eternal sound of the Falls."[11] In addition to the guidebooks, romantic poets and landscape painters also taught travelers how to approach scenic places.

Surprisingly, Schoolcraft did not use the word *sublime* to describe Niagara Falls, even though he would employ the term freely to describe scenes on Lake Superior. He was most impressed by the chasm at the foot of the falls, which he guessed must have been inaccessible until the recent construction of artificial stairs (which seemed to impress him every bit as much as the chasm itself):

> It is in this chasm that the sound of the water, falls heaviest upon the ear, and that the mind becomes fully impressed, with the appalling majesty of the Fall. Other views from the banks on both sides of the river, and from the Island of Iris, in its centre, are more beautiful and picturesque; but it is here that the tremulous motion of the earth, the clouds of iridescent spray, the broken column of falling water, the stunning sound, the lofty bank of the river, and the wide spreading ruin of the rocks, imprint a character of wonder and terror upon the scene, which no other point of view is capable of producing.[12]

Even though he did not use the word, this is clearly the language of the sublime: ruin, wonder, terror, beautiful, and picturesque. Educated people knew how they were expected to respond when they were at Niagara Falls, yet in part because of the high expectations, disappointment was a common response. That fact may help to explain Schoolcraft's first reaction to the falls. He was surprised to see how much writers such as Baron La Hontan, in 1688, had exaggerated the height of the falls. At the same time, however, to the extent that the falls did stir raw emotion, Schoolcraft seemed almost annoyed because that emotion interfered with his objective analysis of the landscape:

> The spectator, who, on alighting at Niagara, walks hastily to the brink, feels his attention imperceptibly riveted to the novel and striking phenomenon before him, and, at this moment, is apt either to over-rate or to under-rate the magnitude of the Fall. It is not easy to erect a standard of comparison; and the view requires to be studied in order to attain a just conception and appreciation of its grandeur and its beauties. The ear is at first stunned by the incessant roar, and the eye bewildered in the general view. . . . It was some time before I could satisfy myself of the accuracy of the accredited measurements of the height of the Fall, and not until after I had made repeated visits, and spent a considerable time in the abyss below. (43)

Schoolcraft fought the subjective response in favor of the objective, scientific approach he was cultivating. In a cryptic sentence, he summed up his impressions of Niagara Falls and suggested that he intentionally kept his head and resisted experiencing what he was *supposed* to experience:

> There appears a great disproportion between the height and the width of the falling sheet, but the longer I remained, the more magnificent it appeared to me; and hence it is, that with something like a feeling of disappointment, on my first arrival, I left the Falls, after a visit of two days, with an impression of the scene, which everything I had previously read, had failed to create. (43)

Here, for Schoolcraft, enlightenment trumped romanticism; most of the eight pages he spent describing the Niagara Falls area were devoted to an analysis of geological structures. To him, "the scenes where nature has experienced her greatest convulsions, are always the most favourable for acquiring a knowledge of the internal structure of the earth" (44). He was especially intrigued with the opportunity to estimate the rate of recession of the falls, in order to shed some light on the age of the continent (47). Although he did not use the term itself, he accepted the fundamental geological principal of uniformitarianism, which assumes that the processes and laws now currently acting to modify the Earth's crust were essentially the same throughout geological time and, therefore, that the geology of the past can be explained by observing phenomena in the present. Schoolcraft proposed that by using accurate maps and by strategically placing a monument that would allow precise measurement, the past rate of recession could be accurately estimated in a few years' time. He added mischievously, "Is this suggestion of too visionary a nature, to merit the consideration of the geological societies?" (48). Ironically, many people in his day—including prominent scholars—feared that too close an examination of the places where people went to feel nearer to God might challenge the Bible's account of creation.[13] Later in his *Narrative Journal*, Schoolcraft alluded to a nontheological debate in geology over transition rocks but stated that he refused to engage the "dogmatism" in current geological theorizing; instead, he would content himself "with the bare recital of the facts."[14]

But even more than theory, Schoolcraft was interested in the economic possibilities offered by geological understanding. Scrutinizing the larger landscape that contained Niagara Falls, he noted that a particular sandstone stratum had provided useful building stone as well as lining for glass and iron foundries. Ever promoting his skills, he stated in a footnote: "Intelligent manufacturers will see the important application of geological science, in tracing the formations of rocks, upon which they are any wise dependent, into the vicinity of their manufactures" (45). The discipline of geology was an infant science in 1820, and its practitioners sought to fulfill many roles. There was also an emerging dichotomy between the theoretical and the applied sciences. With vast tracts of land coming into the public domain, Schoolcraft saw great opportunities for geologists to survey the terrain to accurately identify and locate potential resources, and he believed this vital function could most ably be performed by those who understood geological principles and theories. Other opportunities existed in the emerging institutions of higher learning. In practice, the theoretical and applied sciences would complement each other, just as they do today.[15] Beyond discovering and describing the cosmic and the cataclysmic, geologists fulfilled another function of the mythmaker—explaining the Earth and people's relationship to it, especially how they could use it. Though some areas might be so sacred they should be set aside like shrines, most places contained elements for material consumption and use. At Niagara, Schoolcraft was more inclined to fulfill this utilitarian role of the mythmaker—to show the industrialists how to use the stone and especially to show the economic value of his knowledge. The landforms along the south shore of Lake Superior would evoke a more emotional response from Schoolcraft. In large part, this must have had to do with the newness of the region, the excitement of discovery, and a sense of seeing sights that were inaccessible to most people. Another key to explaining the difference in his responses to the locations seems to be how analogous the landscapes on Lake Superior appeared to be to other "civilized" scenes, real or imagined.

Niagara Falls, 1826

Six years later, on June 13, 1826, Thomas McKenney made his own pilgrimage to Niagara Falls on the way to the Lake Superior country. Unhindered by forced efforts at objectivity, McKenney approached the falls as a tourist, eagerly seeking the sublime experience. He arrived at the falls from the Canadian side and on the way made stops at battle sites and contemplated the violent history of the area, especially bloody contests that had occurred during the War of 1812. Near the falls, he stayed at William Forsyth's Pavilion Hotel, which was one of the best-known establishments on that side of the river.[16] McKenney claimed that the first thing he did when he arrived at Forsyth's was to "go to the upper portico of his house, and look from thence upon this 'hell of waters!'" (93). Later, he revealed that the "hell of waters" line was borrowed from a poem by Lord Byron. Just as James Fenimore Cooper's novels informed McKenney's ideas about Native Americans, romantic poets taught him how to see the land. After what he felt was a feeble attempt to describe his experience of Niagara Falls, he quoted stanzas sixty-nine to seventy-two of the fourth canto of Byron's epic poem *Childe Harold's Pilgrimage*.[17] This was significant because Byron set his poem amid scenes he experienced while on his own grand tour (in his case, of Europe). The fourth canto was completed several years after the first three and was set in Italy. The subject of the four stanzas quoted by McKenney was the Cascata del Marmore. In the second line of stanza sixty-nine, McKenney replaced the word *Velino* with *Niag'ra* and declared that Byron's poem was a "perfect" description of Niagara Falls—even though the English poet had never seen the American Falls.[18] Following Byron's example, McKenney made two visits to his falls, first to view it from the top and then to experience it from below, and like Byron, he seemed to prefer the latter view. Curiously, Schoolcraft had done the same thing and had a similar preference for the abyss over the crest. Both men followed Byron in their obsession with the iris—the rainbow phenomenon often seen at the base of the falls that to some represented Iris, the winged goddess of the rainbow who was a messenger of the gods in Greek mythology.

McKenney struggled to find the right words to describe his experience at Niagara Falls for the secretary of war and the rest of his anticipated audience, "for how can any conception be given for that which there is no parallel, and with which there is nothing to compare it?"[19] He attempted to put the reader at the scene:

> To comprehend the falls of Niagara, you must *see*, and *hear* them—you must therefore behold for yourself—then come along with me to the top of Forsyth's house. There!—what do you think of that?—On your right, and south, and just before you, is that almost semi-circular verge of *seven hundred yards* round, and over which, an unbroken surface of transparent green waters pours without a particle of foam at the turn, and at the rate of, perhaps, *fifteen millions of tons in twenty-four hours!* (93–94)

The italics are in the original text and seem to emphasize how measurements of size and quantity enhanced the sense of grandeur. McKenney then turned to hyperbole, using lines such as "convulsed by the terror and tumult of the scene below!" and "terrors of the approaching deep." To this standard rhetorical device, he added repetition, invoked eternity, and deftly connected the falls to the Great Lakes above:

> ONWARD!—OVER!—are the only words that can convey the impression arising from the sight of the rapids above, and the falls below. They appear to be words spoken by the Eternal when the hurrying, and splashing, and foaming scene of the rapids commenced; and when their waters first made their pitch into the awful profound! The impelling mandate has never been for a moment disobeyed, and it is yet "*onward*," and "*over*," and will be, till the same voice shall speak, and alter the arrangement; or break up the connexion, and the form of it, which now exists between these falls and the great chain of lakes whose outlet is over them. (94–95)

McKenney expressed a sense of omnipresent danger that, according to Edmund Burke, was vital to the experience of the sublime. But if Elizabeth McKinsey is correct that "it was through rhetoric that most Americans became familiar with the idea of the sublime," then McKenney's education at Washington College may have contributed another element to his experience of Niagara, as well as to his way of expressing it.[20] Until well into the nineteenth century, the standard rhetoric text in American colleges was Hugh Blair's *Lectures on Rhetoric and Belles Lettres,* which went through at least 130 printings between 1783 and 1911.[21] Blair's *Rhetoric* contained sections on the use of hyperbole as well as lengthy discussions of "sublimity" and "beauty." His approach was to first instruct students to recognize the sublime in objects in order to prepare them for his lecture on sublimity in writing.[22] Blair argued that for writing to be sublime, its subject had to be sublime, but most important of all, the writing had to "fill the mind with great and awful ideas" and produce "an imagination heated and astonished with the grandeur of the object."[23] To that end, one technique that was commonly used was to emphasize the element of danger, real or imagined.

McKenney accomplished this by relating a story told to him by William Forsyth about discovering a crack in a ledge on which a party of guests at his Pavilion Hotel had been sitting every evening. Forsyth said that when he told the group about the crack and warned them not to venture back onto the ledge, they thought he was overreacting; they had been on the ledge moments before and had noticed the crack but felt the structure was stable. That very night, a terrible sound tore through the air, as if an earthquake had struck the area. In the morning, they discovered that the ledge had broken off.[24] The image of the ledge falling into the abyss helps to heighten the suspense and sense of danger in the following passage, describing McKenney's descent to river level to view the falls from below:

> This going down is fatiguing enough, but you will find it more difficult getting back.—However, come along. This you see is sure enough an awful abyss! . . . Those rocks that over-hang their base, and appear ready to fall on and crush you, and which seem to be brushed by the passing clouds, are about three hundred feet above you; and all these piles of broken rocks, are the fragments that every now and then fall from those projections—and no wonder, for do you not feel how the earth shakes? Now you have the view of this mighty cataract; the verge above, and the pouring over of the water, and the foam below, and the spray flying away into the air, and in its midst that beautiful iris, which, although the spray be so evolved and various, retains its position unchanged; and on your right at your feet, look

> again at the piles of rocks, and above and over you, at the rough projecting and dripping sides of the great mountain of rocks out of which they have fallen, and then at that sheet of white foam on the American side—and how terribly sublime all this is! (97)

McKenney pressed on and attempted to get a view from behind the cascade, but a gust of spray engulfed him and convinced him to turn back. His African American servant, Ben Hanson, immediately ran back to safer ground. When McKenney caught up to him, Hanson reportedly exclaimed, "'*Sir, I do hold this to be a most dangerous place!*'"[25] On returning to the hotel, McKenney dried his clothes, dined, and left on the stagecoach for Buffalo.

McKenney's model for describing the landscape may have been taken from Hugh Blair's work, but his guide to seeing the falls was not a tourist brochure but the previously cited poem by Byron, who described his Italian waterfall right down to the iris. Unlike most romantic poets, Lord Byron considered himself a descriptive rather than an imaginative poet—he wrote about what he saw.[26] Although the Italian cascade Byron depicted was quite different from Niagara Falls and although Byron had never been near the North American location, McKenney considered his poem to be a more accurate description of Niagara than he himself could provide—even with the falls in sight.

Lake Superior

Traveling westward by canoe along the south shore of Lake Superior must have been like traveling the wrong way along a saw blade: the route seemed to run against the grain of the land as well as the prevailing winds. This problem would have been just a minor concern to Schoolcraft or McKenney, though, since they were passengers whose only real task was to write about their experience of moving through the landscape and to record data at their leisure. Indeed, challenging travel conditions only heightened the sense of adventure and caused them to marvel at the skills of their voyageurs.

Schoolcraft's *Narrative Journal* can be read as a reconnaissance survey of geology with a few ethnological observations thrown in, and McKenney's *Tour to the Lakes* might be considered a reconnaissance survey of Indian popu-

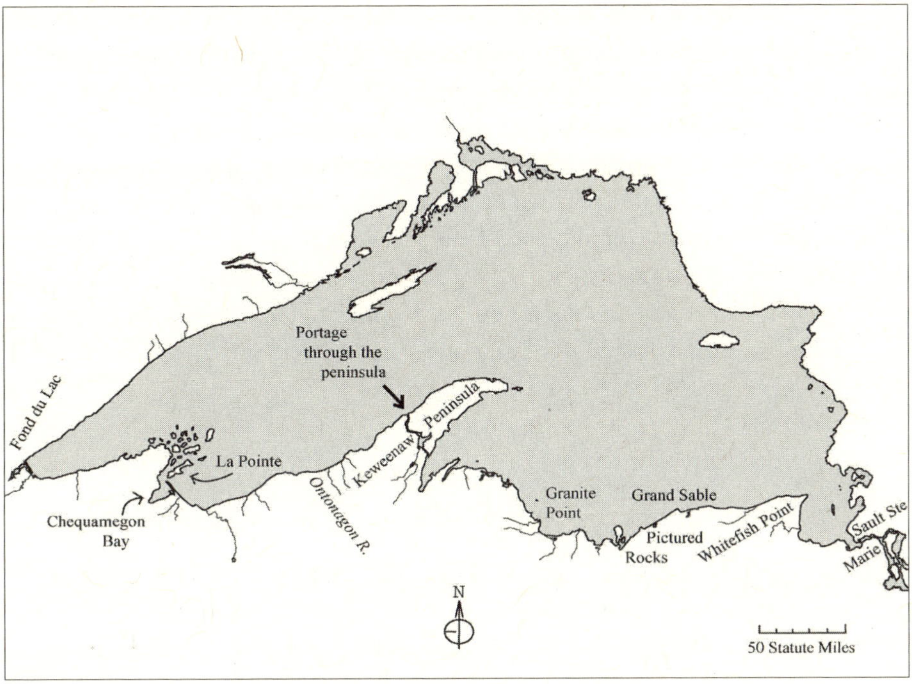

FIGURE 2.1 Key places on the south shore of Lake Superior in the 1820s. Map by author.

lations in Michigan Territory, as well as background to a treaty. Yet I would argue that both texts are best understood as travel narratives in a romantic tradition. Both men aspired to create a literary description of the land. In this vein, a few places along the south shore of Lake Superior are most significant: the entrance to the lake; the dramatic landscape features of Grand Sable (or Grand Sablé) and Pictured Rocks; Granite Point, which was named by Schoolcraft and to McKenney marked a transition point; Keweenaw Peninsula, which seemed to divide the south shore into two parts, with the western portion being more remote and cut off from civilization; the Ontonagon River, site of the legendary copper boulder; the Chequamegon region, especially La Pointe, or Michael's Island, which represented a rare oasis of northwoods pastoralism; and finally, Fond du Lac, at the head of the lake (fig. 2.1).

Once he and his party resumed their journey on June 18, 1820, Schoolcraft said of the entrance to Lake Superior that it presented "a scene of beauty and magnificence which is rarely surpassed, even amid the rugged scenery of the north." He also described this scene as suggesting evidence of the mysterious "convulsions" that apparently had occurred "at some remote period of the creation" and resulted in "so much confusion upon the surface of the earth."[27] Others, including McKenney six years later, expressed apprehension when reaching the entrance to the lake and a sense of passing through a gateway into a potentially dangerous environment. This sense only heightened the experience of sublimity, as long as the travelers stayed safe.[28]

Schoolcraft's Travels

Grand Sable, 1820

On June 20, the 1820 Cass party passed the Two-Hearted River (also known as the Two Heart River) and the Grande Marais and came on the first major landscape feature noticed by most travelers: the Grand Sable. Schoolcraft described it as a "lofty ridge of sand extending nine miles along the shore," with an average estimated height of 300 feet. Though he considered the views of the Grand Sable "novel and interesting" in appearance, he spoke of the scenery as if he actually felt threatened by it:

> Although generally commanding, [the views] present a great uniformity, and leave upon the mind a strong impression of bleakness and desolation. Even the few bushes and trees which are occasionally seen, serve to increase this effect by their impoverished growth, while the birds of prey which we observed hovering around these bleak sandy heights, could hardly be considered as ameliorating the dreariness of the prospect. The bald eagle perched upon a shattered tree half buried in the sand, looked upon us in security, from a height of three hundred feet, while the noisy raven, and the slow sailing falcon, were perpetually upon the wing.[29]

The "bleakness and desolation," the sense of impending doom, and especially the bird of prey "perched upon a shattered tree half buried in the sand" signal that Schoolcraft had momentarily passed from disinterested scientific observer and entered the terrain of the darkly sublime. Even when he switched to a scientific voice and attempted to analyze the geology of the scene, he dwelled on the top of three horizontal layers of sand, which contained "embedded trunks of trees, some of which remain in the position in which they grew, but have been buried by drifting sand nearly to their tops, and thus killed." He also hypothesized that at "some former period," water must have submerged the highest point of the landform (105).

At least some members of the party had a very different response to the landform. While Schoolcraft clung to the safety of the shore, the expedition physician, Alex Wolcott, climbed the ridge of sand, discovered a lake, and brought back rocks for the mineralogist, which appeared to Schoolcraft to be of volcanic origin; he described some pieces of "granite aggregates" being "semi-vitrified," with a surface possessing the "smoothness and gloss of common glass."[30] Charles Trowbridge, too, gave a very different version of the party's encounter with the Grand Sable. According to his journal, he and others were "gratified with a sight of La Grande Sable or Sand Banks, a place much spoken of by voyageurs." He also recounted that "one of our Indians whom curiosity induced to ascend them had much the appearance of a child when running on the summit of the hills, and when he returned to the canoe he was almost exhausted with fatigue."[31] James Doty, the official secretary for the expedition, wrote that "a person passing long their base looks at their summits with astonishment. He can scarcely believe it possible that such a quantity of sand could by any means have been collected and raised to such a height."[32]

Pictured Rocks, 1820

On his 1820 visit, the Grand Sable may have disturbed Schoolcraft, but the Pictured Rocks—La Portaillé to the voyageurs—had a very different effect on him (fig. 2.2). He described the scene as

> a series of lofty bluffs, which continue for twelve miles along the shore, and present some of the most sublime and commanding views in nature. We had been told, by our Canadian guide, of the variety in the colour and form of these rocks, but were wholly unprepared to encounter the surprising groups of overhanging precipices, towering walls, caverns, water falls, and prostrate ruins, which are here mingled in the most wonderful disorder, and burst upon the view in ever-varying and pleasing succession.[33]

FIGURE 2.2 "Pictured Rocks, Lake Superior," from Schoolcraft, *Narrative Journal* (1821). Collection of the author.

What made the Pictured Rocks "sublime" and the Grand Sable merely "bleak and desolate"? Apparently, on his first visit to the Grand Sable, Schoolcraft felt sensations of oppression and danger that pressed too closely for him to enjoy the presence of the sublime there, but at Pictured Rocks, even the "wonderful disorder" delighted him. The sand dunes seemed big, useless, and formless, but to Schoolcraft and others, the Pictured Rocks resembled cultural landscapes. In the rock forms, Schoolcraft imagined that he saw "towering walls" and "prostrate ruins." It seems that one aspect of Grand Sable that disturbed him on his initial visit was the utter lack of anything remotely analogous to human constructions; what he saw instead was an immense and unstoppable wall of sand that could even swallow up whole trees, smothering them.

In contrast, the Pictured Rocks from a distance presented "the terrible array of dilapidated battlements and desolate towers." Schoolcraft's guide to viewing this scene was found in the work of another romantic poet. He quoted stanza eleven from the first canto of Sir Walter Scott's *Lady of the Lake* and then stated:

> All that we have read of the natural physiognomy of the Hebrides—of Staffa,—the Doreholm, and the romantic Isles of the Sicilian coast, is forcibly recalled on viewing this scene, and it may be doubted whether, in the whole range of American scenery, there is to be found such an interesting assemblage of grand, picturesque, and pleasing objects.[34]

He described one feature, which they named the Doric Arch, as resembling a "work of art."[35] In fact, Schoolcraft was so impressed with this rock formation that he used it to illustrate the ornate title page of the 1821 edition of his *Narrative Journal* (fig. 2.3). The picture, a copper engraving, shows a mantle held up by four columns; it is framed by the lake in the foreground and surrounded by live conifers and leafless deciduous trees, and a larger rock formation is in the background.[36] James Doty compared the impact of the Pictured Rocks with that of Niagara Falls. The rocks, he wrote,

> present the most appalling spectacle I ever witnessed. From the deep caverns underneath a roar like that of a cannon is continually reverberated, occasioned by the waves rolling in. In passing under them the sensations exceed those excited on viewing the Cataract of Niagara.[37]

The print of this scene published with the first edition of Schoolcraft's book suggests how much context affected the perceived sublimity of a scene. Not only were the Pictured Rocks far more inaccessible than Niagara, they were also set in a landscape that seemed wilder and more untamed. By the 1820s, Niagara had become too pastoral and accessible to be terribly sublime. Yet paradoxically, Doty, like Schoolcraft, was reminded of human artifacts by the scenery at the Pictured Rocks. He noted that they named the particularly striking arch formation the Doric Arch because of "the resemblance which it bears to that order of architecture."[38]

Charles Trowbridge described the Pictured Rocks as "one of nature's works of grandeur and sublimity." After a sketchy geological description, he stated,

> On the whole, the natural color & height of these Rocks the numerous caverns, arches, variegations and the beautiful cascades which here abound, render it one of the most romantic and picturesque views possibly imaginable. The traveler is lost in amazement, and the insignificance of man is portrayed in the most striking manner.[39]

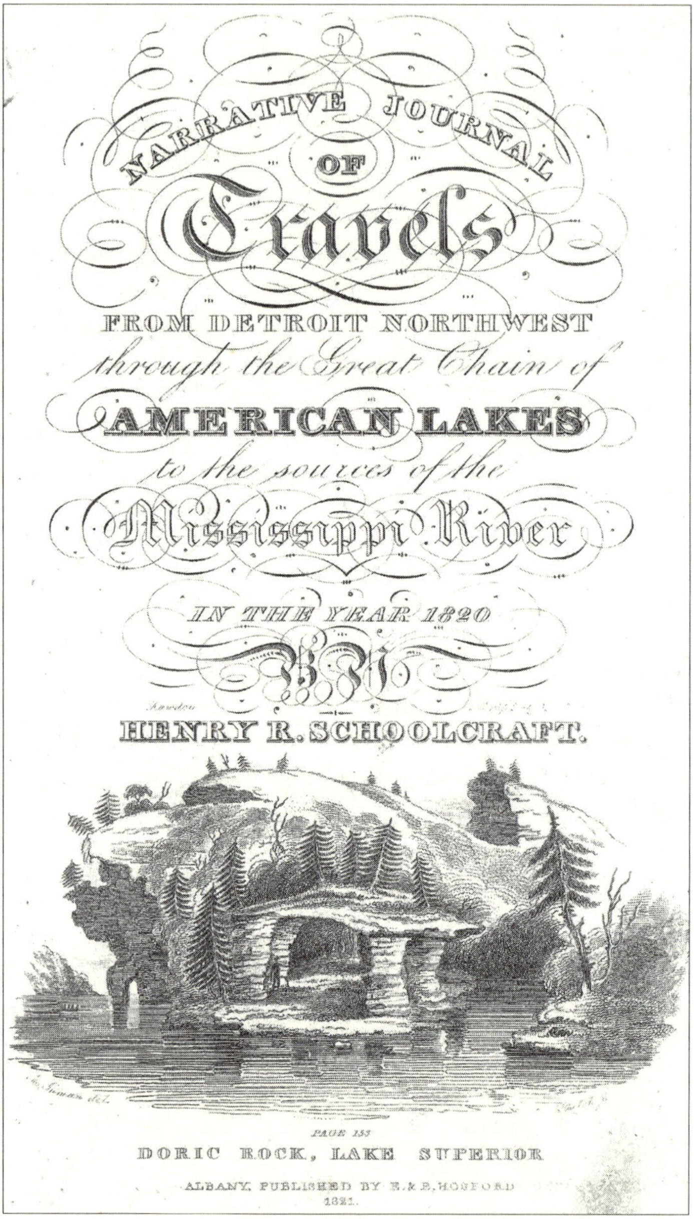

FIGURE 2.3 "Doric Rock, Lake Superior," front plate of Schoolcraft's *Narrative Journal* (1821). Collection of the author.

The landform they named the Doric Arch—known by the voyageurs as Portail Arch—reminded Trowbridge of the arch of a fireplace. "What renders it more curious," he noted, "is that no other rocks are nearer to it than ½ a mile, and it is plainly seen at the distance of one mile from the shore. It is said by those of our company who have seen the Niagara falls, that the scenery there will bear no comparison to the Pictured Rocks."[40]

Keweenaw Peninsula, 1820

To Schoolcraft, the most striking topographic feature on the south shore of Lake Superior was Keweenaw Point, which projects about 40 miles into the lake near the midpoint of the south shore. Rather than take the 90-mile paddle around, the 1820 Cass party took the shortcut through the base of the peninsula via Lake Portage. As they went, they passed through a narrow channel that Schoolcraft assumed was made by voyageurs "of former days." They made their camp on the other side and waited while the soldiers and voyageurs labored until dark and again the next morning, carrying the rest of their belongings across the 2,000-yard portage. They were windbound that afternoon, so Schoolcraft turned his attention to rocks.

Perhaps his earlier ordeal wandering in the wilds of Missouri had made Schoolcraft more cautious in exploring the unmapped interior country away from the shore, but his chosen approach to fieldwork on this trip to Lake Superior apparently involved as little exertion as possible. His leisurely approach could be productive, though:

> While we were sitting upon a bank of clean pebbles upon the shore, at dinner, and admiring the variety of water-worn pebbles, I picked up a fragment of a beautiful carnelian, and this gave a hint for making a search, in which a great number were afterwards found by different individuals of the party. I also discovered, while loitering along the shore, a mass of native copper, of nearly two pounds weight, attached to a water worn mass of serpentine rock, and a number of smaller pieces.[41]

Eventually, even the soldiers, voyageurs, and Indians turned collectors and found some of the finest specimens. Schoolcraft was especially impressed by the interest shown by the Indians, who, he recorded, seemed to think that "we posses the skill of turning all minerals either into money or medicine." Despite communication barriers, Schoolcraft claimed that the Indians expressed an interest in helping him gathering specimens almost from the beginning of the expedition, and they bestowed on him the title *Paw-gwa-be-can-e-ga,* which Schoolcraft translated as "the destroyer of rocks" or "he who employs himself among the rocks," roughly synonymous with "mineralogist" (116).

Ontonagon River, 1820

Navigating from one end of Lake Superior to the other was a fairly straightforward undertaking in terms of keeping oriented. Going from east to west along the south shore, one simply kept the shore on the left and, as described before, marked progress by keeping track of the rivers as they passed, recalibrating when one came to unmistakable landforms such as the Grand Sable or Pictured Rocks. On June 27, 1820, thirty-five days after leaving Detroit, the expedition entered the mouth of the Ontonagon River, which was 51 miles from Keweenaw by Schoolcraft's reckoning. The Ontonagon was one of the largest rivers on the south shore and certainly the most famous. According to Schoolcraft, previous visitors Louis-Armand de Lom d'Arce, baron de La Hontan (1666–1715), Pierre François Xavier de Charlevoix (1682–1761), Alexander Henry (1739–1824), Jonathan Carver (1710–80), and Sir Alexander McKenzie (1764–1820) had all published accounts of it and of the gigantic boulder of native copper said to lie near its bank upstream. One of the main objectives of the 1820 expedition was to verify reports of copper deposits and mines along the Ontonagon. This mission would be the first and only time that members of the party would venture far inland, away from the Lake Superior shore.

They landed across the river from several Indian lodges. Schoolcraft, Doty, and Trowbridge all noted in their journals how healthy and well fed the Indians residing there appeared. They seemed to be largely sedentary, able to subsist on local resources. About 4 miles upstream, they had constructed a weir across the river, and with hooks on the end of long poles, they caught great quantities of sturgeon, which they dried. Despite the sugar camp nearby, the evidence that bear and beaver were abundant, the vast numbers of pigeons flying overhead that were easily killed with sticks and stones, and presumably the ready supply of berries, roots, and other foodstuffs, Trowbridge imagined that the Indians subsisted entirely on sturgeon: "This manner of taking their food," he wrote, "is peculiarly adapted to the indolent habits of an Indian, and here they sometimes sit from morning till night imagining themselves, if we may judge from appearances, the happiest mortals in existence."[42] According to Trowbridge, these Indians had little contact with traders and thus had little access to whiskey, which was a rare treat for them.[43]

Although the Indians were suspicious of the party, having heard of the flag incident at the Sault, four of the men agreed to guide the travelers to the large copper boulder that was supposed to lie several miles upstream. Trowbridge was one of those chosen to stay and regulate the camp, and he expressed disappointment in losing "the anticipated & so much wished for pleasure of seeing that wonder of the North western world."[44] Among those who did go were Governor Cass, Captain David Bates Douglass, Dr. Wolcott, Lieutenant Æneas Mackay, Secretary Doty, and Mineralogist Schoolcraft. They traveled in their two smallest canoes, but the current grew strong as they ascended the river, and after paddling up a series of rapids, their guide announced that they would have to continue on foot.

Schoolcraft recorded the temperature at 90 degrees in the shade. The terrain turned out to be rugged, and the party had to hurry to keep up with their Indian guides. The governor became so exhausted that he headed back toward the canoe to wait, while Douglass, Wolcott, Doty, Schoolcraft, two voyageurs, and two guides continued on (Schoolcraft does not say whether MacKay went with them or with the governor). All were exhausted by the time they finally reached the copper boulder. There, they found the size and purity of the boulder had been greatly exaggerated, but it was impressive nonetheless. Despite the overstated accounts, Schoolcraft was certain that the mass of copper, "viewed in connexion with the mineral appearances of the surrounding country, leaves little doubt that extensive mines of this metal exist in the vicinity."[45] He described the setting in terms more romantic than geological: "The masses of fallen earth,—the blasted trees, which either lay prostrate at the foot of the bluffs, or hang in a threatening posture above,—the elevation of the banks,—the rapidity and noise of the stream, present such a mixed character of wildness, ruin, and sterility, as to render it one of the most rugged views in nature" (123). But after quoting from another poem by Scott (*Rokeby,* stanza seven of canto two), he questioned the area's value beyond the copper and asked whether it was a place for people at all:

> One cannot help fancying that he has gone to the ends of the earth, and beyond the boundaries appointed for the residence of man. Every object tells us that it is a region alike unfavorable to the productions of the animal and vegetable kingdom; and we shudder in casting our eyes over the frightful wreck of trees, and the confused groups of falling-in banks and shattered stones. Yet we have only to ascend these bluffs to behold hills more rugged and elevated; and dark hemlock forests, and yawning gulfs more dreary, and more forbidding to the eye. Such is the frightful region through which, for a distance of twenty miles, we followed our Indian guides to reach this unfrequented spot, in which there is nothing to compensate the toil of the journey but its geological character, and mineral productions. (123–24)

Figure 2.4 seems to convey Schoolcraft's sense of a forbidding landscape. The foreground shows the entire party reaching the rock in three canoes. (Of course, only some members of the group actually reached the boulder, and they did so on foot.) The human figures are dwarfed by the landscape. The sides of the valley close in on the scene, accentuated by dark trees sliding down the slopes. Most ominous of all is the immense bird of prey in the upper right edge of the scene, looking down on the tiny human figures below. Even though the picture partially contradicts Schoolcraft's text, it succeeds in capturing his mood in describing the place. No doubt, his perception was influenced by his fatigue. All members of the Cass party who went on this trip were exhausted by the heat and the pace over difficult terrain.

On returning to their canoes, Schoolcraft and the others who had seen the boulder were alarmed to find that Governor Cass, his attendants, and an Indian guide had not yet made it back to the boats. They fired signal shots in all directions and waited as nightfall approached. Schoolcraft described the apprehension the men in his group experienced: "The feelings of the party may be imagined upon this occasion, seated, as we were, in the midst of one of the most awful solitudes, and in a region which had impressed every individual with an indescribable feeling, that was manifested in a general anxiety to depart from it. I was perhaps alone in the wish to continue our examinations." At long last, the missing governor and the others were discovered by

FIGURE 2.4 "Mass of Native Copper on the Ontonagon River," from Schoolcraft, *Narrative Journal* (1821). Collection of the author.

the men who were sent upstream in a canoe to look for them. They had gotten lost (126).

Back at base camp on June 29, they distributed presents to the Indians, who, Schoolcraft reported, later "danced upon the sand for our amusement"; he was unimpressed and wrote: "It is perhaps all we could expect from untutored savages, but there is nothing about it which has ever struck me as either interesting or amusing, and after having seen these performances once or twice, they become particularly tedious, and it is a severe tax upon one's patience to sit and be compelled, in order to keep their good opinions, to appear pleased with it."[46] Others in the party had a very different response. Trowbridge was intrigued by the variety of dances and the style and skill of the dancers.[47] Both he and Doty mentioned a speech given by a young Indian man, who claimed to be the son of a powerful chief who had told him to respect the Americans. According to Doty, the young man's "countenance, his address, his whole appearance was so modest and unassuming that there were none present who did not admire and respect him. A flag and a medal were given to him, with which he appeared much pleased, and pledged his friendship for our country by giving us two fathoms of wampum."[48] Nevertheless, the entire party seemed happy to leave the Ontonagon River and continue their journey. Schoolcraft did not write much about their trip from the river to Fond du Lac. His focus turned to the vast territory west of Lake Superior and to the source of the Mississippi.

McKenney's Tour

Grand Sable, 1826

On July 14, 1826, Thomas McKenney caught his first glimpse of the Grand Sable. His response was similar to Trowbridge's and Doty's six years before. Indeed, from McKenney's account, it is clear that Schoolcraft himself, who participated in both expeditions, perceived the Sables very differently on this trip; in fact, the region was his home by then. After the fog dispersed on the following day, the group canoed to the Point au Sablé, which represented the beginning of the immense dunes. McKenney said he had never seen anything "so bleak or so barren," yet he found the "mountain of sand" to be a "great curiosity." He, Schoolcraft, and Ben Hanson went ashore together "and resolved on attempting this dangerous and sloping height."[49] McKenney's description of this attempt shows how he utilized his body, as well as his mind, to experience the environment:

> We, (Mr. S., myself, and Ben,) began to ascend this steep, and went up by pressing our feet and hands into the sand. When about two hundred feet up, a portion of the mountain, (about twenty feet square,) breaking loose, began to slide down with me towards the lake. I crossed the breach diagonally and got on a part that was firmer. I had not been there long, nor ascended more than twenty feet, when that gave way also. I made another attempt, and found this to yield, whilst above me, and in the line of my ascent, a large projection shot out some ten feet over my head, when I resolved to return. Mr. S. and Ben found firmer footing, and reached the top. From where I was the canoe looked like a toy, and the men in it like Lilliputians. Mr. S. reported the view into the lake from the top to be grand.[50]

According to biographer Herman J. Viola, at the beginning of the trip, McKenney's health had been so poor that preparations were secretly made for the disposal of his body,[51] but his health improved markedly, and he seems to have been robust by the time he reached the Grand Sable. Although he did not make it to the top, he climbed high enough to get a view of the area. His narrative suggests that all three men had fun climbing the sandpile. Their intimate experience with the landform contrasted strikingly with Schoolcraft's experience six years earlier, underscoring how subjective the human experience of the environment can be: with a sunny day, playmates, and an absence of the hovering birds of prey, what had seemed oppressive under different circumstances was transformed into a gigantic sandbox. Nevertheless, McKenney did contrast the "*Saharrah*" of the Grand Sable with the "agreeable" and "refreshing green" of the surrounding forested landscapes.

Pictured Rocks, 1826

Unlike the members of the 1820 Cass Expedition, McKenney must have had high expectations when he visited the Pictured Rocks on his way to Fond du Lac in 1826. He described "the picture of desolation and barrenness" of the Grand Sable, so different from the lush maple forest that lined the shore until the party arrived at the Doric Rock, which appeared "to have been sent in advance to announce to the voyageur the surprising and appalling grandeur which awaits him ahead." From that vantage point, the Pictured Rocks looked to McKenney like a "line of towers and battlements." In the Doric Rock, he saw an altar and next to it an urn, which he had the artist, James Otto Lewis, include in the sketch that would accompany his book (fig. 4.21). While the artist sketched, McKenney sat in the canoe trying to capture the display in words: "The place seems to have been provided by nature for a place of offering, whether to Diana, or which of the gods or goddesses, there is no way of ascertaining." He was intrigued by the remains of campfires scattered about the rock and assumed that Indians used the area as a "place of resort."[52]

The next day, a Sunday, McKenney and the others sent Hanson ahead with one of the barges and took Lewis in their canoe in his place so that they could stay behind to make more detailed sketches. Just after sunrise, they paddled along a rock face that reminded McKenney of a wall. He described it as being "higher than the capitol at Washington. It makes a sharp angle, the edge of which is as well defined as the north or any other corner of that splendid building. It staggers one's faith to believe that any thing short of architectural skill, and human hands, could finish off such an angle" (227). He thought that another formation resembled "a castle with its towers and battlements and embrasures. It would seem to have been put out thus in advance to protect the interior line of walls upon its right and left, and to have been built by giants!" (227). At that point, the weather changed abruptly and forced their canoe out into the lake. The situation became so grave that the voyageurs stopped singing. McKenney marveled at their paddling skills in keeping the canoe from being driven under a wave. Nevertheless, they had to continually bail out the water with a large sponge. At last, they reached calmer waters near Grand Island, and McKenney relaxed enough to imagine human constructions again:

> The appearance of the south-eastern shore of Grand island, in going up between it and the Pictured rocks, is strikingly magnificent, not only in regard to its extent, but to the mimic cities that line its shores, and high up above the lake. The appearance would deceive any one who did not know that the island was not inhabited. Buildings, of various forms and dimensions, appearing to be of stone, and brick, and wood, with spires and steeples, are as regularly shewn in this distance of ten miles, as if they were real; and serve not a little to soothe one, even with a knowledge that all of this is owing to the broken up rocks, similar in their character to the *portaillé,* or pictured rocks, opposite to them; because the fancy will not let go its hold of images of domestic life, and the pleasures of the social state. I could not keep my eye off these deceptious appearances, nor, for the life of me, dismiss those feelings of ideal bliss, the reality of which would be so heightened, could we in truth be thus near the abodes of men. (228–29)

The Doric Rock marked one end of the Pictured Rocks, and Grand Island marked the other. At the point in his narrative where McKenney caught up with the rest of the party on Grand Island, he claimed that "this island, and perhaps this very spot, has been rendered famous. The feeling of chivalry has been indulged here; and although the occasion to which I refer, has been given to the public, and read, doubtless, by thousands, I cannot refuse it a place in this journal" (230). He then recounted the story, published by Schoolcraft five years before, of the thirteen Chippewa youths who went off to defend their band's honor by fighting a doomed battle with the Sioux. Even in recounting Indian stories, the Americans were already adding their layers to the storied landscape.

To McKenney's eye, Granite Point, several miles west of Grand Island, marked a transition. Until Granite Point, the terrain, except for the Grand Sable and Pictured Rocks, had been generally level and "monotonous."

> [But] now the scene has changed; and although the mountains rise into the peaks, and roll and vary in an almost endless succession, and as far as the eye can see, and afford so much gratification to the beholder, they are all barren, and thinly clad with stinted growths of pine, and cedar, and hemlock, and which is not sufficient to cover their granitic nakedness. . . . The eye has been confined by low flat shores, fringed with wood, it could not pass these, and these have generally bounded our vision, here the unprisoned eye passes out into the distance, and roves delighted over immense tracts of undulating country, until the light loses itself in the blue mists that cover the summits of the far distant hills. (234)

At 11:00 a.m. by McKenney's clock, they ate a breakfast of boiled corn, potatoes, tea, and crackers. Then Dr. Zina Pitcher, Schoolcraft, and McKenney set off to explore Granite Point. McKenney decided to cross a little river to get a better view. Rather than get his feet wet, he called to one of the voyageurs to carry him across (he noted in his journal that the usual method of getting into and out of the canoes was on the backs of voyageurs). But the voyageurs had gone to visit the bargemen, so McKenney's servant, Ben Hanson, "who was washing some towels in the river close by, hearing my call, came to inquire what was my pleasure." Hanson took him on his back, slipped in the sand, and pitched McKenney headfirst into the river. The latter reported that after he got into dry clothes, Hanson insisted on trying again—and this time succeeded (237–39).

Keweenaw Peninsula, 1826

To avoid the arduous task of carrying the cargo of the heavily laden barges on the 1826 treaty expedition, the party decided to bypass the portage and take the long way around the Keweenaw Peninsula. While Governor Cass rode on the sluggish barges, McKenney and Hanson accompanied Schoolcraft in his canoe. They quickly lost sight of the barges and made camp on the end of a point. McKenney's sense of reverie from Granite Point had left him, and at the tip of Keweenaw, his mood turned dark. Complaining that his "head ached intolerably," he asserted that "nothing can be more uninteresting or monotonous than the shores of this part of Point Kewewana" (241). He griped that

> not a bird warbles to cheer us. Not a living thing presents itself to vary the solitude. Nothing is heard but the roar of the waves on the shore, nor seen, but the forests that line it, the lake, and the sky. Whether stormy or calm, the roll of the wave is heard. It never ceases. This is the music of the shores. Now and then the cry of the loon is heard—but nothing sings, save in some places an occasional and stray warbler . . . and the mosquitoes. (242)

This radical change in mood was probably influenced by his headache and exacerbated by his growing sense of being cut off from civilization.

Ontonagon River, 1826

Fortunately for McKenney, the 1820 Cass party had visited the copper boulder on the Ontonagon River, so there was no need to do so again in 1826. Otherwise, he might soon have considered Keweenaw Peninsula a fond memory and a place he wished he could return to, for venturing far inland from the familiar shore could be a disorienting and terrifying endeavor. McKenney's experience at the mouth of the Ontonagon River was comparatively benign and pleasant. By that time, the Indian town on the west shore of the river had been deserted: apparently, the inhabitants had moved to another site several hundred yards upriver. McKenney wrote of the remains of lodges with flagstaffs still in place and also provided a description of the legendary copper boulder—"the largest mass of native copper, it is believed, in the world"—but he did not see it for himself. After spending time with the group of Chippewa and the resident trader, observing the women and children, and smoking "almost to suffocation" with the men, he composed his last note for the day: "We are now a little short of two hundred miles from the Fond du Lac, and feel, after our long and baffling voyage so far, to be quite in its neighborhood" (257).

The Keweenaw Peninsula was a psychological barrier as well as a physical one. It was there that McKenney began expressing homesickness, a sense of loneliness, and of a growing anxiety at being separated from family, friends, and familiar society. This territory was different. It was *baffling,* and he did not quite know what to make of it. But encountering groups of Indians who were obviously hungry and poor convinced him that it was an essentially barren land—barren not just in resources but also in terms of society. Without a sophisticated knowledge of the complex associations and expectations of the middle ground and of its seasonal round, McKenney perceived the hungry Indians simply as beggars. He misunderstood their relationship with him, believing that they depended on him, while in fact, the opposite was closer to the truth. If the Cass party had suffered a mishap and lost the provisions they were carrying to Fond du Lac, the consequences would have been much more serious for them than it would have been for the Indians. The Indians were far more adept at living off the land. Even though most of the Chippewa McKenney described seem to have been doing just fine, and in some cases prospering, it was the apparently starving or drunken Indians that stuck in his mind. What was to be done with this place and its inhabitants?

Michael's (Madeline) Island, 1826

McKenney may have found part of the answer to that question on Michael's Island, which would remain the unrivaled social and economic center of the Chequamegon region until the mid-1850s.[53] To McKenney, the island was an oasis of culture in an otherwise bleak and barren country. As his group approached the shore, he could barely express how grateful he was to see that "it looked green, and had the evidences of civilized life, in houses, horses, and cattle, and fences, which I had not seen since I left the Sault." The first thing he did on setting foot on the island was to ask Michael Cadotte, a local trader, if he had any milk, to which Cadotte replied, "Oui Monsieur." McKenney gushed:

> I never enjoyed this article before. It tasted like nectar—and I thought I would never get enough of it. . . . We were received by this worthy French trader with great cordiality. His houses were thrown open for us, and all he had was put freely at our disposal. . . . This is the only spot that has brought gladness to my heart, the associations of home and civilized society, during a voyage of four hundred miles—since we left the Sault. It

> looks like a fairy scene, and every thing is enchantment. Yet the houses are of logs; but they are lathed and plastered. Tame crows appear common in this part of the world. I notice four here that fly after the family as if they were part of it, and had never been wild.[54]

Cadotte's father had been an important trader at the Sault. His mother was Chippewa. In the midst of a landscape that to McKenney seemed barren, Cadotte's home suggested a modest vision of northwoods pastoralism. The next day, while the voyageurs caulked the barges, McKenney took the opportunity to walk around and examine the cleared grounds of the island. He waxed poetic about the fences, the fields, the chickens and cows, the comfortable homes, and the gardens with potatoes, onions, cabbages, and peas. He did not want to leave as soon as they had planned (263). For him, the island was a refuge: "'*O blest seclusion from a jarring world*'"[55] Nevertheless, McKenney thought that he would not be happy there for long. He remarked that there was no orchard and that "no fruit of any kind grows in those regions, except the wild strawberry, the sand cherry, and the whortleberry. And little grain except oats." However, he also noted that "potatoes are grown, and of the finest quality; they are the bread of the traders." In addition to the peas and cabbages, there was also squash "and, where the trader is a Frenchman, there is sure to be some garlic" (264).

McKenney recognized how strategic this location on Chequamegon Bay could be, and he suggested that a government agency there could exert influence on the "void" between the agency at the Sault and the one on the St. Peter's River (currently known as the Minnesota River), "a void which is too often filled up with cruelties, that need to be checked by the presence of some nearer or more central power" (265). He noted that a priest would make a round from Montreal to Fond du Lac every couple of years, and in the meantime, "the scattered remnants of traders, and some few Indians, who have only traditions, when all is left to nature again" (262). Later, on interacting with some Indians east of the Brule River, McKenney remarked:

> Nothing can exceed the poverty and wretchedness of these people!—and their love of tobacco and whiskey. One of the old men who came ashore out of one of these canoes, said he had eat nothing for two days, and yet his first request was for tobacco. In general, it is for whiskey. Tobacco is the Lethean antidote for all their exposures and wants. An Indian loves to

> soothe his brain with it, and as if seeking to do this, never smokes without blowing the fumes, in streams, from his nostrils, as well as his mouth. (269)

Since Michael Cadotte's mother was Chippewa and he was closely associated with the region's Indians, he represented additional proof to McKenney and Cass that Indians—or at least "half-breeds"—could be civilized. In part, it may have been the example of Michael's Island that gave the commissioners the idea to insert one of three additional articles in the treaty that would soon be signed at Fond du Lac (on August 5, 1826) and eventually approved by President John Quincy Adams. Article 4 of the treaty began: "It being deemed important that the half-breeds, scattered through this extensive country, should be stimulated to exertion and improvement by the possession of permanent property and fixed residences." The lands would, however, be in the form of French long lots and clustered on the shores of the St. Mary's River (481).

Article 5 of the treaty was intended to relieve the apparent poverty of the Chippewa, and in recognition of the "sterile nature of the country they inhabit, unfit for cultivation, and almost destitute of game," a $2,000 annuity in money or goods was to be paid at Sault Ste. Marie. Article 6 provided $1,000 annually to fund a school for the "improvement of the Indian youths." In article 7, it was explained that, although Commissioners McKenney and Cass had not been authorized to add the three articles, the "necessity . . . could be fully apparent, only from personal observation of the condition, prospects and wishes of the Chippeway." It was also recognized that the president and Senate might choose to delete the three articles, and if they did so, the other articles would stand (481). Although the document was framed as a peace treaty, the main objective was to secure mineral rights to the Indian lands. That objective was achieved, but significantly, the land title and jurisdiction would remain unchanged.[56] The Indians were at a disadvantage. Cass went to great effort to intimidate them by making a dramatic landing, enacting military drills, and making it clear that their "New Father," the president of the United States, could destroy them if he were angered. But the truth was that many Chippewa were poor and dependent on manufactured goods. They were not in a position to bargain.

Before McKenney left Michael's Island for Fond du Lac, he looked across the channel toward the hills on the mainland and tried to picture

> those beautiful heights of Georgetown. . . . If the area occupied by Washington were a lake, and the hills south-east of the eastern branch, were eighteen miles distant, and as high in proportion to the distance, the resemblance would be *perfect*. It was so agreeable to fancy the likeness, that I found no difficulty in bringing those hills nearer, and in putting a city like Washington where the lake is. Le Point served very well for the southern shore of the Potomac, and some of its bluffs answered for Arlington house. (265)

In thirty years, other men would arrive, look at the same scene, and see a city—a future metropolis with a rich agricultural hinterland. The model for the city would be New York and later Chicago, and the model for the hinterland would be the productive lands farther south and east. Imagination would play a crucial role in the promotion and development of the place, and it reflected the ideology of the people who visited there and later invested their money or lives in the future of the place. In 1826, such a vision lay beyond even the wild imagination of Thomas L. McKenney, and before it could seem even remotely plausible, at least three things needed to be done. First, a thorough assessment of the region's resources had to be made; then, the land had to be surveyed to facilitate ownership of private property; and finally, locks had to be built at the Sault to assist ship transportation. Gradually, all of these requirements would be fulfilled, and two more treaties would be concluded with the Indians, who, in the end, would not be removed but rather would be allowed reservations. By midcentury, the middle ground was dead and buried, but its spirit persisted.

Ordering the Landscape

3

BY THE 1840S, despite centuries of European visitation and habitation and decades after the establishment of U.S. sovereignty, the Eurameri-can impact on the landscapes south of Lake Superior was not so different from the Native American impact in that it was concentrated in dispersed areas, mostly close to the lake. Vast interior areas remained remote, little known, and rarely visited. The situation would change dramatically when geologists began to systematically find and describe the marketable resources and when the ordinance surveyors walked, measured, marked, and described every square-mile section of land. In the process, the surveyors explored, recorded, and mapped the entire region, laying groundwork for the industrial development of the south shore of Lake Superior and in particular the Chequamegon Bay and Penokee-Gogebic regions (fig. 3.1).[1]

As Clarence Glacken said and Norman Thrower demonstrated, "different ways of subdividing land have influenced road patterns, settlements,

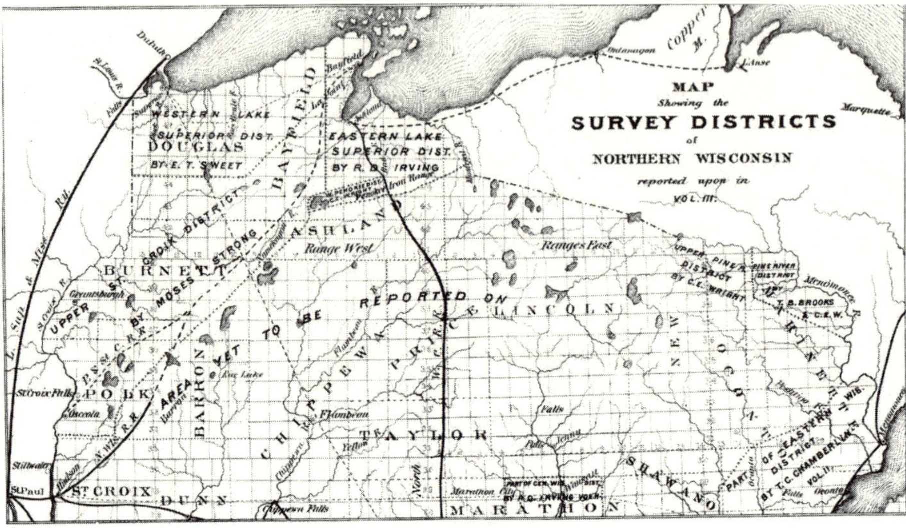

FIGURE 3.1 “Map Showing the Survey Districts of Northern Wisconsin,” from Chamberlin, *Geology of Wisconsin* (1880). Collection of the author.

methods of cultivation, taxation, litigation, even personal comfort and attitudes toward the environment.”[2] The Northwest Ordinance of 1785 declared that land would be surveyed before settlement, that the survey lines would be oriented to the cardinal directions, and that townships would be 6 by 6 miles square, each with 36 square-mile sections. The word *ordinance* is complex and especially appropriate for describing the act that initiated the Public Land Survey (PLS). In essence, it means the “action of ordaining, ordering, or arranging: the fact or condition of being ordered or arranged.”[3] Obviously, the ordinance reflected an effort to impose order not only on the land but also on the people who would inhabit it: an ordered landscape implied an orderly people. The word also has military connotations, as in “arrangement in ranks or rows; esp. in order of battle; battle-array or mode of battle-array; also a display of military force,” which is particularly apt in that the surveyed lands often had resilient and sometimes resistant inhabitants against whom military force was threatened if not used.[4] Finally, like Manifest Destiny, the word *ordinance* has strong religious connotations, as in “a dispensation, decree, or appointment of Providence or of Destiny." A 1669 quotation drives the point home: "The Ordinance of God, whereby every creature is governed and guided." But the Ordinance Survey also had more unambiguously positive motives, the most famous of which was to facilitate Thomas Jefferson's vision of a country of independent yeoman farmers. The various congressional arguments over the size of plots that would be made available reflected concern about the amount of land a single family needed to support itself and to prosper.[5] So, the paradox of the Northwest Ordinance was that it was intended to impose order on the people as well as on the land—and by force if necessary—even as it facilitated landed independence for the masses.

Government-funded geological surveys and the federal public land surveys often complemented each other, but they were generally separate enterprises even when it would have been more efficient to combine them. In the 1840s, Douglas Houghton, the innovative physician, geologist, and entrepreneur, convinced Congress to link the PLS, which divided the land into townships, ranges, and sections to facilitate ownership, and the geological and natural history survey, which (in addition to contributing to general geological knowledge) located, identified, and assessed local resources and suggested how they could best be exploited. Tragically, before he could complete his experimental combined survey, Houghton drowned in Lake Superior, and thereafter, the PLS and the geological surveys were done separately.[6] The first rigorous geological survey of the Wisconsin lands south of Lake Superior was carried out before most of the land had been subdivided by the Ordinance Survey. This situation complicated the mapping and precise location of phenomena.

The Cass Expeditions had established U.S. hegemony over the Lake Superior region and formalized treaties with the Indians, and Schoolcraft's and McKenney's narratives of those expeditions displayed a complex blend of romanticism and cultural chauvinism. But the work of practicing geologists David Dale Owen and Charles Whittlesey represented a new way of seeing the land. Drawing on a growing body of geological knowledge and theory and exhibiting the increasing professionalism of the discipline, Owen was a master coordinator of the large-scale geological survey. Whittlesey was a brilliant field geologist, well versed in geological theory yet remarkably unencumbered by its dogma when empirical evidence suggested alternative explanations. Owen and Whittlesey accurately located and identified the resources that would contribute to the industrial development of the region. Taken together, their works provided a manual for the development of the region, fodder for boosters, information for speculators and settlers, and an important model for future surveys.[7]

The Owen survey was completed between 1847 and 1850, but the public land surveyors took decades to finish surveying the same area. The PLS complemented the geological surveys by laying out first the township and range lines and then the interior sections. This process facilitated the transfer of the land to private ownership. Only when the first geological survey was complete and land parcels were described and ready to sell would the Chequamegon region be ready for settlement. State geological and natural history surveys tended to follow the federal surveys and were part of larger patterns of settlement and national expansion. Typically, the federal surveys were conducted in the territories, in anticipation of statehood and settlement. A primary objective of the Owen survey was to determine if there were mineral deposits in the area, which, under the law, were to be reserved.

Geologists had to be lobbyists as well as entrepreneurs, for they had to convince federal and state legislators to make money available to conduct the surveys. The most successful arguments they mustered involved military reconnaissance and economic development. Few legislators were enlightened enough to vote to fund surveys merely to advance scientific knowledge, yet that was often the main, albeit almost subversive, objective of some geological surveyors. Then as now, it was one thing to impress politicians and quite another to impress scientists. Before President Jefferson sent Meriwether Lewis and William Clark west to find a waterway to the Pacific Ocean, all geological surveys were funded privately by wealthy amateur geologists. Lewis and Clark's 1804 expedition provided a model for funding later reconnaissance surveys.

The 1820 Cass Expedition had military objectives and was funded by the secretary of war's office, whereas the 1847–50 Owen Survey was funded by the Treasury Department and had economic objectives. The reconnaissance surveys established sovereignty and made a cursory assessment of the land; the federal geological and natural history surveys made more detailed and scientifically more rigorous assessments. The ordinance surveys organized the public domain to move into private ownership, and the state survey

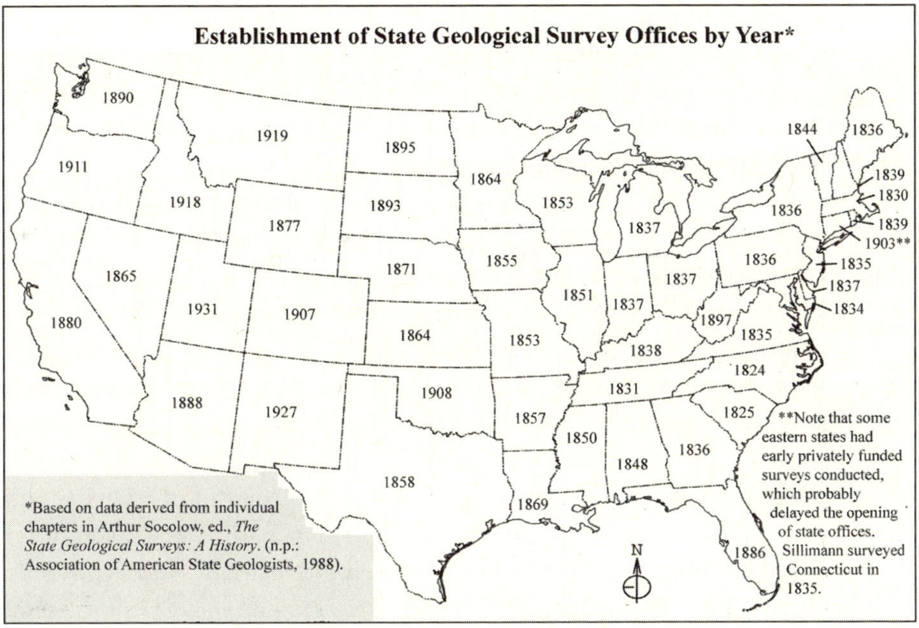

FIGURE 3.2 Establishment of state geological survey offices in the United States by year. Map by author.

offices conducted more detailed and sophisticated assessments of the land (fig. 3.2).[8] Such was the usual order of the surveys, and this pattern was followed on the south shore of Lake Superior. The best surveyors, especially in the territories, were well organized and businesslike, but most important, they were able to function far from help and comfort in often-difficult terrain. The most effective surveyors, such as Douglas Houghton and Charles Whittlesey, shed their city clothes, put on their wilderness costumes, got in and out of their canoes unaided, and enjoyed the camp life.

On the fourteenth day of August, 1845, Charles Whittlesey stood at the top of the portage from Lake Huron to Lake Superior. He was exactly two months shy of his thirty-seventh birthday and about to begin a fifteen-year relationship with the landscapes south of Lake Superior, which would culminate with a special emphasis on the Chequamegon Bay and Gogebic Iron Range regions. His service interpreting the land would be interrupted only by his service in the American Civil War. At this moment in his life Whittlesey was poised on the edge of his first venture onto Lake Superior, a two-month journey along the south shore with frequent forays into the interior country.[9]

Whittlesey was employed as a geologist, and for him, the journey was to be a voyage of discovery—a chance to see new country and, by utilizing his understanding of geological forces together with observation and reason, to unlock its secrets. It was also a chance for him to participate in the frontier experience and to test his own mettle in an extreme landscape. From his vantage point atop the portage, Whittlesey assessed his surroundings. To the east toward Lake Huron, he saw a "flat, wet, marshy piece of land." Westward, the country appeared to be "low and swampy" as far as he could see, but the view was obscured by a thick timber, "principally of spruce, pine, white cedar, birch, and hemlock." As if impatient to see where he would soon be traveling, he hiked to the west for about a mile, where he found a "low eminence rising out of a cedar swamp, composed of masses of rolled granite and other primitive rocks, in size from a small pebble to a diameter of ten feet. The timber among them had been lately blackened by a raging fire." To Whittlesey, "the trunks of [the] charred trees, some standing erect, some leaning against others, and many prostrate on the rocks, contrasted hideously with the white and nakedness of those immense granite boulders which covered the surface." From his vantage point, he could see, on the Canadian side of the lake, a high mountain range extending out of sight, which he found "extensive and gratifying." In the foreground, across the rapids on the St. Mary's River, he could see the white houses of the Hudson's Bay Company's stockaded headquarters. Far down the St. Mary's River, he spotted houses along the banks, with farms extending up the "mountains" in the French long lots. "Here" Whittlesey wrote, " the traders, voyageurs, missionaries, factors, Indian agents, and Indians, reside promiscuously—such is the foreground of the view. Behind and beyond rise the mountain ranges, in that pure atmosphere perfectly distinct at the distance of twenty miles."[10]

Like Allouez, Schoolcraft, and McKenney, Charles Whittlesey would chronicle his journey through this rugged terrain and thereby add a new layer to our understanding of the region. And as his predecessors had done, he would use his descriptive powers to convey key insights about both a place and a time, while providing clues as to why he saw the land and its inhabitants as he did. Whittlesey's writings are especially fertile grounds for understanding the region at the moment just before it was rapidly and irrevocably transformed by urban industrialism. Furthermore, through his work on the 1852 Owen survey, he provided a direct connection to the boosters and promoters and developers who would soon enter the scene. Whittlesey was witness to far more than the land. He also saw changes in the land and the people bringing about those changes: the public land surveyors, the speculators, and the pioneering industrialists.

Below the Sault, significant industrial and urban development was already well under way. But above the rapids of Sault Ste. Marie, even nineteen years after Thomas McKenney's tour, the Lake Superior region remained largely terra incognita—still a middle ground between Indian and European cultures. The French influence remained strong, and voyageurs in birchbark canoes continued to be the backbone of transportation. But Whittlesey's 1845 trip and his contribution to the seminal 1852 Owen Survey represented a break with the tragic-romantic era of Schoolcraft and McKenney. The latter were both employed by the War Department, but Whittlesey was hired first by a Detroit businessman and then by the U.S. Department of the Treasury. Whereas the Cass Expeditions had established U.S. sovereignty over the region and obtained mineral rights from the Indians, Whittlesey's activities, as well as the Public Land Survey he observed in progress, were penultimate steps toward opening up the region to settlement and urban industrial development.

Members of the 1845 party included J. R. Dorr, a Detroit speculator who was funding the expedition; D. P. Bushnell, also from Detroit and the former Indian agent at La Pointe; an "old soldier who officiated as cook"; a whaler back from the Northwest coast; and a company clerk.[11] Whittlesey had been hired as a geologist to locate promising copper lands, but as revealed in his essay on the expedition, he was interested in far more than rock formations and economic possibilities. His opening paragraph hinted at a major transition that was occurring in the region: the world of the Indian, fur trader, and voyageur was fading just as an expansive industrial world was gaining a secure foothold.

The rapids atop the St. Mary's River would remain an impediment to transportation until 1855, when the Soo Locks finally opened. As late as 1852, the Kentucky statesman and western booster Henry Clay argued against funding the locks: "It is a work beyond the remotest settlement of the United States, if not the moon."[12] In 1845, to embark on Lake Superior in a 4-ton yawl seemed daring and even reckless—or at least that is how Whittlesey portrayed it in his essay. The yawl could not be pulled out of the water as quickly as a canoe when the weather changed. But in fact, schooners had been navigating Lake Superior for several years, initially to transport the fish salted and barreled by the American Fur Company and later to begin moving the copper ore that was already being mined on Keweenaw Peninsula. After the Soo Locks finally did open, records indicate that 195 ships made the passage in the first season. In 1895, almost 2,000 ships passed through the locks.[13]

By the 1840s, Whittlesey had come a long way from the log cabin of his birth in 1808. In 1813, his family moved from Connecticut and settled in Ohio. At nineteen, he attended West Point, graduating with honors in 1831. He then served in the Black Hawk War, resigning his commission as soon as it was over. For the next few years, he turned his attention to the study of civil and mining engineering and geology. He also opened a law office in Cleveland and was part owner and coeditor of the *Whig and Herald* until 1837, when he was appointed to the Ohio survey. This post was his first appointment as a geological surveyor. Although Whittlesey was later credited with identifying the state's coal and iron deposits, the project ended in disappointment for him when the legislature prematurely cut off funding after two years. Between 1837 and 1845, he published at least sixteen articles on topics as diverse as copyright law, military history, agriculture, economic geography, elevations in the Northwest, Indian tribes in the Northwest at the time of the Revolution, and vegetation and manures, as well as "A Dissertation upon the Origin of Mineral Coal." Until he died in 1886, Cleveland would be Whittlesey's home base. Yet he seemed to develop a special attachment to the Lake Superior country and to enjoy working in a rugged environment as if the physical challenges heightened his intellectual stimulation.[14]

Charles Whittlesey would play at least three crucial roles in the development of the Lake Superior region. First, he would help to popularize it. His 1846 essay, "Two Months in the Copper Regions," initially published in the *National Magazine*, was aimed at an educated but wide audience.[15] As will be discussed, Whittlesey not only painted a vivid picture of the area but also offered an example or model of how to visit the place that surely played to the popular imagination regarding the frontier. Second, through his extensive geological survey work in the region, he located and described the major resources and pointed the way toward their exploitation while also expanding the scientific knowledge of the place. The third way in which Whittlesey played a role in the development of the region was by convincing his brother Asaph to be one of the first Euramerican settlers. Asaph was among the founders of Ashland, on Chequamegon Bay, and an influential citizen of the region, active in state politics.[16]

As Whittlesey was heading into the Lake Superior country, a party of government surveyors was coming out after spending three months in the interior running a tier of townships into square-mile sections, from Mackinaw northward to Lake Superior. The surveyors' garments were in "shreds and fragments," and they were taking a few days off to repair them. In that rugged country, the survey work was difficult. According to Whittlesey, it was "only by physical energy, and great powers of endurance, that the contractor can realize anything from the prices allowed by Government for its original surveys. They provision themselves by carrying all on their backs, from the depots on the shore."[17] He claimed that the surveys could not have been completed in this terrain without the participation of the "hardy class of Frenchmen and half-breeds, cousin-german to the Canadian voyageur, called 'packers.'" These men typically carried loads of 50 to 70 pounds. They loaded and unloaded the boats, and most important, they could "travel alone in the recesses of the forest without fear of losing their way." Furthermore, they were "patient, cheerful, and obedient; in fact, they are on land what the voyageur is upon the water" and had a "capacity for food" that corresponded with their "ability to endure fatigue" (284).

Clearly, the packers impressed Whittlesey. He expressed deep admiration for their knowledge of and mastery over the environment and believed that they were, at least in part, a product of their environment. He was familiar with the work of George Catlin and probably other frontier artists. Just as the novels of James Fenimore Cooper had influenced the way Thomas McKenney perceived the Indians and camp life on the Cass Expedition, Catlin provided a context for Whittlesey to see the survey party. He wrote that the packers were

> a subject for Catlin, the Indian sketcher. More hale, hearty, and jovial fellows, never broke into the limits of civilization. The northern atmosphere had tinged their cheeks with red, they were all young and active men, glowing with that high animal life, that extreme buoyancy of spirits, which is a stranger to the inhabitants of cities, to those who toss upon feather beds, and live upon soups and comfits. (285)

He contrasted the packers with the eastern gentlemen from the Atlantic shores whom he observed sitting around other campfires nearby, with their

> genteel caps and surtouts, shivering in the raw wind of the morning. Poor fellows! impelled by the hope of wealth to be found in the copper region, they had rushed at steamboat rates to the extremity of navigation, of taverns, and permanent habitations. (286)

In contrast to the shivering urban gentlemen, the laborer of the *pays d'en haut* (upper country) possessed, according to Whittlesey, remarkable powers of endurance: "If circumstances prevent a return to the camp, or the rendezvous, he can lie at the foot of a tree, sleep till daybreak, and resume his tramp without complaint."[18] The packers and voyageurs were at home in the Superior country. They knew the land, how to travel in the forest without getting lost, and how to navigate the great lakes in fragile bark canoes. Perhaps most astonishing was their ability to inhabit two cultural worlds: Amerindian and European. The voyageurs and packers played an indispensable role in the region, mediating between the two worlds.

On the Huron River, Whittlesey's party slept in a lean-to left by surveyors. As they traveled west along the south shore of Lake Superior, beyond the Ontonagon River and as far as the Porcupine Mountains, they were able to read the marks left by the surveyors and know their precise location within the larger Land Ordinance system. At one point, Whittlesey noted that they were "one town, or six miles, north of St. Mary's, and twenty-five towns, or 150 miles west." Their ability to track their progress in this way was important because, according to Whittlesey, the only decent map for navigation was the one Henry Wolsey Bayfield had made twenty years before, and they soon found that their copy was a cheap imitation (301). Furthermore, he noted, "the maps for the copper region, instead of assisting the explorer, were for the interior so erroneous—a fault worse than deficiency—that mistakes equal to a day's travel frequently resulted from a reliance upon them" (321). Getting lost so far from help could be a serious problem.

On September 27, 1845, Whittlesey and his party made camp at the foot of a rapids about 10 miles up the Ontonagon River, 1 mile north of the Ordinance surveyor's correction line, between townships fifty and fifty-one, and 1 mile east of the range line between thirty-nine and forty west. The next day, Whittlesey and Patrick, the whaler, crossed the river and walked due west along the correction line. When they hit range forty-one west, they turned left and headed south. They soon discovered that the region south of the correction line had not yet been surveyed, but they continued on anyway. The sky clouded up, and it began to rain; the downpour continued for four days and five nights. Because of magnetic fluctuations, their compass was not reliable. At that point in his narrative, Whittlesey described what it was like to be lost:

> With the mind in a state of perplexity, the fatigue of travelling is greater than usual, and . . . weakens not only the power of exertion, but of resolution also. The wanderer is finally overtaken with an indescribable sensation—one that must be experienced to be understood—that of *lostness.* At a moment when all his faculties, instincts, and perceptions are in full demand, he finds them all confused, irregular, and weak. When every physical power is required to carry him forward, his limbs seem to be yielding to the disorder of his mind; he is filled with an indefinite idea of alarm, apprehension, and dismay; he reasons, but trusts no conclusion; he decides upon the preponderance of reason and fact as he supposes, and is sure to decide wrong. If he stumbles into a trail he has passed before, or even passed within a few hours, he does not recognize it, or if he should at last, and conclude to follow it, a fatal lunacy impels him to take the wrong end. (318)

Moving beyond the surveyed lands could be disorienting and risky for ordinary men. Especially difficult were the ravine lands and the cedar swamps, "eye-sores" to the explorer or surveyor. Whittlesey said he had experienced "lostness" twice before, once when he thought he was going to take a simple 3-mile walk. He emphasized the importance of having dry matches, food, clothing, and a compass at all times. "Much of the comfort of a trip in this region depends on the outfit," he stated. He recommended carrying hard bread, beans, and salt pork because they were relatively light and compact; tea, coffee, and sugar might not be necessary, but "for the expense and trouble," they were "the greatest and cheapest luxuries that can be had under any circumstances" (342). Most important, he said, one had to take a lot of food—at least 2 pounds per day per person, with more to give to those without. Whittlesey argued that "in this high latitude, with its pure and healthy climate, where the enervating effects of heat upon digestion are unknown, men may eat with impunity what would be fatal to them at the south" (296). He gave detailed instructions on what other items were needed:

> A pocket-compass is necessary for each party. For a pack there is nothing better than a knapsack and straps, without the boards. Ordinary clothing is of no use, for it will disappear in a short time. The surveyors wear trousers made of heavy cotton ticking, and a sort of pea-jacket made of the same. This or medium cotton duck will stand wear, and although moisture comes through, the rains do not. It thickens when wet, and turns long storms better than any thing except oil-cloth. A vest is unnecessary, and instead of suspenders the pantaloons are kept up by a broad belt, on which the tin-cup may be strung. A low, round-crowned, white beaver hat is much worn, but perhaps a light cap of oiled silk, made soft and impervious to rain, is better. For the feet, moccasins or light brogans made of good leather, and plenty of woollen stockings. In the wet season, cowhide boots, made of good but not heavy leather, and very large, but in the shape of the foot. A flint and steel for emergencies, and matches for ordinary use to strike a fire. Without something waterproof around them, the matches will acquire moisture in long spells of wet weather. If you carry a map case, they may be put in a second case, around which the map is rolled. A belt with a leather pouch and a buckle, to carry the hatchet in, is a very great convenience; for nothing is so likely to be lost as a hatchet. We were three days without one in very bad weather, having dropped it on the route. (343–44)

Whittlesey also suggested that taking a tent was a good idea, especially in warm weather when the mosquitoes were abundant and hungry. But he added that "a good, large, heavy Mackinaw blanket is beyond comparison the most necessary article to the voyageur and woodsman" (344). His closing words were aimed at recreationists: "With all these preparations, the lover of exercise and adventure may count upon as much enjoyment on a trip through the Lake Superior country as he will find at home. If he is badly provided, he will be inefficient and uneasy, will suffer many privitations, and perhaps injure his health."[19] To enjoy the camp life, one had to shed the trappings of city life and adopt the ways and dress of the woodsmen—the voyageurs, packers, and guides who in turn had adopted some of the ways and dress of the Indians.[20] Figure 3.3 shows Whittlesey posing in his frontier costume, complete with moccasins.

FIGURE 3.3 Charles Whittlesey, geologist of Ohio, in his frontier field garb, 1858. Courtesy of the Wisconsin Historical Society (WHi-36627).

The voyageur was the personification of romanticism, combining physical and intellectual mastery of sublime environments along with the moral philosophy of the more rakish of the romantic poets—including a love of wine, women, and song. In his 1665 journal, Father Allouez documented how effectively the voyageurs navigated in Indian territory, comfortably inhabiting the middle ground between the European and Indian worlds. The voyageurs were as at home in the upper country with the Indians as they were in the village back at Trois-Rivières. Both Schoolcraft and McKenney had marveled at the endurance and skill of their voyageurs in the 1820s, and they often portrayed them overcoming almost impossible odds and deftly reading sky and water, anticipating storms and swells. Both men also described the way in which the voyageurs approached a village: they would pause to put on their finest clothes, including brightly colored sashes, and then paddle at full speed toward the landing, singing at the top of their lungs. Those on shore might fire guns in the air to welcome them. Like other observers, Owen and Whittlesey also commented on the voyageurs' endurance and especially on their mastery of the landscape.

Unlike Indians, who were often both romanticized and denigrated by the same author, voyageurs were consistently romanticized in the works of most writers. In truth, the voyageurs led difficult and dangerous lives, and not unlike the romantic poets, they tended to die young. An old voyageur was an ironic figure. On Madeline Island in 1826, Thomas McKenney spoke to a decrepit, diseased old voyageur, aged beyond his sixty-nine years, who had been reduced to a mere fisherman. When asked about his former life as a voyageur, the old man slapped his hands and responded, "in the animating and single belief in his supremacy as a *north-western voyageur,*" that he had been "the greatest man in the north-west."[21] Later writers, most notably Grace Lee Nute, largely relying on firsthand accounts from the romantic era, have continued the tradition of romanticizing the voyageurs. Nute even opened her classic history of the voyageur with an epigraph that beautifully expressed this image:

> Said one of these men, long past seventy years of age: "I could carry, paddle, walk and sing with any man I ever saw. I have been twenty-four years a canoe man, and forty-one years in the service; no portage was ever too long for me. Fifty songs could I sing. I have saved the lives of ten voyageurs.

> Have had twelve wives and six running dogs. I spent all my money in pleasure. Were I young again, I should spend my life the same way over. There is no life so happy as a voyageur's life!"[22]

The little crosses marking fallen voyageurs along portages and rapids were evidence that the life was a hard one. It is impossible to state exactly how much romanticism colored the perception of those who observed the voyageurs, but it is safe to say that it must have been a significant influence on many contemporary observers. Like the Indians, voyageurs are part of the bedrock mythological storyscape of the Lake Superior country. The final irony was that voyageurs and packers played a vital role in completing the surveys that spelled the end of the world as they knew it.

One way to read Whittlesey's 1846 essay is as a guide for those who were daring enough to seek recreation in remote country, far from soft beds, taverns, and civilization in general. Although there was something sublime about the rugged life in the woods and on the great lake, the region was best enjoyed with certain comforts. But the urbane woodsman shared an affinity with the voyageur. By partially adopting his dress, from moccasins and a broad belt to a silk hat and a Mackinaw blanket, the adventurer could not only better adapt to the environment but also imaginatively participate in the frontier. In this regard, Whittlesey's essay contrasts sharply with Schoolcraft's and McKenney's accounts of their journeys in the 1820s. Neither Schoolcraft nor McKenney gave any hint in his narrative that he thought others might follow his example. That Whittlesey's essay seemed to assume others would follow him reflected the increasing accessibility of Lake Superior, as well as changing attitudes toward recreation. Although the "official" closing of the frontier in 1890 is often cited as the stimulus for the elite passion for roughing it, Whittlesey's essay confirms that some men self-consciously sought to participate in the frontier long before it was perceived as an endangered commodity.[23] Just fourteen years earlier, in 1831, Alexis de Tocqueville reported that frontiersmen thought he was mad when he explained he wanted to go into the wilderness for pleasure. Roderick Nash cites de Tocqueville's account as evidence that Americans, at least on the frontier, did not yet appreciate wilderness as the more urbane Europeans did.[24] Many scholars have accepted Nash's interpretation, yet they seem to have overlooked evidence that some people, including geologists and laborers such as voyageurs, very self-consciously sought to have a wilderness experience. It is possible that those who traveled with the voyageurs learned to appreciate the camp life as much from the laborers as from the romantic poets.

For example, Schoolcraft's and McKenney's narratives contained frequent references to the apparent delight the voyageurs experienced in working as well as playing in their environment. They sang as they paddled and portaged and engaged in contests of strength. And when their employers participated in a trip, they seemed to regard it as a recreational experience—a chance to see the sites, to rough it a little, to shoot game birds, to catch fish on a fly, and to sit around the campfire. For his part, Charles Whittlesey certainly aimed his essay, to some degree, toward American wilderness enthusiasts, as the following passage reveals. Describing his experience on August 16, when wind forced his party ashore just past the Two Heart River, he wrote:

> Notwithstanding the sand-flies and mosquitoes, it was comfortable to lie down once more upon the green grass and fragrant wintergreens of that shore. The weather was warm and hazy. Some wandered through the sand hills and swamps; some, wrapped in blankets as a defense against the flies, sought in vain for sleep; others, with the fish-hook and artificial fly, rowed up the creek in pursuit of speckled trout. A good dinner and supper of these fish was the result of the expedition.[25]

Whittlesey listed the game he had seen (including partridge, red squirrels, bear, moose, reindeer, lynx, and rabbits in abundance) and also made note of the game he had not seen (such as turkey, deer, and black squirrel).

Elsewhere, he recounted how a storm forced his party to take refuge west of the Grand Sable (probably at Point au Sable). Avoiding travel the next day due to the weather, they invited another party to join them at 1:00 p.m. for an "entertainment." The group feasted on soup, boiled ham, bread, and pickles—the latter being such a treat that they christened a nearby brook Pickle Creek. They sat on camp stools and bundles, drank tea and coffee from tin cups, and ate a quantity that "probably exceeded that of ordinary dinners, as much as it does at the annual meals of the Aldermen of New York and London" (295).

Charles Whittlesey's biographer wrote that "the wild life of the woods threading the streams, with a guide and voyageurs, had great attractions for him."[26] Educated at West Point, disciplined by his military experience, and learning what he could from the inhabitants of the land, Whittlesey moved through the landscape observing, describing, and defining with a competence hitherto unmatched in the region.[27] He played an essential part in the industrial occupation of new territory by providing answers to three basic questions: What are the resources? What is their extent? And where are they located? But he also made significant contributions to geological science and to the understanding of the land and how it was formed. In part based on his fieldwork in the Lake Superior region—and despite the fact that, in 1843, a committee of the Association of American Geologists and Naturalists had settled the North American glaciation debate in favor of the iceberg theory—Whittlesey is credited with numerous firsts. He was the first glacial geologist in North America; the first to describe the "forest bed" in drift (which would help prove that there was more than one period of glaciation in North America); the first to map end moraines and the extent of glaciation in North America; the first to argue that glaciers could erode lake basins; the first to come up with a regional classification of drift; the first to explain the origin of kettle holes; the first to trace drift in the subsurface; and the first to calculate that during the time of maximum ice advance, the sea level was 350 to 400 feet lower. In 1838, Whittlesey declared that drift was stratified; in 1859, he argued that it was possible for glaciers to move over level ground, which would explain all glacial phenomena, and that kettle holes resulted from the action of glacier ice and not from icebergs; and in 1864, he presented evidence that glaciers had carved some bays and rock-bound lakes.[28]

Each point in Whittlesey's journey can be followed by reference to either township and range or place-name. Although he was with a party whose primary concern was to scout out potential copper claims, his keen insights helped to geographize the landscape. And his passion to unlock the secrets of the landscape guided his appreciation of scenery, as expressed, for example, in his description of the Grand Sable. Schoolcraft and McKenney were awed by the Pictured Rocks, but Whittlesey preferred the Grand Sable: after passing Grand Marais, he was struck by how

> the low, regular, dreary shore of sand suddenly changed to a lofty wall of the same material, rising from the water's edge as steep as it will lie, to the height of 400 feet. . . . The *Grand Sable* struck us with more force, because of the sudden transition from a low uninteresting shore, to a bold, lofty,

> regular scarp, four times the height of the tallest trees. But there was upon this Sable no trees or other vegetation, either on the face towards the lake, which was nearly perpendicular, or upon the summit; all was one pile of sand, yet so clear, so regularly stratified and so beautifully variegated by colors, white and red, that the prospect was not dreary, but rather sublime. . . . To me this sight was more grand and curious than the Pictured Rocks. Whence came this mass of sand?[29]

The landscape was full of *mysteries* to discover, investigate, and describe. For a moment only, Whittlesey allowed himself to respond to the Pictured Rocks as he was culturally expected to, referring to the "frightful aspect" of the passage near Grand Island and the high vertical walls

> in places worn into large caverns, in others, colored in fantastic yet grim figures, half real and half imaginary, yellow, green, and black; shapes neither animal nor in the likeness of anything else that is natural, but so near the natural to give rise to the idea of monsters, griffins, and genii. Such are the Pictured Rocks, before which the Indian thinks of his Manitou, and the Frenchman crosses himself with profound reverence. (298)

But after describing the scene in romantic terms, Whittlesey the clear-headed empirical geologist promptly deconstructed it. Referring to a diagram in which he broke the geological elements of the Pictured Rocks in six parts, he wrote:

> The soft conglomerate (No. 1) yields to the incessant wear of the wave, which, rolling in from deep water, strikes with great power. When the undermining process has extended a few yards, the hard stratum next above falls, and with it the superincumbent mass. Much of this dissolves in time, leaving the fragments of No. 2 [compact sandstone] visible in the clear water, in great blocks, at various depths beneath the surface. The colors are furnished by the dripping solutions of iron, in the state of oxide, carbonate, and sulphate; by moss growing upon the face of the rocks, and probably by the green carbonate of copper. The niches, caves, and angles, follow naturally from a rock of different degrees of hardness, acted upon by the same disintegrating force. (299)

In this and other writings, Whittlesey displayed his skills of careful observation, coupled with a disciplined imagination that allowed him to visualize changes in the rocks, the formation of the landscape, and the larger implications of those changes.

Cultural and Scientific Changes after the 1820s

In the introduction to his seminal 1852 work entitled *Report of a Geological Survey of Wisconsin, Iowa, and Minnesota; and Incidentally a Portion of Nebraska Territory,* David Dale Owen compared his own survey with Lt. Stephen H. Long's 1823 survey of the Red River valley. He noted how inadequate the geology of the earlier survey had been: "At the period when Mr. Keating made his observations on that expedition, the science of Geology was, comparatively, in its infancy; and he did, doubtless, for his time, as much as could be expected."[30] The same could be said for Schoolcraft's geological report from the 1820 Cass Expedition. It was a low-budget, seat-of-the-pants undertaking with little support from the larger operation (no dawdling just to study rocks), and typical for his day, Schoolcraft was largely self-trained.

Throughout the nineteenth century, corps of practicing geologists were employed by federal and state governments to survey the public domain. In the early decades of the century, the academic training of the geologists tended to be focused more on letters and the classics and less on arts such as chemistry and mineralology. As the century progressed, the arts, or applied sciences, especially geology, gained in academic respectability. By the 1840s, many geologists were well prepared to conduct geological surveys. Two of the most exceptional practicing geologists of the period were Owen, based in New Harmony, Indiana, and Whittlesey, based in Cleveland, Ohio.

Henry Schoolcraft represented the era of romantic or literary science, but Whittlesey and Owen represented the era of the scientific survey and were part of the evolving scientific establishment. Owen studied and lectured in Europe, and both he and Whittlesey made significant contributions to the scientific literature. Both men were, in some ways, ahead of their time. Owen threw himself into methodological issues, attempting, for instance, to convince his colleagues to use consistent symbology in their reports and geological maps so that they could better communicate and to facilitate comparison and the discerning of larger geological patterns. Whittlesey, by contrast, dived into the landscape itself, and with few tools besides a hammer and a well-trained mind, he compiled an impressive list of geological firsts, often contradicting the accepted views of his peers in the process.

The premier scientific journal of the time in the United States was the *American Journal of Science*, widely known as "Silliman's journal" for its founder, Benjamin Silliman. Silliman's career began in what might be called the romantic, classical period when science was a gentleman's hobby and many practitioners were self-trained. He was appointed as Yale University's first professor of geology in 1819, even though he had never taken a class in the subject. Nevertheless, he turned out to be a good choice for the job. As a mentor to young scholars and especially as the founder and first editor of the *American Journal of Science*, Silliman was influential in the early development of science and especially geology in the United States.[31]

Silliman's journal was associated with the annual conference held by the Association of American Geologists and Naturalists. The organization's fourth gathering, held at the New York State Geological Museum in Albany, New York, for the week beginning April 25, 1843, illustrated the state of science during that period. The conference was attended by an eclectic group, including some of the most prominent scientists of the day. On the afternoon of the third day, David Dale Owen presented a paper entitled "On the Geology of the Western States." His colleagues were so impressed by two 18-feet-long charts he had prepared to depict the rock strata over a large territory that they asked him to present a special session on the construction of the charts. Owen utilized techniques he had learned in his training as an artist to quickly make detailed images that could be clearly seen in daylight or candlelight. His most important contribution at the meeting, however, was his plea to his colleagues that they adopt uniform means of describing geological structures, to facilitate communication with their European colleagues and with each other. Unfortunately, Owen was about fifty years ahead of his time in this regard.[32]

On the fifth day of the meeting, John L. Hayes read a report prepared for a resolution by the association on the "probable influence of icebergs upon drift."[33] The information was based on interviews with roughly eighty persons involved in the whale and seal fisheries who had seen icebergs firsthand, as well as "authentic published accounts." Hayes testified to the "enormous mechanical power" of icebergs and said that, like glaciers, they could transport blocks of earth and rocks. Furthermore, icebergs could be grounded in very deep water and stay in place for many years. From Hayes's report, five inferences were drawn: icebergs may have caused the striations observed in rocks in North America; icebergs must have been involved in forming accumulations analogous to glacial moraines; icebergs had an influence in forming drift in North America; erratics, especially on hills with valleys, were probably deposited there by icebergs; and based on observations of modern icebergs, drift or erratics were not likely to be found far from their source.

Another speaker, C. T. Jackson, noted that it was formerly supposed that the drift phenomena had been created by the flood recorded in the book of Genesis; however, he said, most geologists now believed the drift had occurred prior to the creation of man: "Hence we must conclude that man was not formed until the world was finished and prepared for his abode. The geologist sees in the diluvium not proofs of Divine vengeance, but evidences of the highest wisdom and goodness of the Creator in thus preparing and commingling the soils of the earth" (320). He went on to argue for scientific method and progress, wherein new hypotheses should be rigorously debated so that, ultimately, the truth would be found based on the salient facts. As for glaciation, Jackson said, "Many eminent men incautiously embraced the new theory, which within two or three years from its promulgation, has been found utterly inadequate, and is now abandoned by many of its former supporters" (321). Joseph Nicollet vociferously agreed with Jackson, but another scientist, Edward Hitchcock, said he could not endorse Jackson's contention that the glacial theory "was already dead and waiting to be buried." Hitchcock argued that geologists generally agreed that drift and striations in rocks had been caused by ice and water—they merely disagreed on the proportions. He predicted that if the truth were ever determined, these phenomena would be found to have multiple causes (325). Nevertheless, the consensus of the meeting was decidedly against glaciation, and as Stanley Totten and George White recently pointed out, this effectively set glacial geology in the United States back by a generation.[34] Though the discipline of geology had become more rigorous, organized, and professional by the 1840s, it was still primitive by today's standards.

The 1852 Owen Survey

David Dale Owen conducted pioneering geological surveys of three states and three territories, published the first connected picture of the geological structures and the mineral resources of the upper Mississippi Valley, and served as a role model for later geological surveyors.[35] By the 1840s, he was internationally known as the leading U.S. authority on (middle) western geology. The son of the utopian Scottish industrialist Robert Owen, he seemed to share his father's progressive social vision. At a July 4th oration delivered in New Harmony, Indiana, in 1845, he expressed concern that the "politico-economical paradoxes" that allowed poverty and hunger to exist in a land of plenty and denied some access to an education threatened the liberties of Americans. But he expressed a faith in the "law of progression" working to bring human liberty to perfection.[36] One of Owen's motives in conducting geological surveys stemmed from his belief that until the people of the western states developed their own manufacturing base, they would be impoverished, sending their wealth eastward for commodities they could well make themselves.

By federal law until 1846, mineral lands were to be reserved, but in that year, the law was changed to allow for the sale of Wisconsin and Iowa lead lands, which had been surveyed by Owen in 1839. Early in 1847, Congress passed acts to create two new land districts that were to be surveyed and sold to the public at a higher price than other lands.[37] Owen's 1852 *Report of a Geological Survey of Wisconsin, Iowa, and Minnesota* provided the first comprehensive description of the geology of the Northwest. In addition, his survey was a model for later territorial surveys conducted by Ferdinand V. Hayden, Clarence King, John Wesley Powell, and George Wheeler, and it made a significant contribution to the scientific literature and became a frequently cited handbook for the development of the region. Publication of the survey was a watershed event in the history of the Chequamegon Bay region because it highlighted the area as one ripe for economic development.

Owen's *Report* was intended as a guide for the settlement and development of the area it covered, and it was certainly relied on as such by the early Yankee and other settlers in the Chequamegon Bay region. The work was also widely quoted and copied by boosters, from Iowa to Wisconsin.[38] But its impact on development of that region went beyond suggesting where the best townsites were, where the best soil for farming could be found, or how best to exploit the region's resources. The most long-lasting influence of Owen's *Report* may have been in the way it helped to codify an aesthetic approach to seeing the Chequamegon region. Both Owen and Whittlesey recognized the scenic and tourist potential of the area, and this is reflected not only in their narratives but also in the woodcut prints that adorn the book. Owen himself composed and sketched many of the scenes.

The 1852 Owen survey encompassed more than 200,000 square miles, an area roughly 750 miles from north to south and 350 miles from east to west. The large map that accompanied the text covered an area from 38° to 49° latitude and from 89°30' to 96°30' longitude.[39] The survey was a major undertaking, and Owen made sure that the final publication would match the quality of the content.[40]

Sitting at his desk at his home base in New Harmony on October 30, 1851, David Dale Owen addressed an introductory letter to J. Butterfield, commissioner of the General Land Office in Washington, D.C.[41] In his letter, Owen emphasized the utilitarian aspects of his survey, which he had just sent off to the press. Even though the land needed to be surveyed before it could be offered for sale, many in Congress saw the geological and natural history surveys as an extravagance. Selling scientific surveys to a reluctant Congress was a tough assignment, which may explain why Owen seemed almost apologetic and even defensive in asserting that scientific knowledge had been gained from the survey:

> It has been my aim, during the entire conduct of this exploration, to make the strictly practical and business portion of the survey the chief end and object of our operations. Scientific researches, which to some may seem purely speculative and curious, are essential as preliminaries to those practical results. Further than such necessity dictates, they have not been pushed, except as subordinate and incidental, and chiefly at such periods as, under the ordinary requirements of public service, might be regarded as leisure moments; so that the contribution to science thus incidentally afforded, and which a liberal policy forbade to neglect, may be considered, in a measure, a voluntary offering, tendered at little or no additional expense to the Department.[42]

Owen emphasized how useful the information in his survey would be to "the present settlers, or to those seeking locations in the district of country of which they treat." He also stressed that, though there was paleontological, mineral, lithological, and stratigraphic information that would be useful to the geologist, the bulk of the narrative was aimed at the general reader.

He and his team had traced out and defined the boundaries of the "trap ranges" from the Bois Brulé to the Michigan border and concluded that "in this part of the Chippewa Land District, there are no copper lands, with sufficient promise of productive veins, to justify the Department in setting them apart as a mineral reservation" (xiv). This statement cut to the heart of the matter, suggesting one of the main reasons the survey was funded. Because it offered evidence that there were no significant deposits of minerals such as copper or lead that, under the law, should have been reserved or sold at a higher price, the survey of 1852 effectively opened up northern Wisconsin to general settlement. With legal obstacles lifted, only the challenges presented by the physical environment remained to impede settlement and development.

The Owen text can be read as a guide to the development of a large region that included the Chequamegon Bay area. Arguably a precursor to W. A. Henry's *Northern Wisconsin, a Hand-Book for the Homeseeker* (1896) and similar publications in other states, Owen's work was used by state agencies, speculators, boosters, farmers, and other settlers.[43] Until later surveys were completed by the state, it was the most authoritative document on the northern Wisconsin environment and its potential for development. For decades after its publication, Owen's *Report* would be widely cited, quoted, and copied.

As capable as the surveyors were, the 1852 survey could support different conclusions regarding the development possibilities of the region. In his introduction, Owen seemed to discourage settlement when he described the extensive "refuse" lands:

> There are portions of the District, chiefly in the vicinity of the sources of the Black and Chippewa Rivers, and of the streams flowing north into Lake Superior, which are, in part, so hopelessly arid, that, in our generation, they will assuredly never be purchased or occupied; in part so covered with erratic boulders, that the traveler can step from one to the other, for miles, without setting foot on the drift-soil on which they lodge, and that a bridle-path for a pack-horse cannot be picked out over the country they

FIGURE 3.4 Detail from the map in Owen's *Report* (1852) showing the region surveyed by Charles Whittlesey. Collection of the author.

> cover; in part, again, so intersected by countless ponds and swamps, that fish, frogs, and water-fowl must, in our day at least, be their only inhabitants.[44]

According to Owen, the so-called refuse lands were "so wholly worthless" that they did not warrant sectioning or even surveying; they amounted to some 15,000 square miles, or about 6 percent of the roughly 250,000 square miles encompassed by the survey—much of it in northern Wisconsin. Owen suggested that not surveying the refuse lands would save more money than the entire 1852 survey had cost.

Skillfully tying scientific to practical economic considerations, Owen showed how different geological formations were associated with different soil types and how each soil type offered a different agricultural potential. Based on Charles Whittlesey's survey, the region south of Lake Superior, from the St. Louis River to the Montreal River and inland to the Penokee-Gogebic range, could be divided into four general types of soil and thus four distinct agricultural districts (fig. 3.4). Owen described the drift soil of what would later be called Bayfield Peninsula and high points of the Apostle Islands as "hardly fit for cultivation." Somewhat better were the red clay, marly soils covering most of the level uplands around the coast and on the islands. The trap soil, located near the foot of "igneous outbursts" and on high ridges and slopes, were described as "next in richness to the alluvial lands," which were unfortunately limited to a small area on the east fork of the Bad River. Furthermore, a large portion of the country was poorly drained—a problem that could only be remedied by an expensive system of drainage, "which cannot be expected to be undertaken in a new country where good land is so easily obtained" (xxxii–xxxiii). Owen expressed guarded optimism that the red clay or marl soils that dominated the Lake Superior basin could be cleared and plowed by the same deep subsoil methods used in Maryland and Virginia and that they "would become sufficiently dry for most kinds of crops and garden vegetables" (xxxiii). A geographically closer analogy was the settlement of five hundred Cree Indians at Prince Rupert's Landing, below the Assiniboian colony. Owen had observed these Indians living in comfortable, whitewashed log cabins, cultivating 5 to 10 acres of land each and raising cattle (xxx).

Owen's depiction of La Pointe and Chequamegon Bay was similar to, though not as dramatic as, McKenney's flowery 1826 description. The text was accompanied by a woodblock print based on a sketch completed by a local Ojibwa named Aindi-bi-tunk (fig. 3.5). The picture was then engraved by N. Orr and cut into wood by C. Gildenmeister. Most of the other sketches in the *Report* were made in the field by Owen himself or by his brother Richard. Aindi-bi-tunk's picture was composed from a promontory of Madeline Island. In the foreground are four Indians huddled in blankets and looking toward the focal point of the picture, "the beautiful village of La Pointe" (xxxiii). The Indians are shown as if on the outside looking in, from the periphery toward the center.

FIGURE 3.5 "La Pointe and Bay of Madeline Island, Lake Superior," woodblock print from Owen's *Report* (1852). Collection of the author.

In his influential 1835 "Essay on American Scenery," Thomas Cole wrote that although the Great Lakes possessed "some of the attributes of the ocean," they lacked "sublimity."[45] Owen may have consciously contradicted Cole when he wrote:

> Lake Superior has, at times, not only the varied interest, but the sublimity, of a true ocean. Its blue, cold, transparent waters, undisturbed by tides, lie, during a calm, motionless and glassy as those of any small, secluded lake, reflecting with perfect truth of form and colours, the inverted landscape that slopes down to its smooth, sandy beach. But when this inland sea is stirred by the rising tempest, the long sweep of its waves, and the curling white-caps that crest its surface, give warning, not only to the light bark canoe, still much used along its shores, but also to sloop and schooner and lake steamer, to seek some sheltering haven. At such times, craft of every description may be seen running before the wind, or beating up against it,

> all making for the most favorite harbour on the lake,—the sheltering bay of Madeline Island.[46]

Owen claimed that Chequamegon Bay was capable of holding and protecting "a numerous fleet of the largest class vessels" (xxxiii). He thought that La Pointe had excellent potential as a townsite, being level and spacious with a good red marl soil ("capable, under a proper system of tillage, of returning to the husbandman a hundred-fold, and of producing fruits and vegetables in perfection"), the most productive fishing grounds on the lake, and a milder and more equable climate than elsewhere in Wisconsin. But he thought that La Pointe would be best suited as "a place for health and pleasure." According to Owen, La Pointe "not only [was] one of the most commanding and accessible situations on Lake Superior, but it present[ed] one of the most agreeable and picturesque lake scenes the tourist can well imagine."[47] In addition to the scenery, the beach was sandy and gently sloping, offering sure footing for swimmers. Furthermore, there were unexcelled sport fishing opportunities within a short distance. Owen had little to say about the potential of the mainland around Chequamegon Bay—the future sites of Ashland, Bayfield, and Washburn. Perhaps the village on La Pointe made it easier to envision future development there rather than on the wilder-looking mainland shore.

Although a large portion of the south shore lands were not promising for agriculture, the findings summarized by Owen suggested that a modest agricultural development was possible. It took imagination to foresee any development at all. This was a rugged country, and even when the land was not forbidding, the insects could be awful. Owen was not prone to complaining, but he did devote a paragraph to describing these pests:

> Venomous insects, in such insufferable quantities, that, at certain seasons, they destroy all comfort or quiet, by day or by night. Among the pineries of Northern Wisconsin, and more or less throughout the whole above designated region, the buffalo-gnat, the *brulot* and the sand-fly, to say nothing of myriads of musquitoes, carry on incessant war against the equanimity of the unfortunate traveler. I and other members of the corps, when unprovided with the necessary defense, have had our ears swelled to two or three times their natural size, and the line of our hats marked, all round, by the trickling blood.[48]

In some areas, he said, he and his crew could not have completed their work without mosquito netting over the head and face. Owens painted an image of an interior region that was almost impassable in areas, with tangled cedar bogs, slippery and steep ravines, and thick and dark forests.

Charles Whittlesey's Survey of the Chequamegon Bay–Penokee-Gogebic Region

Charles Whittlesey was a perfect choice to head the subcorps that completed the geological survey of the Chequamegon Bay and Penokee-Gogebic region. He had already proven his willingness to enter rugged territory, and more important, he had demonstrated his ability to come back out not only alive but also with useful information. Even more so than David Dale Owen, Whittlesey was intellectually engaged with the Great Lakes region, especially Lake Superior. Owen excelled most in orchestrating the logistics of the large regional survey and in painting the larger picture of North American geology, but Whittlesey seemed especially drawn to the smaller region of the western south shore of Lake Superior. Indeed, he had a personal and professional connection with the area that spanned two decades. Had Whittlesey achieved his goal of becoming Wisconsin's first state geologist, the legendary Increase Allen Lapham would have had serious competition as the state's first and most brilliant scientist.[49]

Charles Whittlesey's work represented a break from the overtly romantic science of Schoolcraft's era—but not a clean break. Whittlesey, too, was occasionally inspired by the scenery, and sometimes, he compared landscapes to paintings and even invoked the sublime. But at his core, he was a hard-nosed, clearheaded, fiercely objective scientist. Thoroughly trained in the practical arts at West Point and disciplined by his war experience, he was ideally suited to provide a rigorous and accurate description of the area by the time he first entered the Lake Superior landscape in 1845. His two-month trip on the lake that year broke with the past in several ways. First, he was employed by a businessman rather than the federal government, as Cass, Schoolcraft, and McKenney had been. Second, his party did not rely on voyageurs or Indians. And third and most significant, Whittlesey did not cling to the shore but eagerly extended his explorations inland.

Whittlesey's portion of Owen's *Report* was titled "Geological Report on That Portion of Wisconsin Bordering on the South Shore of Lake Superior" (423–47). Of his five chapters, only the first (and longest) focused on the south shore lands. The fifth chapter examined lumbering on the shores of Green Bay and is relevant to the south shore of Lake Superior because he may have seen the lumbering there as a model for future activity on some portions of the south shore of Lake Superior. Whittlesey devoted his third chapter to the red clay and drift soils so prominent in the region and displayed his characteristic innovation by using data gained from wells dug throughout the region.[50]

He emphasized the importance of the map that accompanied the final report (fig. 3.4). That portion of the survey area had not yet been subjected to the lineal survey, so it was a challenge to accurately describe phenomena in terms of location. Using the map for orientation, Whittlesey divided the Chequamegon and Penokee-Gogebic region into four basic rock classifications: sedimentary, trappous (volcanic origin), metamorphosed (slates), and granitic. He hypothesized:

> Since these four systems of rocky beds and masses underwent their last disturbance, the superficial materials have been deposited, reaching from lake-level, and from unknown depths below, up to the highest summits, 1282 feet above the Lake, or 1906 above the Ocean. . . . They are doubtless of the *Quaternary* epoch, and are connected in their origin with sudden and recent movements and upheavals on the north shore, attended by intense heat, by which causes the ancient waters were powerfully agitated and charged with mud and coarse gravel.[51]

On Whittlesey's map, the immediate hinterland of Chequamegon Bay was divided into three basic zones.[52] Between Bayfield Peninsula to the west and the Penokee-Gogebic to the southeast lay the low red clay marl lands, which laid atop red sandstone and constituted most of the shore or lake bluffs from the Montreal to the Brulé rivers. "Although it is called a *clay,*" he reported, "there is very little of it sufficiently argillaceous to make brick. On Madeline Island, and on the Maringouin Fork of Bad River, there are patches from which bricks can be made, but in general it is too sandy, or too calcerous."[53] Whittlesey observed that the process of laying down clay could be observed over the bottom of the west end of the lake where streams carried down large quantities of the material during every rain and wave action continually dislodged and carried out small particles in suspension. He reasoned that one could estimate the rapidity of sedimentary action based on a comparison to data from a sunken schooner in Lake Erie, near Cleveland. In 1843, the *Acorn* sank in 60 feet of water, and after two months, it had a quarter inch of mud on its deck (428–49).

Whittlesey described Bayfield Peninsula as a mass of hills between Chequamegon Bay and the Brule River. He recognized the landmass as being composed of a recent drift, not uniform, and marked by water action. The central portion of the peninsula contained "large tracts of barren, water-washed land, and moderately coarse gravel . . . [and was] chiefly remarkable for its great elevation and its prodigious mass" (429). Whittlesey also noted the drift terraces, which in some places, he claimed, were so distinct that they could be plainly seen and counted from 10 miles away on a clear day. Although they were not uniform in height, he said, "the impression is very strong on the mind of the beholder, that they are of submarine occupance, that they have been modified by the temporary action of the waves of retiring seas" (428). Whittlesey also observed that the sandstone deposits overlying so much of the Lake Superior basin were laid down after the granites he observed on the Wisconsin, Chippewa, and Montreal rivers, for they rested on them. Further, he argued that since that time, "a prolonged and intense internal gaseous action has taken place, and the trap, hornblendic, and greenstone masses have been ejected, and also with them irregular protrusions of *recent* granite and syenite. The metamorphic slates have been elevated during these convulsions, and the sedimentary rocks thrust away to the northward, and tilted at high angles" (429). He hypothesized that there were four periods of igneous action, which produced four different trappose formations: (1) black and red; (2) greenstone trap, on the west; (3) augite and hornblende; and (4) granite, syenite, and coarse hornblende rocks, north of Lac des Anglais. Further, he stated that "the same materials, under different circumstances of fluidity, pressure, and rapidity of cooling, may take all of these forms." This situation complicated the dating of the formations, so he placed all four trap formations together in an era between the red sandstone deposits and the metamorphic uplifts, "for it is by the appearance of this group that both these systems have been pushed aside, one to the north, the other to the south" (430).

The heart of the region, as described by Whittlesey, was not Chequamegon Bay but rather the Bad River and the iron range at the headwaters of its east fork. He noted that the Indians called the river Mashkeg-zibe, which meant "River of Marshes," whereas the voyageurs called it Mauvais, which was translated to the current "Bad River" (431). Just a couple of miles inland from Lake Superior, what Whittlesey called the Mashkeg Fork flowed into the main stream of the Bad River.[54] At this juncture, there was an Indian village known as the Mission. According to Whittlesey, the Mashkeg Fork had three principal branches—Pike River, Rivière l'Eau Claire, and Rivière la Brache. He identified the headwater at Long Lake.[55] On the other side of Long Lake were the headwaters of the St. Croix River, which connected this region, by bark canoe, to the Mississippi River. The east fork entered Bad River about 7 miles above the falls. Whittlesey and his crew went up Bad River to Long Lake from Lake Superior, whereas Owen approached Long Lake from the other direction with a different group. While there, Owen sketched a picture of the lake from the end of the portage, as shown in Figure 3.6. The scene is that of a typical northern lake ringed with a thick forest. In the background, the clouds imply mountains. Three Indians are in the foreground. On the left, there is a woman with an infant on her back, and in the middle, another figure sits wrapped in a blanket and facing the lake. On a short dock is another man, probably Owen himself, his body oriented toward the lake and his face turned toward the artist. Instead of field clothes, he wears a fine frock coat. A small canoe can be seen, partially obscured by a bush. The trees lining the opposite shore are predominantly coniferous, with some deciduous ones interspersed.[56]

Some 25 miles up the Bad River and near a waterfall was a place called Wood's Farm, named after a resident who raised cattle that fed on sedge grasses and sheltered in the pines. Whittlesey cited this place as further evidence of the milder climate near Lake Superior. Until 6 miles below Wood's Farm, the river's current was sluggish, with the river banked by a wide bottomland. Because the bottomland was thickly covered in maple trees, Whittlesey surmised that the soil was "unsurpassed in richness." He also noted several deserted cabins with small potato patches around them, where "such Indians as

FIGURE 3.6 "Long Lake," woodblock print from Owen's *Report* (1852). Collection of the author.

are not too lazy, and the half-breeds of La Pointe, come in the months of March and April to make sugar." Each tree was said to yield 4 to 10 pounds of sugar, and an industrious family could produce an astonishing three-quarters of a ton of sugar in a good year, but Whittlesey added that "white men affirm that the trees would yield much more if the sap was carefully saved and gathered."[57] Whether he recognized it or not, the sugar making was an important part of the seasonal round. He did note that the sugaring season marked the end of the lean winter period.

During the mid-nineteenth century, waterpower was a key consideration for industrial development, so Whittlesey paid special attention to potential dam and power sites. He reported that the fall at Wood's Farm "consists of a series of leaps, of one to three feet each, over the tilted edges of red sand-rock. The descent, which is very straight, regular, and beautiful, is in all twenty-two feet; affording water for a large amount of machinery." He also noted that "between the 'Maringouin Fork' and the 'East Fork,' there are two principal tributaries of Bad River, in size of less than the other three, but capable of furnishing, by their volume and their rapid descent, an unlimited amount of water-power." Above Wood's homestead, Whittlesey found it is necessary to take a 2-mile portage, on the west side of the river, around the falls and rapids. From there, he and his men paddled an additional 14 or so miles upstream. The second branch from the west apparently had no name, so Whittlesey called it the Maringouin Fork, "in commemoration of the myriads of musquitoes that inhabit its banks, that being the name that the half-breed French give those pests of the Bad River region." He noted that the Maringouin originated near Long Lake and on the south "interlocks with the upper branches of the Chippewa River, among some lakes, enclosed by drift ridges, which are, by barometrical measurement, eight hundred and seventy-one feet above Lake Superior." About 10 miles up, he said, "the 'East Fork' tumbles down from the mountain range of trap and conglomerate into the plain of red clay that occupies the space between the mountains and the Lake." He noted how the waters turned a "thick chocolate-red" color when it rained (432–33).

Whittlesey described a "continuous mountain chain from the Montreal River to Bladder Lake" (now called Mineral Lake), which he considered a continuation of the Porcupine Mountain range in Michigan (434). He named the range Pewabic, which he understood to be the Ojibwa word for iron. According to geologist Henry R. Aldrich, when the draft of the *Report* went to the printer, a compositor misread the word *Pewabic* and set it in type as *Penokie*. To further confuse matters, the range was known as the Penokee range until 1873, when geologist T. B. Brooks published a report identifying it as the Penokee-Gogebic range, to indicate its relation to the Gogebic range in Michigan. Aldrich apparently did not read Whittlesey's report because he credited Brooks with recognizing for the first time, in 1873, that the Wisconsin and Michigan ranges were part of the same system. Whittlesey may have been mistaken that the Penokee was connected to the Porcupine Mountain system, but he was correct when he stated that the Wisconsin range extended into Michigan. Later, the name of the entire range was shortened to Gogebic, though the Wisconsin side is sometimes referred to as Penokee.[58]

From a high vantage point on the most elevated ridges of the Penokee range, Whittlesey looked northwest toward Lake Superior and described a bird's-eye view of the region:

> The country below has the appearance of a flat field, densely covered with evergreens; beyond which is the open Lake, the low Apostle Islands, originally part of the same plain, not yet removed by the action of the waves, and far in the distance is the outline of corresponding mountains on the north shore. At the northwest, the bold drift-hills that lie between Chegwomigon Bay and the Brulé River, are seen projecting into the Lake at the Detour.[59]

Turning around, Whittlesey looked south, toward the interior, and described the scene in that direction:

> Where the waters of the Bad River and Chippewa River interlock, is a vast tract, sloping gently to the north, full of tamarack and cedar swamps, and lakes and marshes, of little practical value, unless it be in future for its pines. (434)

Analyzing what he could see from the ridges and what he had learned on the ground, he claimed that this land was different. The order of things was not as one would expect:

> In this region we have a state of things in regard to soil, the reverse of what is usual in mountainous countries. The best soil is on the mountain ridges and slopes. The low grounds are generally swampy, and covered with thickets of tamarack, birch, white cedar, balsam, and spruce, and occasionally pine. At the foot of the mountain ranges, where the slope graduates into the low lands, there is an abundance of hemlock, and the ground is covered with moss, and a shrub called ground hemlock, to the continual annoyance of the traveler. Higher up the slopes, and on the summit, the prevailing timber is sugar maple, of a strong, heavy growth, a few yellow birch and pine trees interspersed. The sugar-tree soil is always good. (435)

Whittlesey was especially enthusiastic about the Penokee-Gogebic range:

> The mountain ranges are bountifully supplied with springs, rivulets, and creeks, of the coolest and purest water. Roads may be made with reasonable expense along the ranges; the climate cannot be surpassed for health; and, if the winter seasons are not *too long*, for they are not *too severe*, about one-third of the Bad River country may yet be occupied by men who till the soil. It is well settled, by observation, that the severity of winter is greater on the dividing ridge, forty and fifty miles south of the Lake, than it is between the range and the coast. (435)

That left fully two-thirds of the Bad River country, in Whittlesey's estimation, as refuse lands. For example, he wrote that "the drift-hills that divide the waters that flow into Chegwomigon Bay and the Mashkeg Fork from the waters of Iron and Penokie River, are in general barren and unfit for cultivation" (436). Perhaps the most favorable and marketable aspect of the country was the comparatively moderate microclimate near the lake. Whittlesey succinctly described the lake effect: "The volume of water is so great, as to act as a controlling manner upon the temperature of the surrounding country" (469). Nevertheless, there could be a lot of snow. (Indeed, the iron range is a natural snow belt, where people continue to measure snow in yards rather than feet.) But Whittlesey even put a good spin on that:

> There are no winter rains, but a great deal of dull sky, from frequent falls of snow; yet residents suffer little from cold, owing to the uniformity of temperature. The under surface of the snow, resting upon unfrozen ground, continually wastes away, and causes the mass to settle more or less every day. The agent of the Fur Company, and the miners, travel comfortably from place to place on snow-shoes and dog-trains or sledges, encamping at night in the thick forest. (470)

He ended with a prognosis that could not have been better designed to lure farmers to the region: "I know nothing of the Bad River country, to prevent the successful cultivation of wheat, and a considerable portion of the soil is favourable for that grain" (470).

Despite this optimistic conclusion, however, a careful reading of Owen's *Report* and especially Whittlesey's part of it would caution anyone thinking of settling in the region. The records of the ordinance surveyors only reinforced the understanding that this was a rugged landscape and that eking out a living there would be a challenge and require different skills than needed on the gentler lands in the southern part of the state.

Variations on a Scene

PART TWO

Bird's-Eye: Of or belonging to a bird's eye: as in bird's-eye view: a view of a landscape from above, such as presented to the eye of a bird; a perspective representation of such a view; also fig. a resume of a subject.

—*Oxford English Dictionary*

Cities in the Wilderness

4

IN 1855, three years after David Dale Owen's *Report* was published, the locks at Sault Ste. Marie opened, finally connecting Lake Superior shipping to the rest of the chain of Great Lakes. The locks project cost the state of Michigan $2,000,000, employed sixteen hundred men, and took two years to complete. The locks were 350 feet long and 70 feet wide. Two locks in tandem raised and lowered ships 18 feet, effectively overcoming the obstacle of the rapids that had isolated the Lake Superior economy and culture from the rest of the country. During the first season of operation, 14,500 tons of goods were moved through the locks. Within a decade, the tonnage passing through the locks had increased almost twentyfold to 284,350, and in another decade, it had grown more than five times to 1,500,000 tons.[1] At first, the locks mainly served the Michigan copper mines, but even before the locks opened, town and city sites were planned around the lake. Because of Chequamegon Bay's location on the western end of Great Lakes shipping, coupled with its proximity to minerals and other resources, some of the most promising sites on the lake were in the vicinity of the bay (fig. 4.1). In the beginning, establishing settlements was a risky enterprise. It was not an easy place, and the first settlers had to be hardy and self-reliant. The U.S. public land surveyors (also called Land Ordinance surveyors) often took careful notes about their surveys from which maps were drawn with detail down to the quarter section, showing lakes, streams, marshes, and even cultural features in certain instances. Some of the notes and maps were so detailed that scholars working more than a century later could reconstruct ecosystems and map out vegetation at the time of survey.

On September 27, 1855, Deputy Surveyor Augustus Barber, together with his assistants, chainmen, and axman, finished surveying Township 47 North, Range 4 West, of the Fourth Principal Meridian (fig. 4.2). At the end of his notes, Barber assessed the 36-square-mile township. He noted that the northwestern sections had already been platted as a townsite called Ashland, which consisted of "several dwelling Houses, a Tavern and Store House and three other buildings."[2] According to Barber:

> This Township has a fair quality of land for agricultural purposes and is well situated upon Long Island [Chequamegon] Bay. The timber is mostly small and will be easily cleared off and brought under cultivation. . . . Springs are of a good quality and White River in the South East part of Township is a good mill stream. Native Copper has been found in this Township, but the formation does not indicate a mining locality.[3]

Barber's gently optimistic report barely hinted at how difficult the land could be. Though he and his crew did not encounter much trouble surveying this particular town, other surveyors were not so lucky. In contrast to Barber's report, the 1847 report from surveyor Harry Wiltse described the travails of running the Fourth Principal Meridian line north to Lake Superior (fig. 4.3). Because the terrain was too rugged for pack animals, Wiltse's crew had to carry everything on their own backs. Survey equipment was mandatory, so they could only lighten their loads by leaving behind personal supplies. Therefore, each man was restricted to bringing only the clothes he wore and one blanket. The men did not bring tents, and they subsisted on pork, flour, and anything they could scavenge along the way. Wiltse was able to hire two

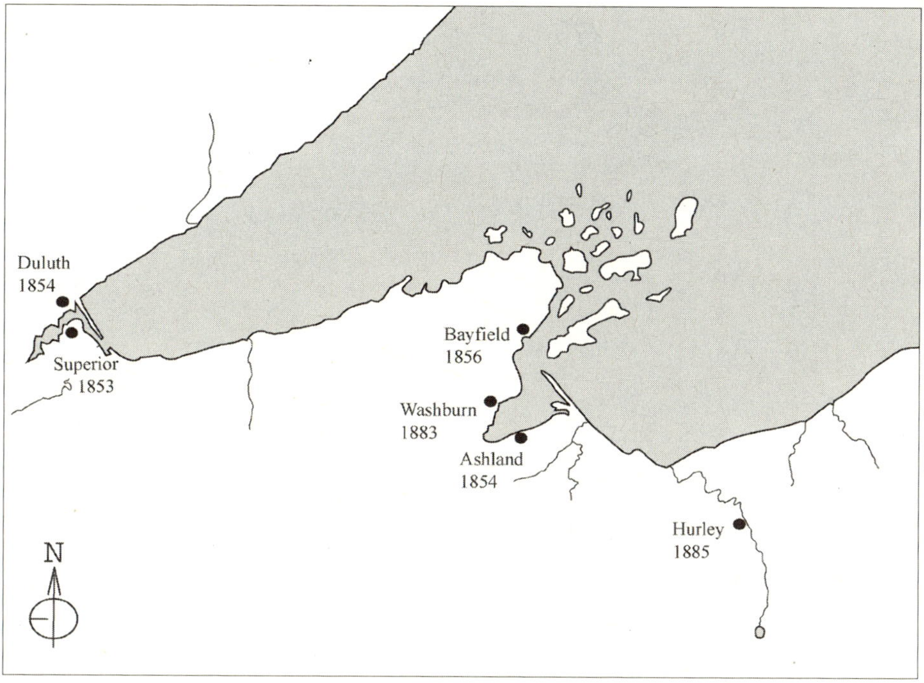

FIGURE 4.1 Early townsites on the west end of Lake Superior and date founded. Map by author.

packers from La Pointe, but both men complained about their loads and refused to carry a pack in addition to supplies. In all, Wiltse estimated that the party had to traverse a line through 175 miles of swamp, much of it obstructed by windfall. For a month in the field, they worked in clothes that were constantly wet, for they were unable to dry them out. As if that were not enough, high water complicated the crossing of rivers, and the men were surrounded by "swarms or rather clouds of mosquitoes, and still more troublesome insects." But the worst part was that they were confined to the survey line and therefore could not choose a more sensible path. Three days short of Lake Superior, they ran out of food and were forced to hike to the shore in search of provisions. There, they encountered geological surveyor Charles Whittlesey, who observed that they were starving and that their clothes were shredded. Wiltse stated that even "after a lifetime of experience in the field,

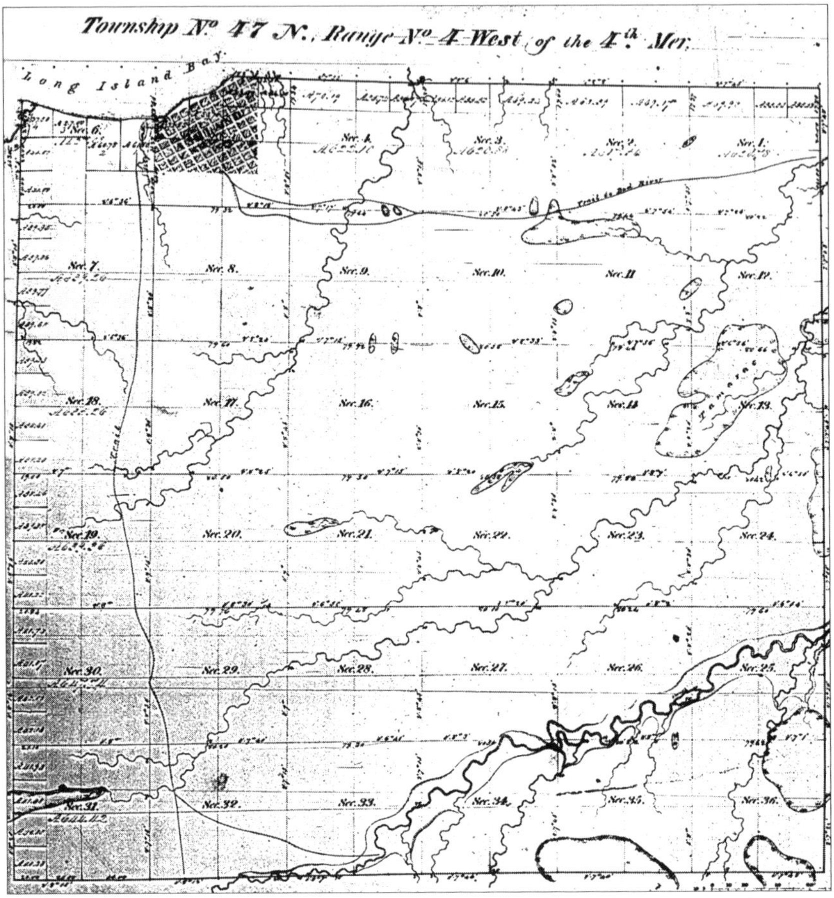

FIGURE 4.2 Surveyor map for Township 47 North, Range 4 West. Courtesy of the Wisconsin Historical Society Archives.

and a great fondness for camp life," he would never contract to do a similar survey "at any price whatever."[4] Crews faced similar difficulties while surveying much of the lands just to the south of Chequamegon Bay, which helps to explain why it took more than two decades to complete the ordinance surveys of the region. Begun in the 1840s, the work continued in piecemeal fashion until the last sections were surveyed in the late 1860s.[5]

Nevertheless, Euramerican settlers were on the land and establishing townsites by the early 1850s. The first lighthouse on the west end of Lake

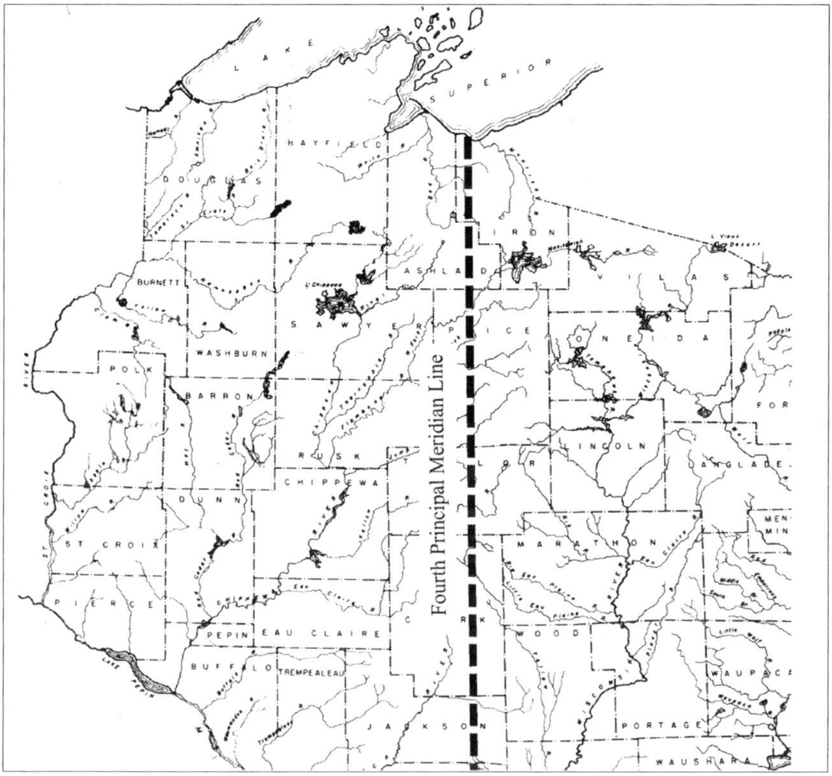

FIGURE 4.3 Fourth Principal Meridian to Lake Superior. Map by author.

Superior was erected on Long Island in 1852 and was built to protect the increasing ship traffic. In 1853, the city of Superior was founded; neighboring Duluth was established the next year. In June 1854, Asaph Whittlesey and his wife and infant daughter moved to La Pointe. Asaph had learned of the region from his brother, Charles, who had surveyed the area for Owen's 1852 *Report*. The fact that Charles convinced his brother to settle there is strong evidence that he had been impressed by the region and was convinced of its economic potential. After a few days at La Pointe, Asaph and his family set out in a rowboat with all of their possessions and landed near the west end of present-day Ashland. On July 5, 1854, Asaph began to build a home, and before long, others joined him. They called their new village Whittlesey. In 1855, different families began to build on land that is now part of the east end of Ashland; they named their settlement Bay City. Eventually, both communities combined under the name Ashland after rejecting the name Equadon, which was purported to mean "at the head of the bay." One source claims that the town was called Ashland because the first tree cut down by Asaph Whittlesey was an ash, but other sources say that early settler Martin Beaser suggested the name in honor of Henry Clay, whose Kentucky home bore the same name.[6] Early settlers seemed to be self-conscious about how they fit into the future frontier mythology. Yet like his brother, Asaph Whittlesey appeared to relish his role as a frontier participant. Figure 4.4, a photograph taken around 1860, shows him ready to snowshoe to Chippewa Falls to catch a train to Madison, where he would take his seat in the state legislature.[7]

Wisconsin became a state in 1848, and several early laws passed by the state legislature affected life around Chequamegon Bay. General laws were passed during the 1850s to protect trees marked by lumbermen and to ensure that laborers on the railroads were paid. An 1850 law forbade the sale of intoxicating liquors to Indians. Section 1 of the Laws of Wisconsin granted the justice of the peace jurisdiction over any offense committed within the county of La Pointe, together with the power to incarcerate an offender for up to three months in the county jail and to impose a fine up to $50. In recognition of the significance of Lake Superior to the local scene—and to plug a legal loophole—section 2 extended the law to cover "persons upon steamboats, vessels, schooners, or any water craft."[8] That same year, acts also authorized the holding of an election to choose a sheriff and county officers, as well as the organization of a court. In 1860, largely due to the efforts of newly elected state legislator Asaph Whittlesey, the large county of La Pointe was divided up and the smaller county of Ashland was formed, with the city of Ashland as the county seat.[9] Also in 1860, an act was passed providing that a road be laid out between Ashland and Chippewa Falls. Another act, passed the following year, provided for a road running from Second Street in Superior to Washington Avenue in Bayfield. Three men were appointed commissioners for the road, two of whom were directed to

> carefully view the ground over which said road is to pass, and lay out and locate a good summer wagon road between said points, not less than thirty feet in width, trees to be well slashed, not less than thirty feet on each side, with a suitable grade, and shall distinctly mark the same; after which they

FIGURE 4.4 Asaph Whittlesey, ca. 1860, dressed for his journey from Ashland, Wisconsin, to Madison, Wisconsin, to take up his seat in the state legislature. Courtesy of the Ashland Historical Society Museum, Ashland, Wisconsin.

> shall make out two correct maps or drafts thereof, and file one of the same in the office of the clerk of the board of supervisors of each of said counties; whereupon said road shall become a public highway; and it shall be the duty of the respective supervisors to open said road, so marked as aforesaid, as soon as possible, and keep the same in repairs, as other highways in said counties.[10]

The act stipulated that the counties would pay each commissioner $3 per day and that up to three assistants would each receive $1.50 per day for their services. The state would contribute no money toward the road. Building a road through the forest was one of many ways that settlers came to know the land even as they shaped it.

Although Owen's federal survey was published in 1852 and the Wisconsin State Geological Survey was first organized one year later, the next comprehensive geological survey of Wisconsin's Lake Superior coastal lands was not published until 1880.[11] The first two state of Wisconsin surveys were completed between 1853 and 1856 and focused on the lead region in the southwestern corner of the state. A third survey, conducted between 1857 and 1862, was never completed. In fact, the legislature abolished the survey in 1862. This survey may have been doomed from the start, when the legislature appointed three prominent geologists as coleaders. James Hall was an eminent paleontologist from New York who was already committed to be the state geologist for Iowa, Ezra Carr was a doctor of medicine who taught chemistry at the University of Wisconsin, and Edward Daniels was the former state geologist of Wisconsin. Almost from the outset, there were conflicts over the contract, division of funds, and control of the project. Meanwhile, in 1861, the legislature appropriated $3,000 to print a report of the lead region by survey assistant J. D. Whitney, while at the same time refusing to fund the publication of a manuscript by Daniels and a work on paleontology by Hall. In the end, very little of the survey's work was published. In part, the legislators were upset because the reports generated by the survey team were too few and too expensive and not nearly optimistic enough to promote the rapid development of the state's resources as they had hoped.[12]

Whether funded by the federal government or the states, public lands surveys were highly political undertakings. Surveyors sold their skills to legislators by arguing that an accurate assessment of the state's resources would facilitate development, and for their part, many legislators naturally saw optimistic resource assessments as a way to draw much-needed capital investment to the state. Therefore, they were loath to finance surveys they saw as overly cautious or even pessimistic—no matter how accurate they were.[13] This situtation created an inherent conflict because many of the surveyors aspired to make their mark in the academic literature yet knew that overly optimistic reports could ruin a geologist's reputation. Furthermore, some geologists cared far more about fossils and academic theories than economic development.

David Dale Owen saw no conflict in this regard. He believed that science served industry and that accurate geological surveys, no matter what their results, were vital to economic development. Charles Whittlesey held similar views. He was a first-rate field geologist and a staunchly agnostic empiricist who was informed but not encumbered by the popular and often erroneous theories of his day. As a result, he frequently came into conflict with more academically inclined geologists. In the early 1870s, Whittlesey became embroiled in a fierce and public battle with professor of geology and paleontology J. S. Newberry over the Ohio Survey. Into this fray stepped James Hall, who had apparently held a grudge against Whittlesey since the time of the Wisconsin Survey that had been terminated by the legislature in 1862. Afterward, Hall was involved in a drawn-out and bitter battle with the Wisconsin legislature to restore his own reputation and get his survey work published, at state expense. Whittlesey quoted a letter by Hall, published in the *Ohio State Journal* on April 2, 1872. In his letter, Hall alleged that Whittlesey had used political influence to get himself appointed to the survey and, further, that he was paid $3,000 for a survey of the northern part of the state that "was not worth twenty dollars." Referring to his contract with Hall, Whittlesey claimed that he was only paid half that amount for work that occupied him for three months; he also said he paid for an assistant and two voyageurs out of his own pocket. Furthermore, he had produced eight chapters and a map, all of which Hall continued to withhold from the state and was threatening to destroy unless the state settled certain claims with him. Whittlesey stood by his work and declared that anyone who examined it could judge its worth. Expressing frustration with the armchair paleontologist, Whittlesey asserted that the lands he had surveyed were country that Hall "has never examined, unless from the deck of a passing steamer; which I have thoroughly traversed on foot, and in birch canoes; but which he [Hall] assumed to know more than I do."[14]

Whittlesey went on to charge that Hall was previously engaged in two other surveys and had entered into contract with Wisconsin with the idea of being absentee leader of the survey, just as he claimed Newberry had done in Ohio. Since Hall was unable, if not unwilling, to personally conduct the necessary fieldwork, J. D. Whitney was hired to survey the lead region while Whittlesey was contracted to survey northern Wisconsin. Angry over Hall's criticism, Whittlesey stated that

> the region it was expected of me to examine; was a wide spread wilderness; occupied principally by Indians; much of it not surveyed into townships; and everywhere inaccessible by the usual modes of traveling. It was only by means of half-breed packers or voyageurs carrying everything in their canoes, or on their backs; that it could be penetrated at all. It was a work for which carpet geologists, had no taste; but who expected of others that as rapid progress; should be made as in the open prairie region; among settlements; with the usual means of conveyance. This territory included nearly half the state.[15]

Volume 3 of Thomas Chamberlin's *Geology of Wisconsin,* published in 1880, partially vindicated Whittlesey. The index listed no less than thirteen references to his work, whereas Hall was mentioned only once and that was in relation to Whittlesey. As for the other two initial leaders of the survey, Daniels was mentioned twice and Carr not at all. Furthermore, R. D. Irving —who resurveyed, for the 1880 volume, the same territory that Whittlesey had surveyed earlier—was impressed with Whittlesey's work. Although Irving thought that Whittlesey had exaggerated the potential of the Penokee (Gogebic) Iron Range, he credited him with conducting the only two surveys of the region, prior to Irving's own, that were respectable. The third volume of *Geology of Wisconsin* further affirmed the value of Whittlesey's work by printing a synopsis of his publications on the region in an appendix, including his 1860 map of the region, as well as a long summary of his relevant works. Irving stated that even though he and Whittlesey differed in their conclusions, "it is evident that Colonel Whittlesey caught the main geological features of the region," despite working under primitive conditions and without the current knowledge of the lithology of the Lake Superior formations.[16] Ironically, Whittlesey's more optimistic assessment of the Penokee range proved to be more accurate than Irving's.[17]

No matter how cautious surveys may have been, boosters found ways to use them to sell their particular places. As soon as speculators advertised a given location, the booster period began. Booster pamphlets published by railway companies, private speculators, and governmental agencies were very effective in creating an alluring image of the Chequamegon Bay region.[18] The boosters were a diverse mix: individuals who had bought townsites, railroad company investors trying to sell the land given to them by the government in order to support construction of the road, the state and counties, and especially local newspaper editors. Each booster had a different angle, but all shared the same goals—to market an optimistic and forward-looking vision of the place, to lure investors and settlers and tourists, and to stimulate the local economy. Betting on the future, they advertised their place in an effort to make their hopes come true. Naturally, they drew on the authority of surveyors' reports to argue for their vision of the development of the place, even borrowing aesthetic conventions. The booster literature reveals a paradox: many boosters promoted wild nature even as they encouraged urban, industrial, and agricultural development of the same landscape. Yet the boosters seemed unaware of the contradiction, and from the 1850s through the 1890s, they continued to simultaneously promote a vision of the Chequamegon Bay region as a pristine wilderness, on the one hand, and a future urban industrial center, on the other.

Geological Imagery in Booster Documents

Comparing the iconography of the texts produced by Schoolcraft and McKenney with Owen's 1852 *Report* and Chamberlin's 1880 *Geology of Wisconsin* strongly suggests that the authors of these works adopted similarly romantic conventions for depicting scenery. Furthermore, the images used in booster media, such as the tourist brochures produced by railway companies and other documents, were strikingly similar to scenes found in geology texts. Like Owen's 1852 *Report*, Chamberlin's *Geology of Wisconsin* was amply illustrated with scenic views of waterfalls and gorges. The waterfall scenes were all depicted from the bottom view preferred by Owen, Schoolcraft, McKenney, and the romantic poet Lord Byron. This approach may have reflected established convention, or it could have been a conscious attempt to

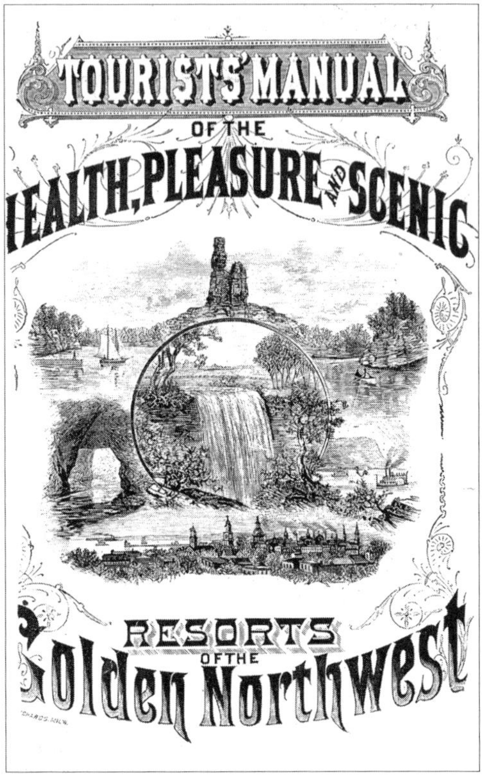

FIGURE 4.5 Cover of railroad company's *Tourists' Manual* (Chicago, Milwaukee and St. Paul Railway, 1880). Courtesy of the Wisconsin Historical Society Library.

appease boosterish legislators while staying true to the facts uncovered by the surveyors. Several pictures in the 1852 federal survey and the 1880 state survey served aesthetic purposes far better than scientific purposes. Conforming with ideas of art as well as developing notions of preferred recreation sites, most of the scenes included water.

Published the same year as the third volume of Chamberlin's *Geology of Wisconsin*, the Chicago, Milwaukee and St. Paul Railway's brochure—given the cumbersome title "Tourists' Manual of the Health, Pleasure and Scenic Resorts of the Golden Northwest, Embracing Descriptions of the Principal Summer Resorts in Wisconsin, Iowa and Minnesota., Together with Game and Fish Laws, Hotel Guide, Excursion Rates, etc.—features a collage of geological and urban images on its cover (fig. 4.5). The centerpiece is a waterfall, a common symbol of sublimity as well as a geological feature. Sitting atop the circular frame around the falls is a monument-like rock formation

FIGURE 4.6 "Red Sandstone, South Shore of Lake Superior," from Owen, *Report* (1852). Collection of the author.

created by erosion. Below the falls is a city on a lake. Other images framing the falls show cliffs, a cave, and a bluff. All of the scenes include water, and with the exception of the city scene, all could have been copied directly from geological survey reports. The key elements of this aesthetic convention are water and rocks.

Figures 2.2, 4.6, 4.7, and 4.8 all show similar scenes as they appeared from water-level vantage points between the years 1820 and 1899. Only the last image is from a booster pamphlet; the rest are from expeditions or geological surveys. The first (fig. 2.2), from Schoolcraft's *Narrative Journal* of 1821, depicts a scene from the Pictured Rocks that had impressed the Cass party so much. On close inspection, a thin waterfall can be seen near the center of the second formation from the left.[19] The picture dramatically reveals the erosive power of Lake Superior's wave action on the soft red sandstone typical of the south shore. Trees cling to the thin soil on top of the formation. Schoolcraft's image is remarkably like one from Owen's *Report* (fig. 4.6). Owen added a boat in the foreground, perhaps to show scale, which has the effect of dramatizing the scene. The observer sees the figures in the vessel as they view the rock formations and is thus drawn into the picture. Images

FIGURE 4.7 "Lake Superior Sandstone, Hemlock Island" from Chamberlin, *Geology of Wisconsin* (1880). Collection of the author.

FIGURE 4.8 "Grand Arch—Sand Island" from *Picturesque Wisconsin* 1, no. 2 (July 1899). Courtesy of the Wisconsin Historical Society Library.

such as Schoolcraft's and Owen's surely inspired tourists to seek out such scenes for themselves. The third image (fig. 4.7), from Chamberlin's *Geology of Wisconsin*, illustrated a serious and rigorously scientific text, yet the scene seems a direct descendant of those provided by Schoolcraft and Owen. The viewpoint is from below, at water level, which makes the rock formations seem larger, looming above the viewer. Only the fourth scene (fig. 4.8) is from a booster publication, George Thomas's 1899 *Picturesque Wisconsin: Legends and History*, a short-lived journal published in Milwaukee.[20] The two issues of *Picturesque Wisconsin* both focused on the Chequamegon Bay area, where Milwaukeean Thomas had—surely not coincidentally—invested in real estate. The publication was aimed at promoting the region's aesthetic resources, in part by elaborating the long and colorful history of the area and by displaying the sublime scenery.

Why would the booster Thomas choose a scene virtually identical to those in academic geological survey reports? To the geologists, from Schoolcraft

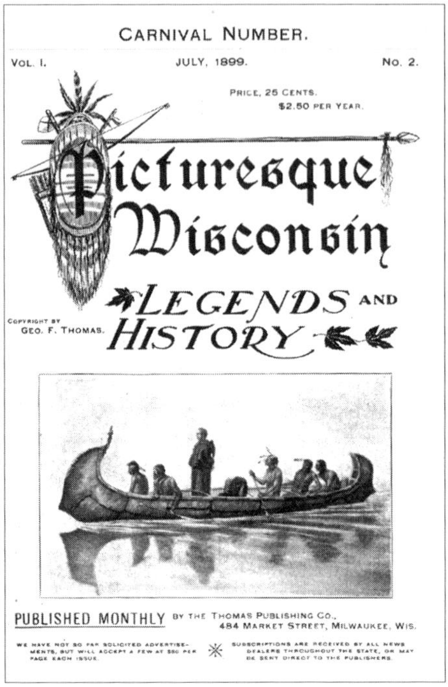

FIGURE 4.9 Cover of *Picturesque Wisconsin* 1, no. 2 (July 1899). Courtesy of the Wisconsin Historical Society Library.

to Owen to Chamberlin, the illustrations were more than interesting scenes: they were evidence of powerful earthly forces and of the growing immensity of geological time. Even in Schoolcraft's day, it was clear that the earth was far older than it was previously believed to be. Near the end of the eighteenth century, James Hutton had taken the first important step toward determining the age of the earth by arguing that geological processes were constant over time.[21] Therefore, he said, processes such as deposition and erosion occurred at a similar rate in the distant past and in the present. If one knew how long it took for a given rock surface to erode an eighth of an inch, one could then calculate how long it took for a milewide canyon to form. Odd rock formations were not only evidence of geological processes and the flow of time but also potent symbols of the gaping maw of time. What could be more sublime?

On the back cover of the first issue of *Picturesque Wisconsin,* Thomas, the editor, optimistically outlined what to expect in future editions. He put a heavy emphasis on the local history of pioneers, voyageurs, and Indians, as well as on Indian lore, information for tourists and sportspeople, and "DESCRIPTIONS OF NATURAL CURIOSITIES, caves, strangely shaped cliffs and

FIGURE 4.10 "The Happiest Hour," from *Picturesque Wisconsin* 1, no. 2 (July 1899). Courtesy of the Wisconsin Historical Society Library.

rocks, noted land marks, old ruins, mounds, mound builders' relics, unusual scenes and freaks of nature."[22] The cover of the second issue shows a Jesuit priest dramatically, if a bit carelessly, standing in a birchbark canoe being paddled by four Indians and a bearded voyageur (fig. 4.9). The message was clear: Wisconsin in general and the Chequamegon Bay region in particular had everything to draw the tourists, from ancient history and Indians to geological oddities and recreational opportunities. Unlike the geological texts, *Picturesque Wisconsin* did not mask its romantic influences. The second issue even contained a contrived scene of Romeo and Juliet experiencing "the happiest hour of all the day, among the Apostle Islands"—sunset near the water (fig. 4.10). The first issue showed a woman "in that lovely vale where the daisies and violets bloom" (fig. 4.11)—two species not commonly associated with the northwoods. Both issues of *Picturesque Wisconsin* included a Wisconsin Central Railway map showing "the direct line to Ashland," graphically illustrating how closely Ashland and Chequamegon Bay were, by then, tied to more urbanized and populous places such as Milwaukee and Chicago (fig. 4.12).

FIGURE 4.11 "In That Lovely Vale," from *Picturesque Wisconsin* 1, no. 2 (July 1899). Courtesy of the Wisconsin Historical Society Library.

Consider the three waterfall scenes depicted in figure 4.13, from Owen's 1852 *Report*; figure 4.14, from Chamberlin's 1880 *Geology of Wisconsin*; and figure 4.15, from Thomas's 1899 *Picturesque Wisconsin*. Recall that Thomas L. McKenney described Niagara Falls by quoting a poem written by Lord Byron. The romantic poet suggested to McKenney a model for how to view a waterfall. Significantly, the preferred view was looking up from the chasm. And

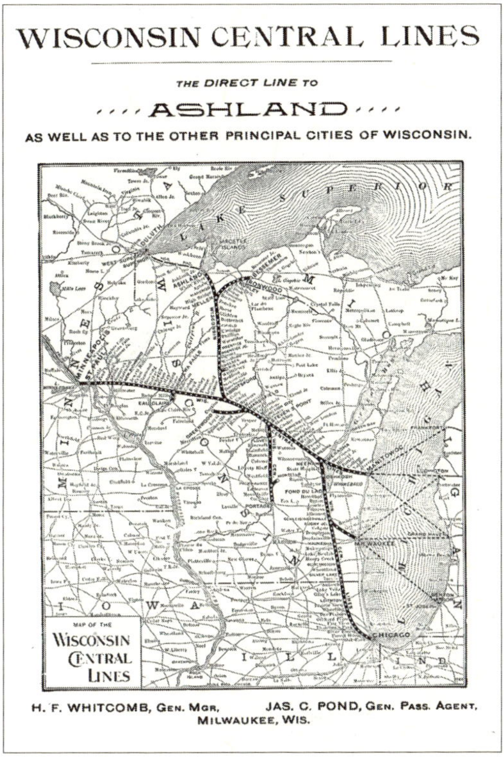

FIGURE 4.12 "Wisconsin Central Lines," railroad map from *Picturesque Wisconsin* 1, no. 2 (July 1899). Courtesy of the Wisconsin Historical Society Library.

Niagara was the premiere symbol of American sublimity. Waterfalls do, of course, have special significance for geologists because they cut away bedrock to reveal stratigraphy and also offer evidence of geological forces. But the two images from geological texts appear to have been composed more for aesthetic purposes than to reveal geological information. Both feature the romantic poet's preferred vantage point, enhancing the sublime feeling of being engulfed by powerful natural forces. Like most popular representations of Niagara Falls, they both show a main body of water dividing into two falls. The scene from Chamberlin's *Geology* is almost identical to Thomas's scene from *Picturesque Wisconsin*, published nineteen years later. At first glance, the two images actually seem to be of the same waterfalls, but in fact, they show different falls on two separate rivers. The photographer of Copper Falls, on the Bad River, chose a vantage point identical to that used in the woodblock print of the Black River's Upper Falls, suggesting similar artistic conventions if not direct imitation.

FIGURE 4.13 "Falls of Caribou River," from Owen, *Report* (1852). Collection of the author.

FIGURE 4.14 "Upper Falls of Black River," from Chamberlin, *Geology of Wisconsin* (1880). Collection of the author.

FIGURE 4.15 "Copper Falls, Bad River," from *Picturesque Wisconsin* 1, no. 1 (June 1899). Courtesy of the Wisconsin Historical Society Library.

FIGURE 4.16 Camping scene from Owen's *Report* (1852). Collection of the author.

Although recreational scenes were not as common in geological survey reports as they were in booster media, Owen's 1852 *Report* contained vivid descriptions of camp life as well as illustrations. Compare the image of the surveyor camp from that work (fig. 4.16) and a camp scene from *Gems of the Northwest,* a promotional booklet published by the Chicago, Milwaukee and St. Paul Railway Company (fig. 4.17). Both scenes center on fire and cooking, both include tents, both are set in a picturesque woods near water, and both depict men at leisure. Like the tourist brochure, the geological text served, in part, as a guide to camp life.

Conceptually, it is useful to argue that there was a direct linear relationship from romantic poets and landscape artists to explorers such as Schoolcraft, to geological surveyors such as Whittlesey, Owen, and Chamberlin, and to promoters such as Thomas and the numerous railway companies in the region. Nevertheless, a model of this type is too simple. Take, for example, the scene of the Bad River gorge, near Penokee Gap, in Chamberlin's *Geology of Wisconsin* (fig. 4.18). It is nearly identical to the scene on the cover of *Summer*

FIGURE 4.17 "Camping Out," an illustration from John Hyde, *Gems of the Northwest, or, What Three Americans Found in Wisconsin, Minnesota, and Iowa* (Milwaukee, WI: Chicago, Milwaukee and St. Paul Railway, ca. 1887). Courtesy of the Wisconsin Historical Society Library.

Resorts on the Wisconsin Central Railroad, published for the railway company in 1887, three years before Chamberlin's *Geology* appeared (fig. 4.19).[23] It is impossible to say if the geologist copied the booster, but the similarity of the two scenes is suggestive. This scene is particularly interesting in that it combines a picturesque natural setting with a human construction—in this case, a railroad bridge.

FIGURE 4.18 "Gorge on Bad River at Penokee Gap, Ashland County," from Chamberlin, *Geology of Wisconsin* (1880). Collection of the author.

FIGURE 4.19 Cover illustration showing the Wisconsin Central Railroad bridge, from *Summer Resorts on the Wisconsin Central Railroad* (1877). Courtesy of the Wisconsin Historical Society Library Pamphlet Collection.

The intermingling of industrial and wild images was common in booster media during the nineteenth century. An especially compelling and symbolic image, much repeated, was that of the railroad steam engine slicing through the wilderness with smoke belching from its stack. The back cover of *Summer Resorts on the Wisconsin Central Railroad* shows a train passing above the wilderness, almost miraculously suspended by the White River viaduct (fig. 4.20). Later booster literature continued the practice of associating natural phenomena with cultural constructions. Figure 4.21, from McKenney's 1827 *Tour to the Lakes,* depicts the "Grecian urn" at Pictured Rocks. This image is especially striking because the artist chose to basically sketch a giant urn in the landscape with trees placed in it like flowers in a vase, all of which had little resemblance to the natural feature. It seems, however, that readers and viewers did not need such over-the-top cues to imagine the constructed object the natural feature was intended to represent. Two typical examples are seen in Figures 4.22 and 4.23, both of which illustrated an essay, published in *Picturesque Wisconsin* in 1899, that was written by the founder and former editor of the *Ashland Press,* Sam Fifield. Fifield's text was full of the romantic imagery of ruins, even where none existed.[24]

At the same time that legislators were seeking to attract investors and settlers to the state with optimistic surveys, speculators, newspaper editors, railways, and state immigration agencies began disseminating booster literature. *Boosterism* can be defined as a rhetorical genre designed to positively alter perceptions of a given place in order to encourage economic development through investment, settlement, and work. Boosters usually stood to profit in some way if their promotional efforts succeeded: speculators could count on selling their lots at a huge profit if a city actually did arise on their site; newspaper editors could expand circulation and advertising revenues if the population grew and business expanded; and railway companies could increase the volume of both passengers and freight if tourism and industry rose, and they also could sell their railroad land grants if they could convince potential settlers to try their hand at farming. Because boosters were often successful in convincing people to invest their money, lives, and labors in their vision of development, boosterism was a critical factor in shaping the American landscape. [25]

A fair amount has been written about city boosterism, and there is a growing literature on the selling of natural retreats. Yet these activities tend

FIGURE 4.20 "White River Viaduct, Wisconsin Central Railroad," from *Summer Resorts on the Wisconsin Central Railroad* (1877). Courtesy of the Wisconsin Historical Society Library Pamphlet Collection.

FIGURE 4.21 "View of the Urn, Lake Superior," from McKenney, *Sketches of a Tour to the Lakes* (1827). Courtesy of the Wisconsin Historical Society (WHi-36628).

FIGURE 4.22 "Temple Gate, Sand Island," from *Picturesque Wisconsin* 1, no. 2 (July 1899). Courtesy of the Wisconsin Historical Society Library.

FIGURE 4.23 "The Devil's Piano, Devil's Island," from *Picturesque Wisconsin* 1, no. 2 (July 1899). Courtesy of the Wisconsin Historical Society Library.

to be presented as two distinct and largely unrelated subjects. For example, Steven V. Ward's *Selling Places* contains one section on "Selling the Resort" and a separate section on "Selling the Industrial Town."[26] Boosters in the Chequamegon Bay area, however, attempted to market their area as *both* a resort and an industrial center . Located near the western end of Lake Superior's south shore and protected by the Apostle Islands, the bay had long been known as one of the safest port areas on the lake. By the late 1850s, railway companies were planning to build roads to the south shore, and many speculators bet that the first connection would be in the vicinity of Chequamegon Bay.

In the late 1850s, Henry Rice, a speculator and former fur trader from St. Paul, Minnesota, bought land on the western shore of the bay and plotted a townsite that he named Bayfield after a friend, British Lieutenant Henry Bayfield—the man who created the first accurate charts of Lake Superior.[27] In 1858, a pamphlet was printed in Philadelphia to promote Bayfield. It boldly stated:

> If one were to point out on the map of North America, a site for a great commercial city, it would be in the immediate vicinity of the "Apostle Isles." A city so located would have command of the *mineral* trade, the *fisheries*, and the *lumber* of the entire north. It would become a metropolis of a great commercial empire.[28]

The pamphlet went on to describe a vision that would be reflected in the rhetoric of future area boosters: a great city was destined to arise on Chequamegon Bay once a railway connection was established. In the beginning, lumber would be cut, transported to the town, milled, and shipped to distant markets. As the "interminable" forests were cut, farms would be established that would provide cheap produce for a growing population. Ultimately, a great industrial center would develop, surrounded by an agricultural hinterland. The pamphlet also promoted the "magnificent scenery." Every summer, it claimed, brought an increasing number of fashionable tourists, "who return delighted with their excursion, and generally improved in health." From that point on, boosters promoted the Chequamegon Region as a natural escape from the ills of city life even as they encouraged massive urban and industrial development of the same region. The boosters seemed unaware of any irony in promoting two contradictory landscapes.

To boosters in the late nineteenth century, everything depended on rail connections. The hope that Bayfield would be the western metropolis of Lake Superior was all but dashed in 1872 when word got out that the Wisconsin Central Railroad had begun work on a route to the townsite of Ashland, which had been nearly abandoned after its founding seventeen years earlier on the southern shore of Chequamegon Bay. The *Bayfield Press,* which had been fiercely boosting Bayfield for two years, promptly started boosting Ashland, quickly relocated there, and changed its name to the *Ashland Press.* The front page of the first edition of the reborn paper displayed a map that optimistically showed five railroad tracks converging in Ashland (fig. 4.24).[29] (Although Ashland would eventually get its rail connections, the first one would not be completed for five more years.) Beneath the map, the *Press* declared: "The scenery and air of our north-western lakes are beautiful and magical; and why people should go abroad and breathe the pestilential air of decaying cities and nations when they can enjoy the inspiring air of home, and see this wonderful wealth of scenery, passes comprehension."[30]

Page one of the newspaper emphasized natural beauty and pristine air, but page two declared Ashland the "future Iron City of Wisconsin" and argued that—once the railroads were completed—it would become the "emporium of the lake region" and the trade center of a "rich mining, agricultural and commercial region." As it turned out, Ashland's future would be far less grandiose than boosters predicted, but the coming of the railroad did accelerate environmental changes. The completion of the first railway to Lake Superior in 1877 was a significant engineering achievement. The White River bridge was 1,560 feet long and 102 feet high and quickly became a favorite tourist stop for those traveling on the Wisconsin Central. At the end of the line, the railway company built the Chequamegon Hotel to house vacationers eager to go as far as the rails would take them—but less eager to go beyond the realm of urban amenities (fig. 4.25).

Among the first tourists to ride the new rails to Ashland was the editor of the Portage-based *Wisconsin State Register.* On July 17, 1877, Andrew Jackson Turner left Portage, located near the center of the state, and joined an excursion party of twenty-eight people traveling north. (Turner was the father of Frederick Jackson Turner, the prominent historian whose "frontier thesis" would have a profound effect on the way U.S. history was presented.)

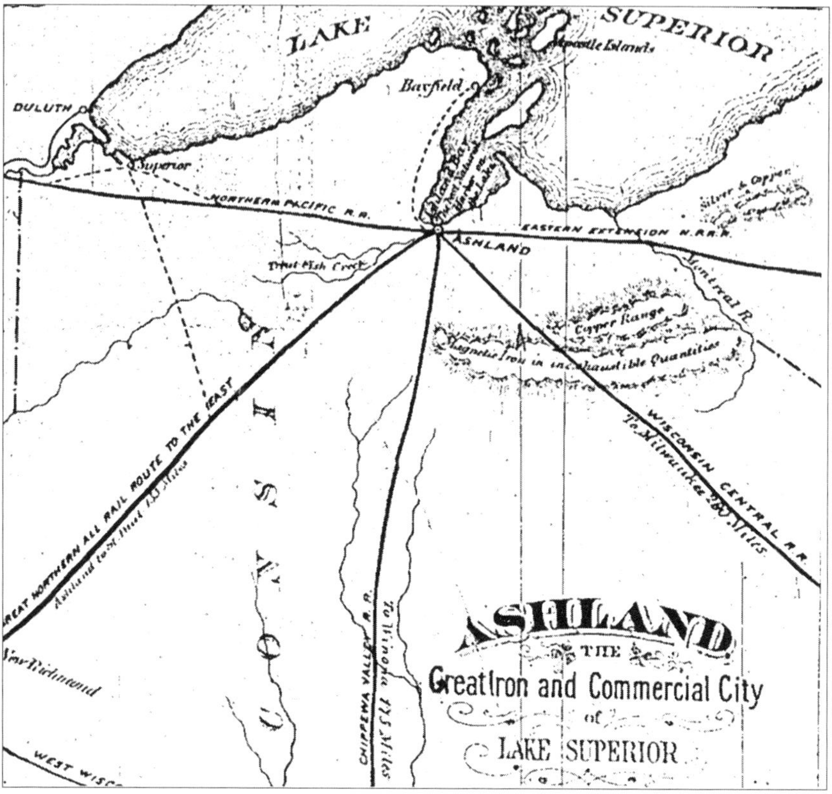

FIGURE 4.24 Map showing five railroads meeting in Ashland, Wisconsin, from *Ashland Press*, June 29, 1872. Courtesy of the Wisconsin Historical Society Library.

Turner wrote about his trip for the Portage newspaper. Although he did not mention it in his piece, he sat on the board of directors of the Wisconsin Central Railroad Company, so his article may be interpreted as a not-so-subtle piece of boosterism. He described the scenery as viewed from the northbound train. For 20 miles beyond Stevens Point, he passed through the cutover lands, which just a few years before had been dense forest. Turner labeled the last 100 miles of the route "wilderness," even though pinelands were rapidly being cleared to supply the sawmills that had been established along the line and homesteaders had begun "to open up farms and homes." He predicted that the removal of the rich pine groves would ultimately reveal

FIGURE 4.25 The Chequamegon Hotel, from Chicago, Milwaukee and St. Paul Railway, *Tourist's Manual* (1880). Courtesy of the Wisconsin Historical Society Library.

the "greatest wealth of this portion of the state"—the agricultural lands. According to Turner, "Probably no portion of Wisconsin offers as great inducements to actual settlers as the country bordering the Central road." He claimed that the soil was so rich and the potential market so huge that "a settler can go into these woods with a certainty of eventual success."[31] Turner was not alone in seeing the deforestation in an unambiguously positive light. Seven years earlier, the *Bayfield Press* stated that the "primeval forests will in time give place to cleared fields and meadows," adding that the rich soil awaited "only the hand of culture to transform a wilderness into fields of maize and waving grain."[32] Another writer for the *Register* even suggested that clearing off the timber could result in a warming of the climate so that eventually even corn could be grown commercially in the region.[33]

The day after Turner and his party arrived in Ashland, they toured the town. He observed that lumber mills lined the shore and were sending large quantities of their products to Chicago, Canada, and even Europe as quickly as trees could be cut. But Turner's party was on vacation. They came to see more than clearings and townsites: they wanted to see unspoiled nature. While the women went about collecting rocks and other "specimens," the men hiked to the government lookout above Bayfield. From his perch, Turner surveyed the "beautiful landscape"—the Apostle Islands sparkling "like diamonds" to the north and "an unbroken forest of hardwood and pine, in all its primeval grandeur" to the southwest. He concluded his essay by recommending the trip to "all who desire to take a release from business cares and enjoy a new country, replete with magnificent scenery, and famous for its pure bracing atmosphere."[34]

In 1885, eight years after Turner's visit, Ashland experienced an iron boom when mines on the Gogebic range to the south began sending carloads of iron ore to be shipped out through Ashland docks. The Milwaukee, Lakeshore and Western Railway Company ore dock, constructed the same year, was described by local boosters as the largest in the world, and it, too, became an iconic image of the region and a tourist attraction in its own right. Meanwhile, land clearing had continued on such a scale that the Ashland pig iron works went out of business because there were no longer enough local hardwoods available to make charcoal for the plant.[35] The entire region became known as "the cutover," and the lumber companies moved their operations to the Pacific Northwest. By 1930, even the Apostle Islands had been thoroughly logged. A park service surveyor lamented that "the virgin forest [had] been ruthlessly exterminated, mostly within the last 5–20 years" and predicted that it would take fifty to one hundred years for the forest to begin to recover. He claimed that "the hand of man has mercilessly and in a measure, irrevocably destroyed their virgin beauty."[36]

Yet even amid these dramatic changes, the boosters continued to promote Chequamegon Bay as both an industrial center and a naturally pristine resort.

FIGURE 4.26 "Nature's Palace in the Wildwood," from Fifield, "Among the Historic Apostle Isles," *National Magazine* (1898). Courtesy of the Wisconsin Historical Society Library.

In 1898 (a year before his similar essay appeared in *Picturesque Wisconsin*), Sam Fifield—the former local newspaper editor and lieutenant governor of Wisconsin whose boosterism over the previous twenty-six years had done so much to encourage the industrial development of the region—wrote an article describing the experience to be had at his Camp Stella, on Sand Island (fig. 4.26): "Thousands of tourists visit these lakes every year and camp in the forests primeval, miles way from the haunts of civilization. It is here that one realizes the majesty of nature primeval—untouched. Our camp, on one of the Apostle Islands, nestling among towering pines was indeed a captivating and beautiful retreat."[37]

Fifield's sentiments would make more sense today if he had gone through a transformation—if, in reaction to witnessing the primeval forests cut, the waters of Chequamegon Bay sullied by sawdust, the pure air polluted, and the tranquil silences broken, he had become a wilderness advocate. But although Fifield obviously appreciated wild nature and, as editor of the *Ashland*

Press, had even advocated an Apostle Islands park, he also promoted industrial growth. By 1898, large portions of the Apostle Islands had been logged and quarried, but Fifield saw the effects more as interesting artifacts of human activities than of a wilderness despoiled. What could account for this paradox?

The easy answer is that the boosters' bottom line was profit and that if money could be made off the natural landscape as well as from industrialization, then boosters simply hedged their bets by promoting both. But perhaps, as the twentieth century progressed, it was not so much that an appreciation for nature was gained but rather that an appreciation of industry was lost. As John Sears stated, most nineteenth-century Americans "perceived no conflict between nature and industrial civilization."[38]

Indeed, Chequamegon Bay boosters were not blind to the negative aspects of cities and industry. Area newspapers did occasionally warn that the forests might not be inexhaustible after all, and their editors and reporters worried that the decline in the fisheries was due to the tons of sawdust dumped daily into the bay by lumber mills. Furthermore, from the start, Chequamegon Bay boosters criticized the bad air and crowded conditions of other cities. Local newspaper editors would consistently express an optimism that they could avoid the problems of older cities such as Chicago and New York. To Chequamegon Bay boosters, anything seemed possible, so why could not a primeval, healing nature coexist in the same space as an emerging northern metropolis?

Through the last decades of the nineteenth century, Chequamegon Bay area boosters perceived nature through two lenses: romantic and scientific. But geologists were the authorities to which they appealed most directly. As has been shown, the scientists themselves were influenced by the romantics, yet the utilitarian purpose of their published work was economic development. David Dale Owen's survey was funded by the U.S. Treasury Department, and Chamberlin's *Geology of Wisconsin* was funded by state legislators eager to use the work to develop the northern portion of their state. The science in both works was sound, especially for the period, yet both works encouraged a view of nature that included beauty as well as bounty.

The Frontier, the Future City, and the Wild West

5

STORIES ABOUT place can be found in many sources, including oral traditions, personal recollections, local histories, and local newspapers. The latter can be a particularly rich resource. Despite the often questionable reliability of newspapers as historical documents, the very faults that make them problematic—the selective vision, boosterism, and fierce provincialism—increase their value as windows into the making of place. Indeed, there is a growing literature on the significance of newspapers in frontier and post-frontier communities.[1] Newspapers played a vital role in nineteenth-century towns: the editor was a community spokesperson, a mediator among local groups and between the local and outside worlds, and the central promoter for a vision of the future place.

Scholars have taken a variety of approaches toward interpreting this document hoard. Some of the most promising methods analyze the rhetorical devices used in emigrant guides and promotional pamphlets, as well as the use and abuse of regional images to associate the promoted place with a particular or generic type of desirable landscape or, conversely, to "dissociate" with a region to indicate the absence of hazards or disadvantages believed to exist there.[2] Association and dissociation were common rhetorical devices used by northern Wisconsin boosters.

By playing the three interrelated and sometimes competing roles of interpreter, promoter, and watchdog, newspaper editors sought to influence not only material construction but also social relationships.[3] As interpreters, the editors decided what was newsworthy by selectively recording the passing scene and the events of the larger world; as promoters, they strove to put the home place in the best possible light and to guide its development; and as watchdogs, they condemned perceived threats to social and economic order and vigorously defended the image of the place from outside attacks. The *Ashland Press* was representative of countless other small-town newspapers. The motivating force behind the paper was a boosterish vision of the place—what is was, what it could be, and, most important, what it *should* be. The editor of the *Press* sought to shape the emerging city and its hinterland with words.

A pioneer press typically began operating before there was a town. In 1854, Leavenworth, Kansas, was nothing more than a cluster of *four tents*, but it had a newspaper.[4] By the 1870s, the typical country weekly was four pages long, with six to nine columns to a page containing local news, advertisements, miscellaneous tidbits, legal notices, and a column or two of political commentary. Nearly every American village of one thousand or more inhabitants had two such papers.[5] Larger communities with larger ambitions often had a dozen or more competing newspapers. Between 1870 and 1880, the U.S. population increased 30 percent, whereas the number of newspapers increased almost 100 percent to seven thousand. By 1890, there were twelve thousand newspapers in the United States.[6] The high number of papers available during the latter half of the nineteenth century can be explained, in part, by economic and technological factors, but migration and settlement processes also played a role.[7] Newly established communities and those with significant immigrant populations tended to have the most newspapers per capita. Ashland, Wisconsin, fit both of these criteria.

Although the *Ashland Press* preceded and outlasted its competition, it was far from being the only paper in town. During the forty-two-year period

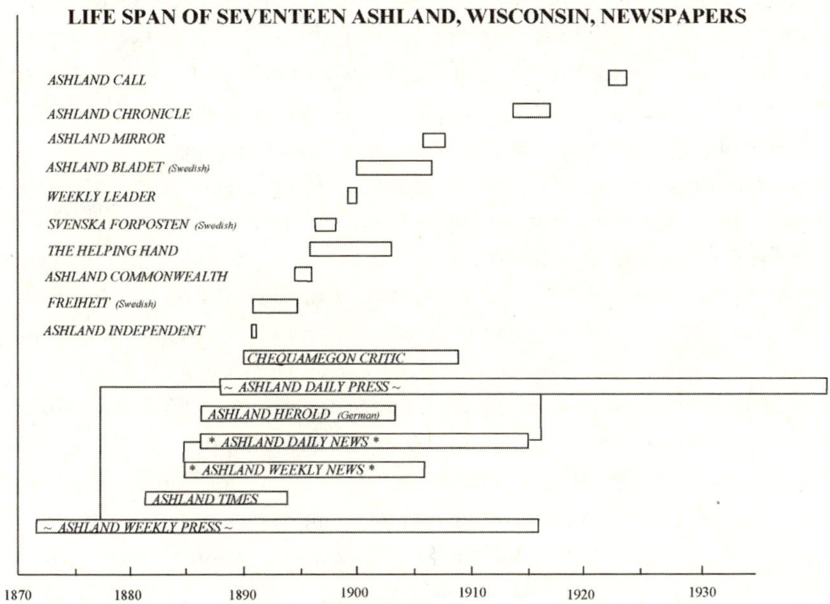

FIGURE 5.1 Life span of seventeen Ashland, Wisconsin, newspapers. Chart by author. Date compiled from Oehlerts and Griswold.

from 1882 to 1924, the *Press* had fifteen recorded competitors, including one German-language and three Swedish-language papers (fig. 5.1).[8] The dramatic growth in newspapers coincided with Ashland's iron boom of the late 1880s, when there was an influx of people into the city and the population peaked at about fifteen thousand. Lest one might think that Ashland was unique, a comparison of newspaper startup data for six other Wisconsin communities of similar size (Janesville, Wausau, Chippewa Falls, Waukesha, Manitowoc, and Watertown) shows that each had as many or more competing papers.[9] Similar data could be shown for other states.[10] Ashland was typical for a city of its size and ambitions.

The first issue of the *Ashland Press* was printed in Asaph Whittlesey's barn in 1872 because masons had not yet finished plastering the walls of the paper's new office. Editor Sam Fifield wryly noted that "there is nothing like being a pioneer."[11] Fifield was self-conscious of his role as a pioneering newspaper editor. He became a major political player in northern Wisconsin yet remained intimately in tune with his adopted hometown. And he played his expected roles so true to script that he is a sterling example of the archetypal small-town editor. In the first issue of the *Ashland Press,* Fifield wrote that the newspaper "is the organ of the people and the community in which it is published. The best, the most accurate, the most lifelike history of the age may be found in the columns of the newspaper."[12] When he died forty-three years later, in 1915, he left his bound files of the *Ashland Press* to the Vaughn Library ("to be kept . . . for public inspection and protected from mutilation") because "within their covers will be found the story of the struggle of the pioneers of the city."[13] In many ways, Sam Fifield was the first *bard* of Ashland. In telling its stories, he created a sense of the place even as he recorded its history.

The most concrete way in which newspapers shaped place was in the promotion of specific building projects. For example, in 1885, the *Ashland Press* argued that the town should have a toboggan slide and a club to promote it,[14] and two years later, the paper announced that the slide had opened and the club had been formed.[15] Countless similar examples in the *Ashland Press* and elsewhere suggest that newspapers could and sometimes did directly influence the material construction of place. But the indirect ways in which newspapers shaped places are potentially more revealing.

Place promotion was the primary function of the newspaper, and the *Ashland Press,* like most papers of its time, can best be understood as a booster organ. The booster motive was clearly and unapologetically spelled out on the masthead of the paper: "Devoted to the Interests of the 'New Wisconsin.'" Promoter Fifield actively tried to influence the public's perception of northern Wisconsin in general and of Ashland in particular. He knew that the more clearly people visualized the area's potential, the more likely they were to make it reality. He promoted the geography of the possible. A good illustration of this effort is the map published in 1872 that was entitled "Ashland, the Great Iron and Commercial City of Lake Superior" (fig. 4.24). The "city," which probably had fewer than five hundred residents, was depicted as *the* railhead on the lake—five long years before the first rail connection to the city was established. Ashland (or Chequamegon) Bay was labeled "the best harbor on the lake," and in addition to an iron range (described as "inexhaustible"), there were two imaginary silver and copper ranges on the map. The map did predict railways that would actually be built, but it could not alter geographical reality: Ashland's harbor was adequate but not the best on the lake, iron ore was exhaustible, and copper and silver resources in the area proved insignificant.

Nevertheless, seventeen years later, most of the railways that were shown on the map had been built, and a short-lived iron boom gave the next editor of the *Press* the confidence to declare that Ashland's advantages were "in many respects, . . . equal if not greater than Chicago, and in one thing Ashland is far ahead of Chicago—she can manufacture iron cheaper, all things considered, at the present time than Chicago can a thousand years hence."[16] Chicago may not have heard Ashland's challenge (or may not have cared if it had), but Ashland did experience a modest success as a transhipment point for iron ore, which passed via railway through its harbor until the 1950s.[17]

In the role of interpreter, the newspaper editor decided which people, phenomena, and events were newsworthy. Newsprint made certain aspects of the world visible—rendering power by mere mention—and at the same time, it left other aspects of the world effectively invisible. Interpretation took various forms throughout the newspaper, and it could be skewed in the interest of promotion, but the interpreter role required the editor to record the common, everyday, lived experience of residents of the place. When the weather got too hot or too cold, the editor wrote about it: to do otherwise would be to risk losing credibility. And even though the *Ashland Press,* like most newspapers of its time, was a booster organ, it still contained a wealth of information that would seem to counter the paper's promotional efforts, especially if one read between the lines.

Local happenings are still a regular feature in many small-town American newspapers. Today, a column devoted to that topic is usually limited to who-visited-who snippets, but until the early part of the twentieth century, the locals column was a weekly or daily record of life in a small town from the editor's point of view. It was also the usual place for the editor to unleash the community watchdog. In the role of watchdog, the newspaper editor vigorously defended the image of the town while at the same time drawing attention to and condemning what was deemed inappropriate behavior within the community. It was acceptable for the *Press* to criticize Ashland, but the editor might respond harshly to outside critics. When Duluth newspapers denigrated Ashland's harbor, for example, the *Press* responded promptly with a volley of statistics to "prove" that the harbor was the last to freeze shut and the first to open, whereas Duluth's harbor was frozen shut practically the entire year. Similarly, when the *Cincinnati Enquirer* published sensational stories about white slavery in the "hell-holes of the North Woods," the *Press* pointedly suggested that the reporter should actually visit the place of which he wrote. When a Chicago detective apprehended the "notorious fugitive" and "seductrice" Maude Cassidy, who was hiding out in Ashland, the *Press* quoted the detective as saying how surprised he was to find such a clean and orderly city after reading the distortions of the region printed by the Chicago papers. He even promised to set them straight when he returned to his hometown.[18] Elsewhere, the *Press* described Chicago as the "city of sin," black with mud and crowded with people.

Closer to home, the paper did its part in exposing local problems. It publicized thefts, condemned the "loose morals" and "barbaric habits" of the lumbermen, threatened to reveal the names of those catching more than their share of fish off the city dock, admonished people to clean up their yards ("for it will soon be cholera time!"), and warned readers of mysterious strangers seen about the area.

Even when the editors and writers at the *Press* denounced anarchists and socialists in other cities and advocated the deportation of those they labeled "foreign trouble makers" or when they praised their local ethnic groups for their complacency, they revealed their fear that "outside agitators" could disrupt the socioeconomic order of their emerging home. The editor was well aware that the key to building the "New Wisconsin" was labor, even more than capital. Working people would materially transform the northwoods into the kind of place envisioned by the northern Wisconsin newspaper. Thus, when attacking labor unrest, the *Press* seemed careful to praise the common worker, suggesting that though the worker might be misled, he or she was more than welcome in the northwoods.

Newspaper editors in the nineteenth and early twentieth centuries had a remarkably consistent vision of what emerging places should be like and what it would take to make them. They knew that they could shape the place with their words, and they actively tried to do so. But they also recorded the world about them as it unfolded, even when it contradicted their vision. Their multiple roles compelled them to not only promote their place by magnifying the positive but also to reveal the worst elements of that place. Newspapers could be as chaotic and as paradoxical as the reality they sometimes tried to reflect as well as direct. But it is for this very reason that newspapers may be a better indicator of what a place was like—the hopes, happenings, disappointments, and sorrows—than any other single index or medium. For this reason, newspapers have survived and continued to record, distort, and shape places that are never as ordered or as predictable as social scientists would like to think. Throughout the years, newspaper editors have drawn on a rich cluster of theories, myths, and partial truths to promote their place, and in doing so, they have made their own contributions to the mythmaking process.

Popular Narrative Models in Chequamegon Bay Newspapers

As noted earlier, boosters' stories were often recorded in railway company pamphlets and in state and university publications. But most important, they were disseminated through local newspapers. These stories offer key insights into the creation and re-creation of place. Three popular narrative models that recurred in local newspapers between 1870 and 1896 were especially important to the development of the Chequamegon Bay region.[19] The first was the "future city" model, whereby city boosters sought to convince others (as well as themselves) that—due to the inevitable confluence of natural advantages, economic and social forces, and, most crucially, the imminent arrival of the railroad—theirs would be *the* site of the future metropolis of Lake Superior. The social vision of the boosters, although progressive and even utopian, was too narrow to be fully inclusive, especially in regard to their Chippewa neighbors. The second was the "independence on the land" model, also known as the Turnerian model because of its similarity to Frederick Jackson Turner's frontier thesis and because the prime example of the model came from the pen of Turner's father, Andrew Jackson Turner. The third was the "Wild West" (or "cosmopolitan frontier") model, which was most dramatically represented by the coverage of Buffalo Bill Cody's 1896 visit to Ashland, Wisconsin. Cody's story line began as the classic struggle between "savagery and civilization"—between Indians and whites—but by 1896, it had evolved into something more complex. Ironically, this last model best expressed the heterogeneous human geography of an area such as Chequamegon Bay, and it appeared to envision a place for the Indians. It seems natural to think of these three models in a progressive way, just as Frederick Jackson Turner did in his seminal essay, "The Significance of the Frontier in American History."[20] According to Turner, the frontier was typified by recurrent reevolution: as the frontier progressed westward, settlers regressed temporarily to a primitive state, built homes, created an agriculturally productive landscape, and finally built towns and cities.

But as William Cronon argued in *Nature's Metropolis,* the city boosters had it right and Turner had it backwards: frontier growth *began* with the city rather than ending with it.[21] When what could later be identified as a Turnerian narrative of independence on the land appeared in nineteenth-century newspapers, the purpose was clear—to encourage the settlement of the future city's hinterland and to sell railroad property. The success of the railroad, together with the growth of a farming hinterland, was considered vital to the success of the city. By the 1870s, the independence on the land narrative had been widely used for decades by railroad companies, state immigration boards, and newspapers to encourage settlement. Frederick Jackson Turner himself, in his 1893 essay, quoted a long passage from John Mason Peck's 1848 *New Guide to the West* to illustrate the three waves of settlement: first came the pioneers, then the settlers, and finally the "men of capital and enterprise."[22] But in the Chequamegon Bay region, as elsewhere, the men of capital and enterprise came first, for it was their stories of independence on the land that lured pioneers and settlers alike. Both the city boosters and the country boosters, who were often the same people telling different stories for different purposes, offered coherent narratives. Although the city boosters offered a more accurate description of city-country relationships, the country boosters' frontier stories were more enduring.

In his essay entitled "Frederick Jackson Turner and Buffalo Bill," Richard White analyzed how Turner and Cody worked with the available frontier narratives for different purposes. According to White:

> Turner and Buffalo Bill, in effect, divided up the existing narratives of American frontier mythology. Each erased part of the larger, and more confusing and tangled, cultural story in order to deliver up a clean, dramatic, and compelling narrative. . . . Turner took as his theme the conquest of nature; he considered savagery incidental. Buffalo Bill made the con-

> quest of savages central; the conquest of nature was incidental. Yet both Turner's and Buffalo Bill's stories, it must be remembered, taught the same lessons.[23]

In both Turner's and Cody's narratives, the frontier was almost gone. Each of these men worried not only about what this would mean for the nation's future but also about what the end of the frontier meant for manhood. The frontier was conceived of as a manly place, where even an effete and urbanized male could go to reclaim his masculinity. Cities were the antithesis of the frontier: "They emasculated men, robbed them of their true manhood, and thus cities and machines became defined as feminine."[24] Ironically, both Turner's and Cody's frontiers were very much products of the city. Indeed, the racial warfare theme—between "savagery and civilization"—on which Cody originally built his reputation represented what anthropologists Brian Ferguson and Neil Whitehead called the "bloody edge of empire" as the rapidly urbanizing country expanded its territory.[25] This edge was the meeting point between conflicting storyscapes, where the new one was writing over, absorbing, and erasing the old. The new storyscape was being written in the city.

In his *Gunfighter Nation,* Richard Slotkin contrasted the Wild West with the White City as both appeared at the 1893 World's Columbian Exposition in Chicago.[26] On the surface, the Wild West and the White City were polar opposites representing savagery and civilization, but as Slotkin has pointed out, there was quite a bit of civilization in the Wild West and more than a little savagery in the White City. Chequamegon Bay was a remarkably civil place before cities were established there. It was never a "savage frontier." Indians and whites had coexisted peacefully for more than a century. Indeed, local Indians were able to resist a presidential removal order in the 1850s in part because no one could argue that they were a threat to their white neighbors. Despite the sometimes ignoble behavior of the whites, northern Wisconsin Indians had always upheld their part of the 1854 treaty and had been civil in their interactions with whites.[27] In contrast, the faster the city grew, the wilder it got. By the boom years of 1886 and 1887, labor unrest, riots, prostitution, drunkenness, and thievery were of serious concern to the editors of the *Ashland Press.* Brawls were so common as to be considered almost unnewsworthy.[28]

Conflicting Storyscapes

In his classic *History of the Ojibway Nation,* William Whipple Warren preserved remnants of the first stories told along the shores of Chequamegon Bay. One story related how Menabosho—the Algonquin demigod who made the earth anew after the deluge—was hunting the great beaver in Lake Superior, which was then but a large beaver pond. The beaver hid in Chequamegon Bay. To capture him, Menabosho built a large dam. Occasionally, he would throw a fistful of mud into the lake, each of which formed an island. The dam reached almost to Madeline Island. But the elusive beaver broke through the dam and escaped into Lake Superior.[29] According to Warren, it was from this story that Chequamegon Bay got its name, meaning "place of the soft beaver dam." Perhaps the most important story recorded by Warren told of how the Ojibwa were led from the "great salt water toward the rising sun" to Chequamegon Bay by the Great Megis (seashell) to find refuge from their oppressors.[30] In the seventeenth century, French Jesuits recorded a multiethnic Indian village on the shores of the bay. The villagers were refugees from the Iroquois Wars at the far eastern end of the Great Lakes.[31] They came to be known by other Native Americans as the Ojibwa—meaning "those who write," referring to their practice of preserving their traditions on birchbark scrolls.[32]

In the Chequamegon region, Chippewa oral traditions were replaced by written texts and birchbark scrolls gave way to newspapers, but stories continued to be told. The retellings added to the constructed meaning of the place, which was manifested in behavior; the results are visible in the landscape and in the relationships among the people. The newcomers told very different stories about Chequamegon Bay than did the Chippewa, the Jesuit priests, the fur traders, or the explorers.[33] One of the first stories the new settlers told themselves involved a great metropolis that, because of certain mysterious and quasi-scientific forces, was certain to emerge on the shores of Chequamegon Bay. The only question was precisely where. Two places seemed most promising: the future sites of Bayfield and Ashland.[34]

By 1860, residents began to leave Ashland in favor of Bayfield, which possessed a deeper, more sheltered harbor. By the end of the decade, only one family remained in Ashland. But this was a volatile period, and hopeful cities' fortunes could change almost overnight. The first edition of the *Bayfield*

Press to hit the stands was dated June 13, 1870. Two years later, the paper became the *Ashland Press* when the Wisconsin Central Railway began construction to Ashland instead of Bayfield. But the railroad did not arrive until 1877, and Ashland never did become a metropolis. Disappointments only led to more stories, and Ashland was a place of many stories. In 1892, the population was under ten thousand but was enough to support nine newspapers, two of which were dailies.[35] Today, only the daily *Ashland Press* survives.

As noted earlier, the frontier newspaper was primarily a booster organ. In part, the goal was to encourage outside investment, but more important, the press aimed at reassuring residents that they were right to stay—that no matter how things looked at the moment, the future was bright and prosperity was right around the corner. The editors tried to attach positive nicknames to their cities—hopeful names such as "the Metropolis of the New Wisconsin," "the Embryo City," "the Iron City," "the Future City," and "the Garland City of the Inland Sea."[36] They also tended to list so-called natural advantages that would assure the growth of a large city. As Cronon observed in *Nature's Metropolis,* the boosters articulated a coherent set of theories concerning the growth of cities.[37]

In the November 26, 1870, *Bayfield Press,* editor Hank O. Fifield asked and answered a question that was on the minds of many at the time: "What Natural Advantages Are Required to Assure the Permanent Growth of a City." Undoubtedly influenced by contemporary booster theorists, Fifield asserted that "there are certain fixed laws which govern the location of a large population, as surely as other laws control the general course of emigration; and that these laws are never held in abeyance except by the pressure of some unusual advantage which will control and unite many diverse interests."[38] Furthermore, in contrast to the many mining boomtowns "in the territories" that grew quickly only to be abandoned, a potential city needed more than one thing going for it. Fifield listed six conditions that had to exist in a place for it to attain permanent growth. First on his list—and implicit in the rest—was *location.* The right location would be "a point for the easy concentration and distribution of the agricultural and mechanical products of a large area of territory." The place had to be accessible by land and water and therefore required a large and safe harbor with a "reasonable length of the season of navigation." Bayfield, of course, possessed the best harbor on the west end of Lake Superior, the most interior of the Great Lakes. Second, heavy building materials such as timber, stone, and brick had to be close at hand to lessen the cost of transporting such supplies. This second condition would, of course, rule out much of the Great Plains. Third, for a city to be enduring, it should not be limited to exporting resources; it had to develop its resources into a manufacturing base. Fifield expressed the hope that coal might be discovered near Bayfield to facilitate the manufacture of iron and lumber. (A closer reading of Owen's 1852 *Report* would not have encouraged much hope that abundant coal would be found, but Owen did point out that local hardwoods could provide charcoal.) Another prime condition was that an enduring city needed a rich agricultural hinterland in the immediate vicinity, so that cheap and abundant food could assure "the uniform prosperity of all classes." Although Owen's *Report* offered conflicting analyses of the agricultural potential of the region, it did suggest that the red marl soil that dominated the Lake Superior lowland around Chequamegon Bay had potential, if properly cultivated. Furthermore, the proximity to the lake moderated the climate and resulted in a longer growing season.

But physical geography was not enough, according to Fifield, to assure permanence. Social issues also needed to be addressed. Citing the "destruction of human life" and the "material loss inflicted by each recurring epidemic in our large cities," Fifield offered his fifth condition—that there had to be abundant pure air and water and good natural drainage. His sixth and final condition was that there had to be enough space for business and residential areas. Fifield articulated the pragmatic political motive behind his last two considerations:

> It is daily becoming more apparent to those familiar with even our smaller cities that much damage has been experienced by neglect of this consideration. The condition of the laboring classes, so intimately affecting political and social morals, is gaining deserved attention and study. To change it in cities already built will task the abilities and energies of the whole country. Many of its worst phases may be averted in cities yet to be, by giving attention to the subject of space, sunlight and pure air, and assuring the laboring classes assessable, pleasant homes instead of sickly dungeons.[39]

Fifield concluded by arguing that Bayfield was one of the few places that actually met all of the six conditions he set forth "and more." Finally, he expressed confidence that with human initiative, Bayfield would soon see "the fulfillment of the promises Nature has lavished on this beautiful spot."

Fifield did not say so, but he must have been influenced directly or indirectly by social and economic theorists of his day.[40] Although his emphasis on location, resources, and climate suggests the influence of booster theorists such as William Gilpin and Jesup Scott, his expressed concern for the "condition of the laboring classes" resembled the language of social theorists such as Karl Marx and Friedrich Engels. This may seem odd, since Fifield was clearly a booster and boosters were almost by definition the cheerleaders for capitalism whereas Marxists led the booing section. Yet Fifield sought to envision a *permanent* city, in contrast to older industrial cities that already seemed to be coming apart at the seams because of filthy living conditions and labor unrest. In Fifield's vision, capitalism could grow unimpeded if, in addition to having the right location and resources, cities could also provide affordable food and a healthy living environment for the workers on whom economic development would ultimately depend. This progressive vision is remarkably in tune with the ideas of the utopian industrialist Robert Owen, whose son, David Dale Owen, had conducted the first comprehensive economic geological survey of the Chequamegon Bay region.

At heart and in keeping with the thinking of other booster theorists, Fifield's argument was essentially a geographical one. The "certain fixed laws" to which he appealed can be boiled down to the synergy of site, situation, and resources, all of which are bound to location. Together, they became "the promises of Nature," which required only the addition of human initiative to assure their realization. The general "fixed laws" were customized to fit the particular place being boosted and to argue for its superiority over other competing places. In the case of Bayfield, having a combination of "all of the above" was better than having a "single unusual advantage," to avoid the fate of the mining boomtown. On that end of Lake Superior, the possession of the best harbor seemed to be the most compelling factor in terms of supporting one site over another.[41] But what is most remarkable about rhetoric of this sort is how common it was. Similar rhetoric could be found in countless newspapers across the Midwest, from true future metropolises such as Chicago to would-be cities that never made it off the map.

The natural advantages that the booster touted usually fell into three broad categories: resources, transportation routes, and global climatic factors.[42]

FIGURE 5.2 Map of William Gilpin's "Isothermal Zodiac," from Gilpin, *Mission of the North American People* (1873). Courtesy of the Wisconsin Historical Society Library.

The specific advantages that happened to be found in a given place were, of course, deemed most significant; the basic structure of the booster's argument was easily transported from one place to another. In Bayfield (and, within two years, in Ashland), the vital resources were usually expressed as a triumvirate—a triple combination either of fish, lumber, and brownstone or

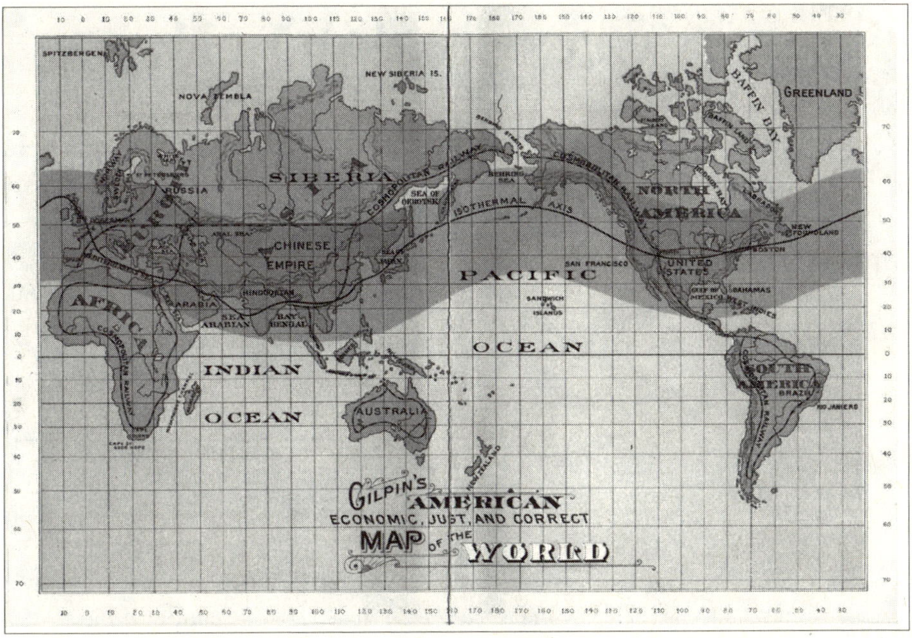

FIGURE 5.3 Map of William Gilpin's "Cosmopolitan Railway," from Gilpin, *Mission of the North American People* (1873). Courtesy of the Wisconsin Historical Society Library.

of iron ore, fertile soil, and scenery. And, of course, Bayfield's (and soon Ashland's) strategic geographical position made it a vital link in a transportation network that would, according to promoters, transform the region, nation, and probably the world once completed.

The most mysterious of the natural advantages believed to give rise to great cities was climate. Inspired by the German geographer Alexander von Humboldt, booster theorist William Gilpin argued that nature controlled where great cities could arise.[43] He adopted von Humboldt's idea of an "Isothermal Zodiac" through which passed an "Axis of Intensity," whichwas essentially the 52° isotherm (fig. 5.2). It was no coincidence that this zone was also seen as the ideal habitat for the white race. In this climatic belt, so the argument ran, all of the great centers of civilization had arisen. The next world metropolis was expected to develop somewhere near the center of the United States along the favorable isotherm, and a "cosmopolitan railway" would spread the influence of this city around the globe (fig. 5.3).

The Ashland Press.

SAM. S. FIFIELD, Editor and Proprietor. (DEVOTED TO THE DEVELOPMENT OF THE "NEW WISCONSIN.") TERMS: $2.

VOL. 5. ASHLAND, WISCONSIN, SATURDAY, JUNE 2, 1877.

MAP SHOWING THE TEMPERATURE OF ASHLAND, AS COMPARED WITH OTHER SECTIONS OF THE UNION.

THE TEMPERATURE OF ASHLAND.

Its Comparative Warmth in Winter.

The Coolest City in the United States in Summer.

A few Facts, Verified from the Official Statistics of the Signal Service Weath-

the latter. For this reason, the isothermal line given above is not quite as favorable to Ashland as it would be if based upon observations taken at the same instant of local time.

WHY IS ASHLAND WARM IN WINTER?

The peculiarities of Ashland temperature are chiefly traceable to the influences of the Lake breezes. The severity of all northerly and westerly winds is greatly modified by the temperature of the vast body of comparatively warm water over which they must pass. Lake Superior is, in some respects, different from any other body of fresh water

Ashland and Vicinity.

—Butterflies.
—June Bugs.
—Balmy June.
—Mosquitos, ugh!
—Bacon and greens.
—Hot, hotter, hottest!
—Brilliant northern lights.
—Magnificent ice cream at VACHON'S.
—CHARLY DAY has a nice boat for sale.
—The lemon ice at VACHON'S is superb.
—Fearful weather for lard, butter and fat men.

Special Meeting County Board of Supervisors.

A special meeting of the County Board of Supervisors of Ashland county, was held pursuant to adjournment, at the office of the County Clerk, this 28th day of May, 1877, at 10 o'clock A. M.

S. S. VAUGHN, Ch'm., presiding.

Members present, S. S. VAUGHN and J. A. DAVIS, Deputy County Clerk.

There not being a quorum present, the meeting adjourned till 7 o'clock P. M.

The Board reconvened at 7 o'clock.

From our Regular Correspondent.

Bayfield Items.

—DAVID COOPER'S new house will soon be ready for him to occupy.

—The potatoe bugs are here again, offering chromos for early potatoes.

—Our fruit trees are in full bloom and there will be a good crop of small fruits.

—AL. ANGUS has finished painting the Court House, and it looks as neat as wax.

—Fishing among the islands is reported good, and such lots of speckled trout! O, my!

FIGURE 5.4 Isotherm map, from *Ashland Press*, June 2, 1877. Courtesy of the Wisconsin Historical Society Library.

The problem for a city such as Ashland was that the isotherm needed to be extended northward—which seems to be just what editor Sam Fifield tried to do (fig. 5.4). The front page of the June 2, 1877, *Ashland Press* displayed a "map showing the temperature of Ashland, as compared with other sections of the union." To give a "correct idea of Ashland's average temperature," the map was based on data for the "entire month" of February 1877. The map placed Ashland on essentially the same isotherm as Milwaukee, Detroit, Cleveland, Erie, and Rochester and not far north of New York and Chicago. The message was clear: Ashland was the most likely place on Lake Superior for the next great metropolis to rise. The isotherm map was, of course, controversial in Bayfield, which lay just outside the isotherm; it was also the subject of some derision in Duluth and Superior.[44]

Fifield did not take his own map too seriously. On the same page that declared Ashland "the coolest city in the United States in summer" was a local gossip column full of complaints about the heat and mosquitoes and a warning that people should clean up their yards because cholera season was approaching.[45] Some boosterism was tongue-in-cheek. A decade later, in 1887, former editor Hank O. Fifield returned to Ashland after a long absence and was astonished at how much the town had actually grown. As a regular subscriber to the *Ashland Press*, he should have been prepared for this, but the paper quoted him as saying, "'You always used to blow about Ashland and lie so like the devil about it, we reserved our opinion.' He thinks now that we have reformed."[46]

Much of the booster rhetoric was little more than wishful thinking, and from the beginning, the boosters wished for a railroad. As mentioned earlier, the front page of the June 29, 1872, *Ashland Press* displayed a map showing four railway lines serving Ashland, even though the first rail connection would not be made for five long years (fig. 4.24). When the last rail was finally laid on June 2, 1877, the paper declared: "The Sunlight of Progress Has Penetrated the Wilderness of the New Wisconsin at Last!—ASHLAND AND LAKE SUPERIOR UNITED BY IRON BANDS WITH THE WICKED WORLD." And that the *latter* would be better for it.

Selling Independence on the Land

The emerging railway network not only connected Ashland to the world but also linked it to its rural hinterland. Examples of agricultural boosterism became increasingly common in the *Ashland Press* after the first rail connection was completed. Much of the boosterism came from the railroad companies, which had experienced economic difficulties with their northern Wisconsin lines.[47] Part of their predicament related to their vast holdings of unsold land. In addition to railroad land advertisements, there were frequent editorials and letters to the editor (often unsigned or with an obvious alias) extolling the opportunities for settlers on the cheap and fertile railroad lands. In one of those amazing historical coincidences, among the first people to ride the new rails to Ashland was the editor of the *Wisconsin State Register* and the father of Frederick Jackson Turner—the person who would almost single-handedly turn a generation of American historians toward investigating the significance of the frontier.

As mentioned in the last chapter, Portage newspaper editor Andrew Jackson Turner, on July 17, 1877, joined a party traveling from Portage and Madison to Ashland on the first railway to reach Lake Superior's south shore, the Wisconsin Central. Figure 5.5 shows the route from Portage to Ashland.[48] Although the bulk of Turner's article in the *Register* described a perfect vacation full of breathtaking scenery, boating, hiking, Indian dances, gourmet cuisine, and gracious hosts, the first column was devoted to describing the landscape between the two towns.[49] What Turner portrayed was nothing less than frontier progression *northward*. A wilderness of "almost interminable forest" was being cleared south to north by lumbermen, and in their wake, pioneers were opening up farms:

> Contrary to the general understanding, what appears to be an unbroken forest, except the track for the railroad as you pass over it, the "woods" on both sides of the road are rapidly filling up with homesteaders and others who have purchased of the railroad company, and already many good homes have been built and excellent farms opened. A vast tract of country remains open for settlement, and probably no portion of Wisconsin offers as great inducements to actual settlers as the country bordering the central road.[50]

Turner raved about the superior soil. He was not certain about its potential for raising corn, but he predicted that the former northwoods would soon be the "finest wheat growing portion" of Wisconsin. If settlers were willing to work hard, he said, they could "go into these woods with a certainty of eventual success."[51] According to Turner, the northwoods farmer had a considerable advantage over the prairie farmer because the woods not only offered building materials close at hand but also employment opportunities during the idle winter months. Furthermore, the lumber camps provided a local market for farm produce. Turner listed the "thriving little villages" his entourage passed through on their way north to Ashland.

Fully sixteen years before Frederick Jackson Turner first presented his essay entitled "The Significance of the Frontier in American History," Andrew Jackson Turner and other land boosters had worked out the essential elements of the frontier thesis. For the next two decades, the *Wisconsin State Register*, the *Ashland Press*, and many other northern Wisconsin newspapers sold the cutover using imagery that would become known as Turnerian but is generally

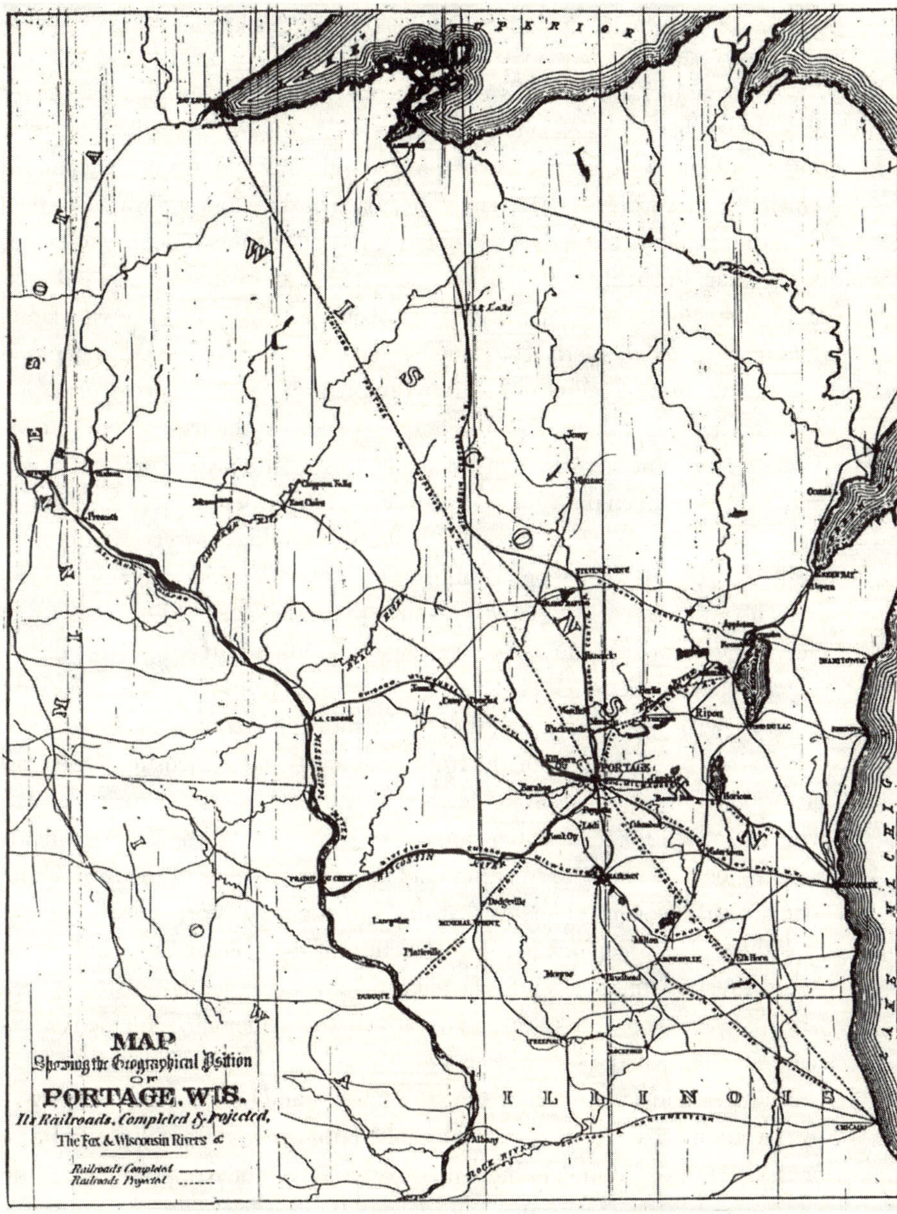

FIGURE 5.5 Railway map, from *Wisconsin State Register*, Portage, July 17, 1877. Courtesy of the Wisconsin Historical Society Library.

associated with *westward* migration. One northwoods letter writer even paraphrased Horace Greeley: "Go *North* young man!"[52]

Andrew Jackson Turner's essay was not merely a travelogue. Like many boosters, he had a hidden agenda, for he was deeply involved with the development of the Wisconsin Central Railroad line that had just opened and on which he had just traveled. He sat on the board of directors and was elected its secretary. In 1879, Turner wrote about the travails of the Wisconsin Central, noting that "probably no railroad in the state has met with so many and such great obstacles."[53] One of the greatest obstacles was selling the vast landholdings granted to the rail company by the federal government to encourage the construction of railroad lines into remote areas. If the senior Turner influenced his famous son, then it seems possible that the frontier thesis may actually have emerged from rhetoric that was essentially advertisement for railroad lands. Even the very idea of a "closing frontier" reeks of salesmanship. The *Ashland Press* warned, "This country is filling up very rapidly. The wilderness begins to blossom. Beautiful farms are already enriching the owners, who look with pride upon the results of their labors."[54] The message was clear—Do not delay! Buy now! Only while supplies last!

Of course, Frederick Jackson Turner was not trying to sell frontier land when he wrote his 1893 essay; indeed, he mourned its passing. Instead, he was trying to sell the *idea* of the frontier as a legitimate focus for American historians. It does not seem far-fetched to suggest that the rhetoric that had worked so well for the frontier salesmen also worked for the frontier historian. When Turner made an argument for the significance of the frontier, he emphasized the same elements that the settlement boosters did. He merely took these ideas a step further, from the effect of the frontier on the individual to the effect of the frontier on the nation: "The existence of an area of free land, its continuous recession, and the advance of American settlement westward, explain American development."[55]

The essential elements of the sales pitch—and of the frontier thesis—can be summarized as follows. For a limited time only, the conditions of free or cheap land and abundant high-wage jobs offered equal opportunity, to the *right type* of settler, for assured success and rapidly achieved prosperity and independence on the land. It would not be an easy lifestyle, but the satisfying experience of homesteading in northern Wisconsin would build a strong, healthy, independent, and manly character and strengthen the nation as well.

Beyond selling a frontier ideal, the land boosters were selling real estate in a particular place. The rhetorical devices of association and especially dissociation were used shamelessly in the newspapers to steer the westering migrants northward. Take, for example, an excerpt from a letter to the editor in the *Wisconsin State Register*, signed "Old Chippewa": "The prairie is a delusion and a snare to any poor man; and those poor fellows who went out west are trooping back to Wisconsin; perhaps leaving behind them in the land of grasshoppers, the wife of their youth, who perished in a frost storm, or bringing with them helpless children whose hands and feet are frozen off."[56] Another example, appearing fifteen years later in the 1892 annual edition of the *Ashland Daily Press*, encompassed dissociation as well as association and held out the lure of independence on free land. It began by describing the recent influx of settlers:

> The hardy farmer who has been ague-stricken in Illinois, smothered with mortgages in Iowa, eaten up by grasshoppers in Kansas, withered up with the drought in Nebraska and the Dakotas, or driven out by fierce competition and low prices in the eastern states, all these classes are represented in new arrivals to Ashland county in the year '91.
>
> The lands are free—free as the air, and Uncle Sam was the donor. Here in the Wisconsin forests the farmer builds his comfortable house . . . clears off his land, and is independent of the world. Pioneers from older states often remark, of the similarity of such life to that of the early settlers in the timber regions of Ohio, Indiana, Illinois, New York and other eastern states.

As recently as the year before, Frederick Jackson Turner had declared the westward moving frontier closed, yet Wisconsinites were still selling their northern frontier. Two other essential elements of the frontier thesis—and of the frontier sales pitch—were equal opportunity and the character-building qualities of the homesteading experience. These elements were related and were basic to Turner's controversial assertions about democracy. The West, or so the story goes, was more democratic than the East. According to the *Ashland Press*, in the East

> an aristocracy is thus built up. The same families who now live in affluence, increase in wealth and power, while those who serve them now for wages can look forward with but little hope for any improvement either for themselves or their children.

> IN THE WEST THIS IS NOT SO.
>
> Brains and muscle win every time.—Industry and frugality are bound to stand on the upper rounds of the ladder. Family and blue blood don't count. There is room for all. . . . No one cares who your father was. . . . The only question is, "*Who and what are you?*" If you are honest, true and manly, come out here. If you aspire to be a *man* among *men*, you will be welcome in Northern Wisconsin. Here is plenty of room and a clear track. You can surely win if it is in you.[57]

The West was the land of opportunity, and the West was where manly men were made. This narrative of positive environmental influences was a common one in the northern Wisconsin newspapers. The benefits came at the cost of a difficult lifestyle, but because of the railroad, that cost was less than it had been in the past:

> Those who now come to Wisconsin have all the pleasure and excitement of pioneer life without the isolation and deprivations of former days. He makes his new home on the line of a railroad within easy access to our large cities and can come and go as may suit his pleasure. The great attractions of this kind of life are found in its independence,—the health and spirit it imparts; and in the constant changes which go on rapidly about you, and which you help produce. You feel that you are of some importance to the world, you see the results spring from your own efforts, and you are conscious of growth in manliness, independence and strength of mind and body. It is gratifying to know that the right kind of men are settling here, and are giving character to the country while at the same time they are developing its wealth.[58]

While the men remade the land, the land remade the men.[59] This notion had taken on new importance in 1877, when Andrew Jackson Turner made his excursion northward. Yet Turner's sunny description of assured success on free land contrasted sharply with other articles running on the page where it appeared—reports and opinions on the great railroad strike of 1877 that was gripping the nation. The juxtaposition of happy vacation and railroad land opportunity with anarchy and bloody conflict seems strange, but it could have been deliberate. It sent a powerful message: the solution to the eastern big-city labor problems was to be found in northern Wisconsin, on "free" land. A closer examination of the strike coverage suggests that the mayhem was blamed on "tramps, thieves, roughs, and criminals generally" and that there was sympathy with the honest, if misguided, workers. Low wages and unemployment were real problems. A small headline in the paper asked, "What shall be done?" and an answer was provided:

> We see hundreds of men who might take their axes and go to the woods, and take up a homestead. . . . The men of property in this state, are the men who in nine cases out of ten gave their time in early manhood to hard labor on the farm. The best employer a man can have is himself. Young man, take an ax and go to the woods and hew out with your own strength your own home, and build your own fortunes. You may—you will—often have weary limbs, but your sleep will not be disturbed with threatened reduction of your wages and strikes.[60]

The northwoods of Wisconsin, the railroad lands, and Ashland's hinterland were described as "the best country for laboring classes in the United States."[61]

The notion of the frontier as a safety valve was another theme shared by land boosters and the frontier historian. The frontier was believed to be a place where troublesome citizens could be sent to remake them into productive Americans: as Frederick Jackson Turner put it, "The frontier is the line of most rapid and effective Americanization."[62]

This was not a new idea. Encouraging Indians to become commercial farmers had long been an important facet of acculturation efforts. According to Edmund Jefferson Danziger Jr., "The white vanguard consisted of religious missionaries and agents of the federal government bent on Christianizing and 'civilizing' the red men of the south shore through formal education and the encouragement of an agrarian economy."[63] That an idea similar to one used to acculturate Indians would be promoted for rebuilding the characters of striking workers was more than mere coincidence. Richard Slotkin has argued that the imagery and icons used to build a myth of the Indians as a primal threat to civilization in order to justify their extermination was readily transferred to striking workers and labor organizers to justify their violent suppression.[64] That the transference could work both ways was suggested by the announcement of Sitting Bull's death in the December 27, 1890, *Ashland Weekly Press*, which began: "That old peace disturber and Indian anarchist has turned his toes to the daisies." But such images were not applied to the local Indians, who were such peaceful neighbors that they had become almost invisible, at least to the newspapers editors. The well-advertised arrival of Buffalo Bill's Wild West show in 1896 would bring the local Chippewa dramatically back into view.

The Wild West and the Cosmopolitan Frontier

By the 1890s, the showman Colonel William F. Cody was taking full advantage of the railway network that had brought A. J. Turner north, and Ashland was one of his stops. Buffalo Bill Cody was an influential person and a central character in promulgating the frontier myth. He, like Frederick Jackson Turner, was a genius at manipulating the icons of the frontier to create a compelling metanarrative. Unlike Turner, Buffalo Bill actually inhabited the role of frontier hero. Richard White was correct in suggesting that Turner and Cody divided up the existing mythology: Turner emphasized free land and peaceful occupation, whereas Cody emphasized bloody conflict, especially with Native Americans. But by the time Buffalo Bill arrived in Ashland, Wisconsin, in September 1896, his Wild West had changed. The Buffalo Bill narrative had come to represent something far more complex than just the conquest of savagery.

In 1896, Buffalo Bill's Wild West traveled 10,000 miles and made 132 stops.[65] His appearance in Ashland was brief; the next day, he performed in Duluth. The local papers considered his arrival on September 11 big news. But almost equal coverage was given to the estimated nine hundred Chippewa who poured into town to see the show. When the Indian agent, Lieutenant William Mercer, heard that so many Chippewa were coming from the Bad River and Lac du Flambeau Reservations, he said he decided that they should be transported and housed systematically, "instead of allowing them to roam about without restraint."Consequently, he arranged for the Indians to be sheltered and fed at the Chequamegon Hotel.[66] Mercer wanted the reporter to take special note of the 123 schoolchildren from Odanah and Lac du Flambeau, pointing out that "they are as nice looking and neat, and as well behaved as the same number of white children would be."[67]

The sight of so many of the local Chippewa in town was so uncommon that hundreds of Ashland residents went down to Front Street to see the "dusky men and women whose presence had converted the Chequamegon into a veritable Indian reserve." At the hotel, as the children played, the reporter imagined that the older Indians "gazed around them at the wonderful changes the hand of civilization and progress had made on the shores of Chequamegon Bay."[68] He did not ask himself why so many of the local Chippewa would travel to Ashland to see Buffalo Bill's show. But the newspaper account of the Wild West cavalcade that marched by the Chequamegon Hotel at 11:00 a.m. offered a clue.

The main attraction of the cavalcade was reported to be the "Congress of Rough Riders of the World." Since the Columbian Exposition in 1893, Cody's Wild West show had become more diverse. By 1896, it included English huntsmen; German, French, Russian, and Irish military units; Bedouin Arabs; Mexican vaqueros; American cowboys; South American gauchos; a "Negro Jockey"; Annie Oakley; and one hundred Sioux, Cheyenne, and Arapaho warriors (fig. 5.6). And after the massacre at Wounded Knee on December 29, 1890, Buffalo Bill's theme had turned from "savage warfare" to reconciliation with Native Americans.[69] In Ashland, according to the *Ashland News*, "the red royalty that roved the continent when Columbus landed . . . marched by the side of his erstwhile foe, now friend, the scout and frontiersman . . . this assemblage of sons of fighting forefathers marched to the spirit of peace . . . formed a collection—all on horseback—that preceded the dawn of universal friendship—the millennium."[70] When the procession passed the Chequamegon Hotel, its leader, Buffalo Bill himself, stopped to meet Lieutenant Mercer and the Chippewa. The Indians lit a peace pipe to smoke with Buffalo Bill, whom they considered to be the head of their traditional enemies, the Sioux. Cody invited the Chippewa to meet with "his" Sioux between shows.[71]

Later, backstage and away from the crowds, the Chippewa and the Sioux, along with Buffalo Bill, Mercer, and the city editor of the *Ashland Press*, smoked the pipe of peace and pledged eternal friendship.[72] Cody biographers who mention the event seem split on whether it was an example of Cody's altruism (because he reportedly refused to publicize the event) or an example of his genius for self-promotion.[73] In the end, that may not matter at all because

FIGURE 5.6 Advertisement for Buffalo Bill's Wild West, *Ashland News*, September 11, 1896. Courtesy of the Wisconsin Historical Society Library.

to the Chippewa and Sioux who participated and to the few who refused to take part, it was a serious and historic event. Cody himself suggested that the meeting with the Chippewa would be a "civilizer for the Sioux" because the former had made so much progress in adopting the ways of the whites.[74]

In 1890, booster theorist William Gilpin prophesied that his grand scheme of a cosmopolitan railway would unite "in one race, one language, and one brotherhood all the peoples of the world." The problem with Gilpin's story, with booster stories in general, and with Turner's stories of free land was that the only role for American Indians was to assimilate or die: in either scenario, they would disappear. But Buffalo Bill's story of a truly cosmopolitan frontier offered a different role for Indians—to ride side by side with the "Congress of Rough Riders" toward a more diverse future.[75]

Despite Buffalo Bill's flaws—and there were many—in the 1890s he offered a vision of diverse peoples riding together, separately but in the same direction, toward a future that allowed differences while emphasizing a common humanity. It all may have been an act, but it was an act with roles that everyone could inhabit and thereby claim a common past. According to Richard White, the performative West showed that the roles of the American frontier could be imaginatively inhabited by anyone:

> In a country as diverse as the United States the long dominance of this central imaginative narrative of the frontier has had significant virtues. In a country with so many variants of actual experience, it is perhaps a good thing to find imaginative coherence in a set of stories that accept change and conflict as givens. When we mount up, when we assume the right to inhabit and retell a common past, then there seems to be a unity among us that transcends, without erasing, our differences.[76]

The 1896 appearance of Buffalo Bill's Wild West in Ashland must have had special significance both for the Chippewa and for the rest of the audience as well because the population of Ashland at that time was almost as diverse as the Wild West. According to the 1895 state population census, out of 12,310 Ashland residents, only 66 percent had been born in the United States, and of these, four individuals were identified as "colored." Scandinavians, Germans, French, Dutch, and others but (according to the census) no Indians made up the bulk of the population. Ashland County had an even higher percentage of foreign-born residents than the city did. More than two decades before, in 1872, an *Ashland Press* writer had remarked: "It would seem necessary for our Ashland merchants to be familiar with several languages to understand the wants of our cosmopolitan customers."[77]

What these diverse people shared were *stories.* All were drawn to the region by stories. The Chippewa were led to Chequamegon Bay and Madeline Island by their megis and the promise of freedom from their enemies, a story often repeated and preserved in the common mythology of the place.[78] The rest of the people, American-born and foreign-born alike, were drawn by stories of a future metropolis on the shores of Chequamegon Bay and of landed independence in its rural hinterland. In his much-maligned essay, Frederick Jackson Turner wrote that "nothing works for nationalism like intercourse within the nation. Mobility of population is death to localism, and the western frontier worked irresistibly in unsettling population. The effects reached back from the frontier and affected profoundly the Atlantic coast, and even the Old World."[79] But it was stories that mobilized the people, and it was stories that would help to unite them—just as other stories could separate them. Stories expressed and shaped beliefs, and they influenced peoples' behaviors toward one another and on the land. In its multiple roles, the local newspaper printed many of these stories and thereby helped build a sense of place even as it contributed to American mythology.

6 Northern Exposures

THE ICE broke up and moved out of Chequamegon Bay in the first week of May 1886. Within days, boats began to arrive at and depart from the competing harbors of Bayfield, Washburn, and Ashland. Just whose harbor had the longest shipping season was subject to endless debate in the local newspapers. The three Chequamegon Bay communities did agree, however, that their bay contained the best harbors and that the Superior and Duluth harbors, at the extreme western end of the lake, always opened last and closed first. Nonetheless, the fiercest rivalry was probably between Superior and its Minnesota neighbor, Duluth. Even after railroads connected the region to the larger world, having the best harbor on the lake was a matter of local pride and was considered vital to the growth of a metropolis. The region remained largely dependent on the lake and subject to its whims. With its open water or ice and with its calm or rough surface, Lake Superior was a constant reminder that human activity was not entirely independent of nature's rhythms. When the big lake froze, parts of the local economy did, too.

Spring thaw allowed iron ore from the just opened Penokee-Gogebic mines near Hurley and also those in Michigan to be shipped through Ashland harbor to the steel mills of Pittsburgh, Youngstown, and Gary.[1] It also meant that coal and other commodities could arrive by water, to be distributed inland. In Bayfield, the Boutin and the Booth fisheries began their open-water season. Brownstone from mines on the Apostle Islands and the nearby mainland was shipped to Milwaukee, Chicago, and elsewhere to build the brownstone structures that were then in fashion. Up and down the coast, logs arrived from the seemingly interminable forests to supply the mills that shipped their finished lumber to build railroads, fences, and buildings not only on the Great Plains and in U.S. cities but as far away as Latin America and Europe. In 1886, Ashland was in the midst of an iron boom, which would peak the following year before things slowed down again. The entire region was buzzing with activity. Warmer weather also brought tourists by the thousands. In August, the Bayfield and Ashland newspapers complained that there were not enough accommodations for all the visitors.[2]

On May 29, 1886, a regular reader of the *Ashland Press* would have learned about a visitor with a special purpose. Henry Wellge, a Milwaukee lithographer and bird's-eye artist, was in town making sketches for a bird's-eye view of Ashland. The next week, he was busy canvassing for subscribers to the work. The *Press* declared the preliminary sketch "a splendid and *correct* view worthy of the artist. . . . It gives a fine view of the harbor and will make a beautiful picture to frame. It not only gives an outline but a detail view of all the public and private buildings, easily recognizable by their owners."[3] Wellge was one of the most prolific of the nineteenth-century viewmakers and in 1886 was at his peak. A week after finishing at Ashland, he began sketching Bayfield, and he completed sketches of Washburn and Hurley the same summer. With his illustration of Superior completed earlier, in 1883, Wellge had created snapshot images of the major population centers of Wisconsin's Lake Superior coast during a critical period in their development. Each finished print seemed to capture the essence of the town and portrayed a wholesome image of northwoods pastoralism. But how "correct" were these views? What sort of record do the bird's-eye views leave for the historical geographer to interpret more than a century later? What can they tell us about the people, their place, and their time? And are they accurate portraits?

Although the future city and independence on the land narratives drew on a larger national mythology, they represented homegrown attempts to describe a distinct location and thus contributed to a unique sense of place. This chapter will contrast the pastoral view of northern Wisconsin communities portrayed in bird's-eye views with sensationalized depictions of those same communities as centers of extreme violence and vice. Both views were imposed from outside. Local boosters seemed to accept the pastoral image of their place, but they fiercely resisted the hellhole image. Neither image really came close to capturing the complex places of the Chequamegon Bay region, but they did influence the way people perceived these areas.

Bird's-eye views were generally reliable records of street patterns, buildings, and neighborhoods, showing the size of a town and how it was situated in the landscape. The main customers for such views were the town residents. Therefore, the lithographs had to be realistic—but not too realistic. The historian John Reps has recommended looking at the views as "flattering, carefully posed, and retouched portraits rather than as completely candid records of reality."[4] Just like other maps, bird's-eye views presented a certain perspective. In a sense, they *lied*—what they left out was as important as what they left in. They were both more and less than they appeared at first glance and represented a biased view of the communities they depicted. The viewmaker tried to reflect the local residents' idealized notion of their town: the town as seen from its best vantage point, emphasizing its structures and its potential and omitting its social conflicts, weedy lawns, rundown buildings, garbage disposal problems, and stray dogs. On the south shore of Lake Superior, each view was distinct and seemed to capture a sense of place that was probably just forming in 1886.

Because the Midwest is relatively flat and had been systematically surveyed, it was an ideal place to practice the viewmaker's craft. Accurate street maps could be obtained and used as basemaps by the viewmaker. The basemap could then be easily adapted to two or three favorite perspectives, which the artist used over and over, boilerplate fashion, to save time. Bayfield and Washburn were situated in terrains that defied regular grids, but Ashland sat on relatively flat ground. The 1886 view of Ashland is a good example of the two-point linear perspective typical of most of Henry Wellge's bird's-eye views (fig. 6.1).[5] If lines were drawn down the middle of the streets and extended beyond the borders, they converged at two points beyond the borders of the print. The first vanishing point was well above the horizon to the right of the view; the second was to the left of the view near the horizon. This technique maximized the potential market for the final prints by pulling up the background so that even the remotest buildings were discernible.

Lithographs, or chromos, have been called the "democratic art."[6] This characterization is especially true of bird's-eye views because the prints were affordable for average people and because they depicted communities of all sizes.[7] Furthermore, due to business conventions and artistic shortcuts, bird's-eye views tended to make all communities look alike. Harbors were always busy; neat and well-planned streets seemed to push the urbanized area outward; boats and trains and horse-drawn carriages were always in motion; and smokestacks routinely churned smoke toward the sky. All towns appeared to be caught in the process of rapid expansion. Sometimes, the impression was accurate.

Bird's-eye views are especially appropriate documents with which to explore Wisconsin's historical geography. According to John Reps, "Nearly all of the artists and publishers who dominated American viewmaking from the end of the Civil War until the turn of the century got their start in southern Wisconsin or found themselves doing business there or in nearby Chicago."[8] Art historian Thomas Beckman has pointed out that Milwaukee had several advantages as a printing center, including its large population of skilled German immigrants; its proximity to cheap and high-quality Fox River valley paper; its comparatively low rents; its central location between the urbanized East and the rapidly growing West; and finally, the magnetic effect of already established immigrants, artists, and publishers.[9] Henry Wellge was a typical viewmaker. He was a German immigrant to Wisconsin, and though he traveled widely to produce the views, he was based in Milwaukee.

Reps classified city views and their makers into two types: outsider and insider. Outsider artists used traditional landscape techniques. They required no special knowledge of their subjects beyond what they could see. They simply chose the best vantage point and drew what they saw. Insider artists, by contrast, required an intimate knowledge of their subjects because their views were drawn from an imaginary perspective somewhere above the horizon. Bird's-eye views were maps, and potential customers were more likely to purchase a copy if they could locate familiar buildings, especially their

FIGURE 6.1 Henry Wellge, "A Bird's Eye View of the City of Ashland, Wis., County Seat of Ashland County, 1886." Lithograph. (Milwaukee: Norris, Wellge and Co., 1886). Library of Congress, American Memory Map Collections, available at http://hdl.loc.gov/loc.gmd/g4124a.pm010190.

own homes. Paradoxically, insider artists such as Wellge were usually outsiders to the communities they drew. Therefore, the insider viewmaker had to spend several days walking the streets and getting to know the town. They made sketches of individual buildings and took detailed notes about terrain as well as architecture. The best viewmakers made very accurate and useful documents of their subjects.

As Wellge's bird's-eye view of Ashland was being delivered to subscribers, a Sanborn Insurance Company map was being produced for the same town. A systematic comparison of the September 1886 Sanborn map of Ashland with Wellge's 1886 bird's-eye view attests to the essential accuracy of the latter. In almost every respect, the insurance map validates Wellge's work. But there are revealing discrepancies. For example, a building shown to have burned down on the insurance map is intact in the bird's-eye view. Perhaps the viewmaker chose to show the building that was or the building that would be rebuilt. Or maybe the building burned after Wellge left and before the insurance company cartographer arrived. Most revealing are the buildings and docks that had not yet been built. The September 25, 1886, *Ashland Press* reported that

> [Wellge's] lithograph is now being delivered to subscribers by J. J. Stoner, of Madison, and is altogether a fair and accurate picture of what Ashland is. The public buildings that are and those that will be . . . are recognizable. . . . The new dock to be built by the Lake Shore Company is also upon the map, and gives a good idea of how things will look in that locality in another summer.

Unlike a photograph, the bird's-eye view recorded not just what was there but what *would* be there (or at least what some people hoped would be there). Consequently, the bird's-eye view was more than a snapshot because it also recorded perceptions, hopes, and expectations. Through Wellge's views, one can take a virtual tour of the extreme northern Wisconsin communities.

The View of Superior

At the western end of Wisconsin's Lake Superior coast is the city of Superior. Between 1890 and 1900, Superior would grow so rapidly that it became the second-largest city in the state, dwarfing its closest northern Wisconsin rivals. But in 1886, Ashland and Hurley were in the midst of the Gogebic iron boom, and Superior did not seem to pose much competition. When the view of Superior was completed in 1883, Superior was a mere village (fig. 6.2). As in most nineteenth-century communities, the dreams of the residents were much larger than the population. Superior's main rival was Duluth, Minnesota. When the Lake Superior and Mississippi Railroad that was chartered to run from St. Paul to Superior bypassed Superior in favor of Duluth around 1870, the major advantage went to Duluth. Superior did not get a rail connection until 1881, when the Northern Pacific passed through from Duluth to Ashland.

In Wellge's bird's-eye view of Superior, the street grid dominates the picture and draws the viewer's eye quickly out of town and across the lake toward the horizon, as if trying to pull the observer's attention away from the sparsely settled streets. There is no land in sight except that occupied by Superior. The city's hinterland is behind the viewer and left to the imagination. Among Wellge's views of Lake Superior towns, this is the only view that looks out toward the lake. This perspective gives little idea of how the community sits in relation to the land, but it does give a sense of activity. Not

FIGURE 6.2 Henry Wellge, "Bird's Eye View of Superior, Wis. County Seat of Douglas County, 1883." Lithograph. (Madison, WI: J. J. Stoner, 1883). Library of Congress, American Memory Map Collections, available at http://hdl.loc.gov/loc.gmd/g4124s.pm010580.

counting canoes and small sailboats, about thirty steamboats and larger sailing rigs are pictured in the harbor or heading toward its entrance. Yet even though the harbor is far from full, the bird's-eye greatly exaggerates the amount of commerce: the total number of recorded ship arrivals in Superior for the entire 1883 season was only twenty-one. In addition to the boats, a total of six trains appear in the view. One occupies the center of the image. Trailing smoke gives a sense of motion to the boats and trains.

Set between a large and sparsely settled hinterland and the biggest of the Great Lakes, Superior was a community on the edge in 1883. By emphasizing the street grids and by filling up the harbor with imaginary boats, Wellge was able to portray an orderly, prosperous, and growing community—the very image that town boosters would have portrayed. The town directory along the bottom of the image is impressive for a village of less than twenty-five hundred people, showing that all of the necessities and many luxuries were available to residents and visitors. Names such as the Kuykendall House, the European Hotel, and the Scandinavian House reflect the influx of foreign-born immigrants. Two lumber mills, a shingle mill, and a brickyard made up the industrial base. A physician, a druggist, grocery stores, meat markets, and hardware stores provided necessities, and saloons, a jeweler, a photographer, and a bookstore met other needs. The presence of churches and schools indicated a growing community. The railroad that traveled through

Superior on its way to Ashland bypassed Bayfield, but there was an overland road between the two communities. During the summer, most people traveled by boat; in the winter, they went by sled and on foot.

The View of Bayfield

Although Bayfield's population was only around fourteen hundred in 1886, it is the only community among Wellge's views that looks complete (fig. 6.3). It appears to be naturally framed by water, wooded hills, and sky. It has no gaping open spaces begging to be filled up. Unlike in the view of Superior, individual vessels and buildings loom large in Bayfield. In the center foreground, a lone figure guides a small sailboat to shore. Bayfield seems balanced, tranquil, and orderly. Smokestack industry, in the form of Pike's sawmill, is neatly segregated from the rest of Bayfield on the other side of the tracks. Although the smoke surely symbolizes progress and prosperity, the lack of numerous smokestacks may not have been considered a shortcoming because of Bayfield's growing reputation as a haven for hay fever sufferers. In August 1886, the *Bayfield County Press* published a report by Madison surgeon Joseph Hobbins regarding several remedies for hay fever. Hobbins considered the most promising treatment to be the "climatic influences as it is found in Bayfield or the shore of Lake Superior and its vicinity in Wisconsin."[10] The doctor thought the most significant factors were ozone and pine aroma.

In addition to pure air, Bayfield was known for water. Before it was wiped out by a flood, an elaborate wooden piping system carried running water to the village. As early as 1858, Bayfield was advertised as the "city of fountains,"[11] and on Wellge's bird's-eye view, it is possible to identify several of these fountains. Although some boosters still hoped that the town would become the dominant metropolis on the Great Lakes, most visitors were attracted by its quiet charms. By 1886, Bayfield was a well-established stop for tourists. Even Mark Twain and his wife made a brief stop there during the last week of June that year, aboard the propeller boat *India*.[12] In the bird's-eye view, touring boats rather than cargo boats dominate the harbor.

The iron ore boom that was beginning to stir Ashland and Hurley had little effect on Bayfield. The *Press* put a positive spin on things: "Bayfield is

FIGURE 6.3 Henry Wellge, "Bird's Eye View of Bayfield, Wis., County Seat of Bayfield County, 1886." Lithograph. (Milwaukee: Norris, Wellge and Co., 1886). Library of Congress, American Memory Map Collections, available at http://hdl.loc.gov/loc.gmd/g4124b.pm010210.

getting there slow but sure having no boom but enjoying a steady, slow growth that means permanency every time."[13] Indeed, Bayfield had not changed much since Portage editor Andrew Jackson Turner spent the better part of his vacation there in 1877. According to Turner, "There is no more charming little village in America. . . . Its beautiful yards, fountains and excellent hotel, all conspire to enchant our party."[14] While booming Ashland and Hurley were becoming famous for their slugging matches, saloons, and prostitution, Bayfield was more like a New England coastal village and was known for its beauty and relative tranquility.

The View of Washburn

Bayfield and Ashland both claimed a history going back beyond their establishment in the 1850s, to the days of Radisson and Groseilliers and the Jesuits. But Washburn was different. As the 1892 *Ashland Press* annual edition put it: "There are no romances of Indian lore in the history of its foundations—no poetical inspirations can be derived from its early history. When Washburn was platted it was strictly a business consideration, and it has been a matter of business ever since."[15] Indeed, Washburn was platted as a terminal for the Chicago, St. Paul, Minneapolis and Omaha Railroad, which arrived in 1883. The railroad docks dominate Wellge's bird's-eye view (fig. 6.4). No fewer than nine trains are depicted coming, going, loading, or unloading.

In general shape, perspective, and proportions of sky, land, and water, the Washburn view is almost identical to the Bayfield view. Otherwise, it could not be more different. Although Bayfield has a finished look, Washburn seems to have barely begun. The directory lists three sawmills, which are pictured to the left of the railroad docks, as well as two newspapers and a schoolhouse. A church is listed, with a large gap before the word *church* as if the viewmaker was unsure of the denomination and planned to fill in that detail later. In 1886, Washburn had a population of around nine hundred. Six years later, it had grown enough to take the county seat from Bayfield (which had taken the seat from La Pointe back in 1858). Wisconsin's Lake Superior coast was a dynamic place. Everything was in flux, and anything seemed possible.

The View of Ashland

Wellge's view of Ashland can be read as the national mythology in miniature—the story of the conquest of culture over wilderness (figs. 6.1 and 6.5). Frontier progression can be seen moving from the forest, which is least developed, to the shoreline, which is most developed. Industry was in the process of transforming the land. The first step involved superimposing a grid on the landscape. Next, the cells of bounded land were cleared of trees. The stumps, like those plainly depicted on the corner of Delaware and Fifth

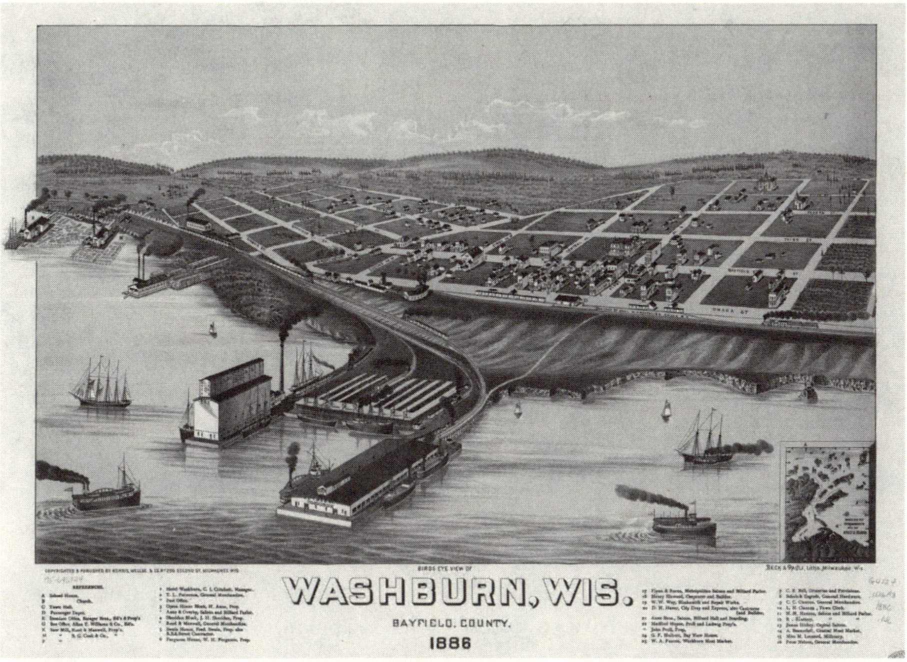

FIGURE 6.4 Henry Wellge, "Birds Eye View of Washburn, Wis. Bayfield County, 1886." Lithograph. (Milwaukee: Norris, Wellge and Co., 1886). Library of Congress, American Memory Map Collections, available at http://hdl.loc.gov/loc.gmd/g4124w.pm010610.

Street, represent former forest that has been cut, the logs hauled to the sawmills on the shore; there, they were transformed into lumber, some of which went into local buildings but most of which was sent to distant markets by boat and rail. After the stumps were removed, buildings filled in the void. When a block went from dense forest to dense buildings, the progression was complete. In Wellge's view, all of the stages of progress are visible.

In the case of Ashland, Wellge might not have exaggerated the busyness of the harbor. Not including small excursion steamers and towing tugs, almost a thousand ship arrivals to Ashland docks were recorded during the 1886 shipping season. Almost 50 million board feet of lumber were manufactured by the mills lining Ashland's shore. Forty-six cargoes of lumber were

FIGURE 6.5 Detail from Henry Wellge, "A Bird's Eye View of the City of Ashland, Wis., County Seat of Ashland County, 1886." Lithograph. (Milwaukee: Norris, Wellge and Co., 1886). Library of Congress, American Memory Map Collections, available at http://hdl.loc.gov/loc.gmd/g4124a.pm010190.

shipped to Chicago and other markets, and more than fifty loads of coal, railroad iron, salt, oil, and other materials were received. The dock on the left margin of the Ashland view (fig. 6.1) shipped 721,981 gross tons of ore, and this was in the era of wooden ore boats that required a whole day to load while the trimmers distributed the cargo.[16]

The View of Hurley

Hurley was connected to Chequamegon Bay through Ashland by the recently opened Milwaukee, Lakeshore, and Western Railway. Most of the Wisconsin iron ore that was shipped out of Ashland harbor came from mines near Hurley. Wellge's 1886 view summarizes Hurley. The story begins with recent history—Hurley in 1885 (fig. 6.6). The left of two insets in the lower right-hand corner of the view shows men felling large trees in a dense forest. The other inset, to the right, shows miners working hard at the Colby Mine. Hurley was a mining boomtown, just recently hewn out of a dense forest. But already, ac-

FIGURE 6.6 Henry Wellge, "Hurley, Wis., Ashland County, 1886," bird's-eye view. Lithograph. (Milwaukee: Norris, Wellge and Co., 1886). Library of Congress, American Memory Map Collections, available at http://hdl.loc.gov/loc.gmd/g4124h.pm010340.

cording to the bird's-eye, there was a schoolhouse, two churches, two newspapers, and two dozen businesses providing everything from bakery goods to eyeglasses. Brown sandstone from the Bayfield Brownstone Company was brought in to build the more substantial structures, creating another link to Chequamegon Bay.[17]

One sawmill and three working mines are visible in the view. The Germania Mine is depicted in great detail in the right background. Most of the Gogebic mines were underground, and some were quite deep. The Montreal Mine, for instance, eventually reached a depth of 4,335 feet.[18] In 1886, the miners would descend into the earth on long ladders. Theirs was a hard and dangerous occupation, arguably worse than being a lumberjack. Like the lumberjacks, the miners lived in isolated camps set up near their work. Both groups spent long periods cooped up in an exclusively male environment. When payday came, hoards of these men would head to town to drink, gamble, and pursue woman. Because most of the miners worked in Michigan across the Montreal River, where law enforcement was more vigorous, Hurley became the "sin center" for the entire Gogebic region.

Hurley's connections to mining were reflected in street names such as Iron, Copper, Granite, and Gold. The inset on the lower left side of Wellge's view shows the north front of Silver Street. This street, so modest and peaceful looking, would soon be notorious throughout the entire region. But that story is not part of the bird's-eye view. The viewmaker's pictures tell a progressive and even heroic story of future cities emerging out of forests—a story of industry and hard work rearranging nature to create ordered, humanized places. The viewmaker's vision was similar but not identical to the local booster's vision. Of course, boosters sold a vision of what their cities could become, whereas the viewmaker sold lithographs. And the secret to selling lithographs was giving people what they wanted to see.

Bird's-Eye Views, Boosters, and Northwoods Pastoralism

Part of the reason why newspaper editors were typically among the most prominent boosters of any given town was due to simple economics. The fortunes of a local newspaper were closely tied to local growth. More people meant more subscribers, and more businesses meant more paid advertisements. Both the *Bayfield Press* and the *Ashland Press* made use of bird's-eye views to promote their towns and to illustrate growth. These works reflected and reinforced a certain viewpoint of the places they depicted. Commercial bird's-eyes, such as Wellge's views, tend to de-emphasize regional distinctiveness. More than any other feature, trees defined the region of which Wisconsin's Lake Superior coast was a part. Indeed, northern Wisconsin seemed synonymous with immense forests. What was striking about Wellge's portrayals of the northern Wisconsin towns was the relative absence of trees. In his view of Superior, for example, the artist avoided depicting trees almost entirely by orienting the perspective toward the harbor; the forest was behind the viewer. In Wellge's Bayfield view, coniferous trees suggested the northwoods environment, but their regular, lined, and gentle parklike appearance was decidedly pastoral—not a word commonly associated with the northwoods. The background forests of Washburn and Ashland were depicted in a similar stylized fashion. Even Hurley, just recently hacked out of the forest, seemed to sit in a park of neatly planted trees.

In the 1880s, local boosters tended to think of the northern Wisconsin forest as a commodity to clear away in order to gain access to another commodity —the soil, which they believed would produce crops as abundant as those grown on southern Wisconsin farms. It would take decades to disprove this notion to the satisfaction of the boosters, but images of northwoods pastoralism were a mirage. Ecologically, this region was different from the rest of the state, and life could be rough on the edge of the "inland sea." Winters were long and summers short. Furthermore, the red marl soils, described with guarded enthusiasm in the early geological surveys, was better for growing trees rather than wheat. On the south shore of Lake Superior, for every natural advantage there were equally compelling natural disadvantages. The commercial bird's-eye views depicted an idealized place that was similar to, if less grand than, the place the boosters strived to be. One might assume that this was the image the boosters themselves would have portrayed in a bird's-eye view. But the 1885 view of Ashland, the "Metropolis of the New Wisconsin," done by Marr and Richards and commissioned by the *Ashland Press,* was a far more realistic portrayal than one would expect from boosters (fig. 6.7).

This view was probably not sold separately but was instead commissioned by the newspaper to illustrate its annual edition, so the artist did not need to show every building clearly in order to entice subscribers.[19] He had the leeway to take a different perspective, which reflected a different purpose. Ashland's shore faces the northwest. Streets run perpendicular to the shoreline (northwest to southeast) and parallel to the shoreline (northeast to southwest). Wellge chose to view Ashland from the west looking eastward. The Marr and Richards view, by contrast, was composed from the north looking south. The two views are almost mirror images of each other in terms of the general shape of land and water, and both use a two-point linear perspective. But Wellge's vanishing points extend far beyond the borders of the print, and the one on the left is far above the horizon. Marr and Richards's vanishing points are just beyond the borders of the print and near the horizon. Their view is less maplike and more realistic.

FIGURE 6.7 Bird's-eye view of "Ashland, the Metropolis of the New Wisconsin," 1885. Courtesy of the Wisconsin Historical Society (WHi-11175).

The different choice of viewpoint profoundly affected the images and resulted in almost antipodal emphases. Whereas Wellge's viewpoint focuses on the heart of the built city, the Marr and Richards view emphasizes empty lots and the new Milwaukee, Lake Shore and Western Railway Company ore dock, about a mile northeast of the center of the city plat. Described as the largest in the world, the ore dock was almost half a mile long and extends into the center foreground of the view. The empty lots highlight the grid pattern. Rather than focusing on the already built landscape, the Marr and Richards view emphasizes undeveloped land, as if trying to lure investors.

The commercial bird's-eye and the locally commissioned one seem to depict two different places. In the former, the city appears to be naturally expanding inland, with the gentle woods presenting little obstacle. In the latter view, completed just a year earlier, the forest looks almost impenetrable and the city seems to be pinched between forest and lake and forced to expand along the shore rather than fight the forest. Indeed, it seems as if it would be easier to expand into the bay than into the forests, as evidenced by the numerous docks. Even though Wellge's use of perspective pulls up the background so that distant buildings can be shown clearly, he still manages to subdue the forest as if the earth curves sharply back just beyond the city. On Wellge's view, the Penokee-Gogebic range is faintly visible in the background. The Marr and Richards view is distorted so that the iron range looms mountain-like in the background. The forest is thick and wild and is penetrated only by rivers and the thin trace of the Wisconsin Central Railway, slicing through the wilderness.

Given the boosters' grandiose vision and their tendency to exaggerate natural advantages while denying natural disadvantages, such a realistic depiction of the natural environment is unexpected. But though one might look at the Marr and Richards view and see wilderness engulfing a thin line of habitation calling itself the "Metropolis of the New Wisconsin," the boosters surely saw opportunities: there was iron in those hills, and immense forests meant an endless supply of timber for Ashland's mills. The boosters firmly believed that the forests would give way to farms, but they also had a strong sense of the distinctiveness of their region. Their place was different from other places, and they knew it. Unlike Wellge's view, there was nothing pastoral about the Marr and Richards view of Ashland. But even if the boosters had a clear-eyed vision of their region, they also had an idyllic notion of what their region could become, which outdid Henry Wellge's pastoral representations. The cover of the 1892 annual edition of the *Ashland Daily Press* suggests the ultimate relationship between the city and its natural environment (fig. 6.8). This unusual bird's-eye view could be interpreted as the final triumph of culture over wilderness. Nature is symbolically erased by civilization, personified as a woman. This image might have been presented as an antidote to another image of the region that depicted northern Wisconsin as a place where the worst elements of frontier life were manifested. In the last decades of the nineteenth century, not everyone thought of the northwoods as pastoral paradise or the site of a future metropolis.

The "Hellholes" of Northern Wisconsin

As early as the 1850s, northern Wisconsin was developing an image as a vacation mecca—a place to escape from the ills of city life, to engage in healthful recreation, and to rejuvenate both mind and body while being soothed by pine-scented air. Railway connections in the 1870s made the area readily

FIGURE 6.8 Cover of the *Ashland Press*, Annual Edition, 1892. Courtesy of the Wisconsin Historical Society Library.

accessible to people as far away as Milwaukee and Chicago. But by 1887, a very different image of the region was being sensationalized in distant newspapers. An article in the *Cincinnati Enquirer* suggested that the darker view of northern Wisconsin may have begun with the arrest of Maude Cassidy on charges of abducting young Chicago women and delivering them to certain dives in northern Wisconsin, where they were pressed into prostitution. According to the *Enquirer*, “The disclosures following the arrest . . . indicated a horrible state of affairs in this almost unknown region.” A Chicago correspondent for a New York news service spent a week investigating the region; he disguised himself as a lumberjack “as it would not have been safe to enter into the country in any other way.” The reporter claimed that while undercover, he interviewed young women who were being kept prisoner in dens of inequity, guarded by vicious dogs and subject to horrific abuses. Those few who tried to escape were tracked down, captured, beaten, or worse: "They can not escape because there is no law in the whole desolate region. Robbery and murder have been carried on there with impunity for years. . . . The country in which the dens are situated is wild and dismal. No one lives there but Indians, the lumbermen, and those that supply their wants." And what the "Pinery Minotaurs" wanted was all forms of vice.[20] Residents on the south shore of Lake Superior might have taken some comfort because these dens were near Marinette on Lake Michigan. But a month later, another article appeared in the same paper. It was entitled "Wisconsin's Hell-Hole" and featured sensational grabbers such as "Hurley, the Worst Town in America," "Made Up of Saloons, Dance-Houses and Gambling Dens," "Women Selling the Clothes on Their Backs to Escape the Place," and "Men Who Do Not Seem to Be Human—Murder No Unusual Thing—Reports of the Vile Dens Not Exaggerated." This article quoted a "prominent railroad official" who claimed that, although he had built roads through new territory for years and had been in the "worst mining and construction camps," he had never seen anything as bad as "the hell-holes of Northern Wisconsin." Ashland, too, had a reputation as a rough town, but Hurley became notorious almost as soon as it was named. There was a saying that the four toughest places in the world were Cumberland, Hayward, Hurley, and Hell—and Hurley was the toughest of them all.[21] These and similar anecdotes paint an alternative "bird's-eye view" of the region that contrasts sharply with Wellge's pastoral view. But which was the most accurate view? There are no easy answers. In the local newspapers, there was ample evidence to support and to refute both images of the region.

The Complex Geography of Place

National tensions were reflected locally and often intensified by news as well as advertising in the local press. In 1877, the *Bayfield Press* carried an advertisement for a revolver intended "for Police, Bankers, and Household use" (fig. 6.9). Apparently to drive the last point home, the ornate gun had an vignette of a small house complete with a picket fence. Playing on fears of outsiders and vagrants, the gun was called the Tramp's Terror, and the

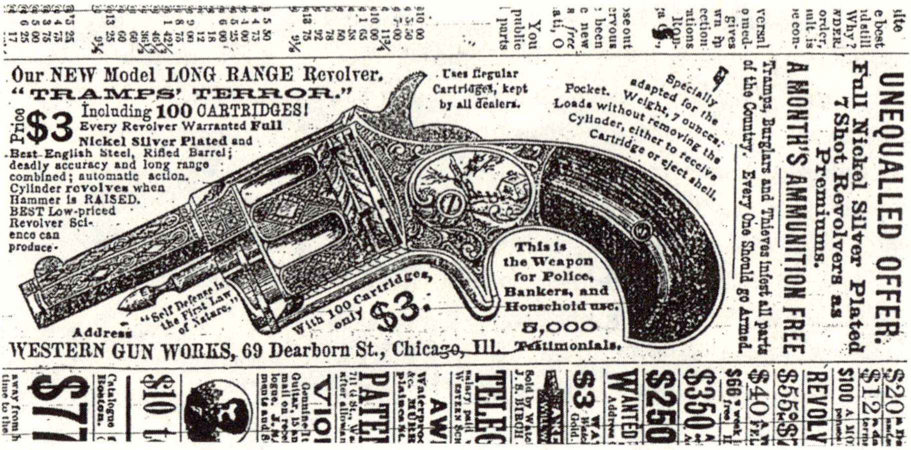

FIGURE 6.9 Gun advertisement, 1877. Courtesy of the Wisconsin Historical Society Library.

advertisement warned that "Tramps, Burglars and Thieves infest all parts of the Country. Every One should go Armed." The gun was "Specially adapted for the Pocket" and could be ordered through the mail by sending $3 to the Western Gun Works, in Chicago.

A recurring source of anxiety was labor unrest. Scanning the Bayfield, Washburn, Ashland, and Hurley newspapers published during the summer of 1886 reveals that much space was devoted to national news. The biggest stories of the summer concerned widespread labor problems. In April, there were riots in St. Louis, resulting in several deaths. In May, the Wisconsin governor called out the Milwaukee Battalion to quell unrest in Milwaukee. But the greatest amount of attention went to the trial resulting from the Haymarket Square riot in Chicago. Eight anarchists were tried for conspiracy after a bomb blast killed seven policemen. The trial was concluded in August, and all eight were found guilty, with seven sentenced to death. Closer to home, the May 29 *Ashland Press* charged that the Milwaukee anarchists cost the state $15,000 and state businesses millions more. The local newspapers generally favored the harsh treatment of subversives. The *Ashland Press* on May 8, 1886, expressed "concern for the future welfare of the country." Under the headline "Riot and Ruin," the *Press* urgued that the socialists, communists, and anarchists should all be "expelled from the country they disgrace"and "returned to the slums of Europe." Even distant labor unrest increased local anxiety.

Frequent strikes were reported in all of the major communities in the region. On May 29, the *Ashland Press* reported matter-of-factly that "several unimportant labor disturbances [had] occurred in Ashland during the past week." Even idyllic Bayfield had problems. In May, the workers at Captain Pike's lumber mill went on strike, demanding ten-hour workdays and $1.75 per day as pay. Pike refused to accede to their demands, and the strike was abandoned. In July, carpenters finishing the new school (which, along with Pike's lumber mill, was prominently displayed in Wellge's view of Bayfield) went on strike on a Saturday. They were replaced on Monday. The newspapers tended to downplay unrest close to home. An advertisement in the *Bayfield Press* summed up the local mood: "The Chicago riots are over but you can buy a hat at Nourse's as cheap as ever."[22]

Reports of labor unrest and hyperbolic gun advertisements are not the only evidence to support a darker view of Wisconsin's Lake Superior coast. Most disturbing are the all-too-common records of individual tragedies. For example, the July 1, 1886, edition of a Hurley newspaper carried a small article that should have sobered the celebrants in the rough-and-tumble frontier town: "Nellie Holk, an inmate of the Mahoney bagnio died suddenly on Tuesday night." She had been "dancing and carousing until midnight when she took a lunch and retired, and in about an hour was found dead by her roommate." According to the paper, two physicians, named Jones and Thomas, "made a certificate that the girl came to her death by self-inflicted wounds, in an attempt to produce an abortion."[23] The brief account in the press raises far more questions than it answers. Who was Nellie Holk? How did she really die? Was it usual for two doctors to perform autopsies? Was foul play suspected? Did anyone care that she died so tragically? And beyond the sad story of Nellie Holk, what is really known about the men who regularly invaded Hurley and who built its reputation? Their lives, too, must have been marred by quiet suffering. Most were miners who spent the bulk of their time outside town, in unreinforced underground mines. Accidents were a regular occurrence.[24]

Life could be difficult in northern Wisconsin. Reports of violence were common. In May, a Bayfield man was arrested and charged with assault and battery of his wife.[25] However, most reported assaults occurred between men, usually drunken men. On May 15, 1896, the *Ashland Press* reported that in a "drunken row" between two men in the Bay City division, one of the brawlers bit the lip off the other. Two days later, the *Bayfield County Press* complained that no police action was taken when "four drunken half-breeds indulged in a rough and tumble fight on the corner of Rittenhouse Avenue and Second Street between four and five o'clock Tuesday morning." Newspaper editors naturally preferred to report problems in neighboring towns. Thus, for example, the June 5, 1886, *Bayfield Press* chastised its neighbor across the bay: "Ashland—'The New Metropolis' is becoming notorious for its slugging matches: indications, it is presumed, of having arrived at a point of representing the dividing line between a pioneer town and a full fledged city. Give her a turn to the right, boys." But was life really more violent in a pioneer town than in a metropolis? It is possible that people in Cincinnati, Chicago, and New York enjoyed reading about Wisconsin's supposed hellholes for the same reason people in Ashland, Bayfield, and Hurley enjoyed reading about labor riots and criminal gangs in Chicago—because the stories distracted them from problems closer to home. During the summer of 1886, every major city in the United States experienced social problems no less disturbing than those reported in northern Wisconsin. And in cities that were already large, it was not enough to hope that they would simply outgrow these problems.

In December 1887, "notorious Maud Cassidy," the Chicago seductrice whose arrest a year earlier may have triggered the sensational reports of northern Wisconsin's hellholes, was arrested in Ashland. She had jumped her $1,000 bail and was caught hiding in a "house of ill fame." Cassidy was quoted defending herself in the *Press:* "The Bonneville girl was not ruined by me. She was at three bad houses before I met her—one at Merrill, one at Florence, and another one at Iron Mountain. The papers have razzle-dazzled me pretty bad, and I don't want to say much. I knew Detective Murtha was here three weeks ago, but I kept shady." According to the *Press,* "Quite a number of the sporting fraternity knew that Maud was in town and where she was located, but they would not give her away. She has a great many friends among her associates, who would gladly furnish her a hiding place." Lest Ashland's notorious reputation grow even larger, the *Press* cornered Detective Murtha and printed his opinion of Ashland:

> I am really astonished to see such fine residences and stores here. I never paid much attention to the matter, but from what I read I formed an opinion of this section that was not the best. I shall make it a point to tell my friends in Chicago and the chief of police in particular what a beautiful, orderly, well governed little city you have here. The people of Ashland so far as I have seen them, are more like the best element we have than any I know of.[26]

Even Hurley was not as bad as its reputation. Lewis Reimann argued that Hurley's social problems were concentrated around Silver Street and that throughout the town's history, it was only a handful of people who gave the town a bad name. The majority of the citizens had always been "sober, law abiding, industrious family people, church going and charitable."[27] The same was true for Ashland and probably for Cincinnati and Chicago as well.

Nevertheless, it was abundantly clear by 1886 that there were deep fissures in the social fabric. The representation of laborers, vagrants, and landscapes in the local newspapers reflected a deep anxiety over the perceived social and environmental chaos that, by the turn of the century, seemed to threaten boosterish order. As William Cronon, David Hamer, and others have pointed out, booster rhetoric from the late nineteenth century expressed a largely coherent notion of progressive development that, backed with certain geographical knowledge, seemed to make it possible to predict how a place would develop.[28] Chequamegon Bay area boosters felt confident in predicting that their lakeshore communities would serve as gateways between abundant natural resources, homegrown industry, and distant markets via water and railways. Activities such as clearing forests and building roads would help impose an order on the land that would allow for development on a scale sure to surpass that of large metropolitan centers in the East. The boosters were well aware that labor was key to realizing their expectations. But the booster rhetoric of attaining working-class independence through cheap land and high wages, a rhetoric that had been used to lure many laborers to the place, contradicted the need for an orderly and dependent labor force.

In the 1870s and 1880s, it was not uncommon for the local newspapers of Ashland, Bayfield, and Washburn to romanticize (or vilify) certain classes of workers, but in the 1890s, representations of laborers were more subdued and matter-of-fact. In 1899, labor news focused on the shortage of men to work in the lumber camps and on the railroad, despite the high wages these jobs offered.[29] Every time fifty or one hundred men arrived from Duluth to help finish the Bayfield transfer line, it was noted in the newspaper. In December, for instance, the *Bayfield County Press* reported that "considerable excitement" was caused on the street after about sixty road workers arrived in town expecting to be paid off. When an attorney by the name of Friend told them that they would have to wait until morning, they surrounded him and made it clear they wanted their pay without delay. After a couple of hours, the matter was settled, and Friend was allowed to go on his way. Unfortunately, he had missed his train. The *Press* sympathized with the laborers and noted that "they were not boisterous in manner but simply wanted what belonged to them."[30]

Much more concern was expressed regarding the unemployed. The September 3, 1894, *Ashland Daily Press* implied that recent fires had been set by "suspicious characters" who had been seen hanging around town: "The bluffs and bay front are lined with tramps and bums. The police would relieve the city of considerable apprehension if they would form a skirmish line, and drive every suspicious character out of the city."[31] Yet even though newspapers might scapegoat those on the margins, a little unruliness on the part of workers was tolerated. Common laborers were rarely mentioned by name unless they broke the law or were gravely injured or killed. Unfortunately, however, individual laborers were mentioned by name almost every week. For example, from September to December, the *Bayfield County Press* mentioned sixteen workers by name. These included three millworkers, two woodsmen, three miners, three railroad men, two homesteaders, and a road worker. Seven were killed, three were expected to die, and six were seriously injured. Of the fatalities, two accidentally blew themselves up in a mining accident, two drowned in the bay, two were felled by trees, and three were run over by trains. The fourth train victim was an engineer who suffered a particularly gruesome death when he was charred to a crisp by live coals. The engineer's case was special because of his higher social status, and it was unusual because the incident was thoroughly investigated, with a coroner's jury finding the company negligent.[32] More often in that time and place, employees were fully responsible for their own injuries. Furthermore, according to Larry Lankton, who has written extensively on Michigan copper miners, few people outside of accident victims' ethnic groups and, to a lesser extent, their work groups really cared about these victims.[33] The only bias in reporting accidents seems to have been related to either the incident's distance from the home city and its drama value. For instance, one of the tragedies listed earlier happened in nearby Iron River. Road workers accidentally felled a tree on top of two homesteaders in a buggy. The *Ashland News* mentioned both men by name, but the *Bayfield Press* only identified the victim who was formerly a resident of Bayfield; the second man was not mentioned at all.[34]

According to the *Press*, "There is hardly a season passes but someone loses their life in Chequamegon bay. The fall of the year is a very dangerous season to be out in sailboats." The individual who wrote the article might have added that it was also a dangerous time to be in a mill, a mine, the woods, or especially near railroad tracks. Even the yeoman homesteader complained:

> O, I'd be a homesteader, happy and gay,
> Living in the wild woods night and day,
> Cutting down the tall trees, digging up stumps,
> Breaking my back, piling up chunks.[35]

Landscapes could be dangerous; they could kill people.

Labor Day celebrations in the last decade of the nineteenth century symbolized the effort to physically as well as psychologically maintain order. Historians Michael Kazin and Steven Ross have argued that the holiday gave union leaders the opportunity to promote a class-conscious movement while at the same time affirming their loyalty to ideals of American citizenship that downplayed class distinctions.[36] But shifting the focus from large cities to the smaller, more tenuous, and peripheral communities opened an important window on booster ideology and attitudes toward workers. Contemporary newspaper accounts suggest that boosters embraced Labor Day as an opportunity to promote a progressive community consciousness tied to a larger national order, while simultaneously allowing the business owners, as well as newspaper editors, to publicly display their support for workers. In doing so, the community's elite symbolically enlisted organized labor to further their progressive goals. The first Labor Day parade took place in Union Square in New York City in 1882, but the day did not become a national holiday until

1894.[37] Although many places resisted the celebration until the 1930s or 1940s, Chequamegon Bay area communities quickly embraced the national holiday. And in the beginning, there was a determined, if doomed, effort to celebrate it properly.

The Bayfield newspaper mentioned the 1894 celebrations that would take place in Washburn and Ashland. Hurley's *Montreal River Miner* announced that a large number from the "range" would attend the Labor Day celebration at Ashland and that the Wisconsin Central Railway would run a special train, with one fare for the round-trip, to transport people to the festivities.[38] Mining company paternalism may have inhibited parade planning in Hurley and Bessemer.

The most elaborate celebration would take place in Ashland. There, the *Daily Press* captured the spirit with the headline: "ALL FOR LABOR DAY." Mayor Hubbell called on all citizens to "suspend business as far as possible" and to decorate their business places to give the city a "national appearance." Speaking for the community, he declared, "We are all interested in the labor of our country, therefore it is proper that all should take part."[39]

The parade was to form at Ellis Park and to begin moving promptly at 9:00 a.m., marching down Third Street to Ellis Avenue, where the marchers were to wait for the miners to arrive from Hurley and Ironwood. Once the miners joined the parade, they were to march to Ninth Avenue, down Second Street, onto Fourteenth Avenue, and then back to the park, where the Milwaukee Knights of Labor organizer, Robert Schilling, and others would deliver their addresses. The speeches would be followed by contests, including bicycle races and footraces, jumping and hopping competitions, hammer-throwing events, a log-rolling contest, and a tug-of-war between longshoremen and millmen. Prizes ranged from a silk umbrella for the footrace to a butt of tobacco for the hammer throw.[40]

The announced order of the line of march reflected a hierarchal order: the color-bearer was to lead the parade, followed by Winninger's band and the speakers in carriages. Next came members of the Central Labor Union, the Miners' Union, the Ore Trimmers' Union, and the Dockmen's Union, who were followed by another band and then the men of the Longshoremen's, Millmen's, and Typographical Unions. Members of less influential unions followed the Railroad Men—the Painters' and Decorators', the Taylors', the

Barbers', and the Butchers' Unions. Finally, just in front of ordinary citizens in carriages, the Unorganized Laboring Men would march.[41] In addition to a workers' hierarchy, the order also suggested a geographical pattern, with the national flag up front followed by union leaders, union men from the docks and mines, and then city workers. The unorganized laborers bringing up the rear would have been lumberjacks, fishermen, homesteaders, and others who worked away from town. Unionization seemed to concentrate in cities and mining camps. Lumberjacks and fishermen rarely organized.[42]

An editorial in the *Ashland Daily Press* declared that Labor Day, like the American and French Revolutions, the freeing of slaves, and expanding voting rights, was "only another evidence of the growing power of the people." According to the *Press,* "Labor Day is no more or less than an object lesson in the power and might of the masses. It is not a day given to marching of armed men in menace. Socialism and communism have no connection with it. It is a day devoted to the dignity and might of labor, as such it is significant of the growth of the equality of mankind."[43] Organized labor was clearly part of the boosters' progressive vision of the emerging place, for only an *ordered* labor force could impose order on the land. Deeply aware that laborers —whether unionized or not—could work against their vision as well as for it, the city boosters embraced and celebrated labor. But labor was not the only entity that could be unruly.

Despite the high expectations before the event, the Labor Day edition of the *Ashland Daily Press* had little to say about the day's festivities. Instead, forest fires dominated the news. Most of the front page that day was devoted to a harrowing account of a railroad disaster just north of Hinkely, Minnesota. After the engine cab and the engineer caught on fire, an air hose burned off, and a passenger train carrying about 250 people stopped dead in the tracks in the midst of a forest fire. According to the *Press,* only half of the people on board escaped and were taken to Duluth. The rest were presumed lost.[44] But the "fire fiend" was not confined to Minnesota. Drought and abundant lumbering debris helped turn much of northern Wisconsin and Michigan into a tinderbox. It is no wonder that fire gripped local attention. Just the week before, a large portion of downtown Ashland had burned, and all the frame buildings between the Vaughn Library and the Ashland National Bank had been lost.[45]

In an extraordinary example of overcoming environmental constraints, Washburn stubbornly celebrated Labor Day despite extensive fire damage and encroaching forest fires on the city's borders. Ignoring editorial protests from Ashland that they should keep closer to home, a dozen men and a hose truck left Ashland and worked to hold back the fires burning on the west end of Washburn. Once Washburn's firefighters had the dock fire under control and Bigelow's mill seemed out of danger, they rushed to join the Ashlanders. A few days later, the *Washburn News* reported that

> a peculiar combination of obstacles seemed to be in the way of a proper observance of Labor Day in Washburn. The committee in charge of the affair had all the arrangements about complete for a rousing celebration, but on Saturday the fire came along and on Sunday night it was even then uncertain whether or not our population would not be compelled to put in Monday fighting fire instead of celebrating Labor Day. However the Monday dawned with matters settled nearly down to their normal state and the committee decided to celebrate the best they could under the circumstances. The Ironwood Band in full uniform arrived here in the morning and in the afternoon the visiting and home bands with the unions of the city paraded our principal streets winding up at Opera Hall where the speaking &c. took place.[46]

The *News* went on to chide the *Chicago Tribune* for reporting that Washburn had been wiped out by fire. A *Tribune* reporter arrived in town to take pictures of the ruins for his paper, but according to the *News,* "He kept rather still or a committee of citizens might have waited on him to have him show them where he got the picture of the ruined town."[47]

Organizers of subsequent Labor Day celebrations would be hard-pressed to match the drama of that first one. Soon, Chequamegon Bay communities were taking turns hosting the event. By 1899, it was Bayfield's turn. The Republican papers, the Bayfield *Press* and the Ashland *Press,* continued to give glowing accounts of the celebration, but the Democratic *Ashland Weekly News* complained about the "lack of entertainment provided by the Bayfield people" and groused that "the attention and interest . . . seemed centered on the ball game between Washburn and Bayfield," rather than on the laborers.[48]

Just as boosters and the local business establishments may have promoted Labor Day to further their own agendas, laborers used the holiday for their own reasons. By 1900, the increasing emphasis on sports suggests that local workers, like their big-city counterparts, used the holiday less to celebrate laborers and more to increase their own leisure hours. At the same time, laborers knew they had a degree of power, and when they used it in an orderly manner—whether under the union banner or through less formal, more spontaneous organization—the local press was usually sympathetic. Everything was intertwined. Booster dreams were hollow without labor cooperation, and thus, laborers found a measure of the advertised independence that had drawn them to the region. More together than at odds, boosters, businesspeople, and laborers attempted to carve out a living from the land and to propel their peripheral place toward the economic and cultural heart of the nation. For a variety of economic as well as environmental reasons, they missed their mark. But in such a rugged landscape, between a sometimes treacherous lake on the one side and recurring forest fires on the other, people living on the shores of the Chequamegon Bay region were given forceful reminders that they were all in it together.

What was it like to live on Wisconsin's Lake Superior coast in that era? The answer is complex. By 1886, the place was not as pastoral as a bird's-eye view, as deplorable as a hellhole, or as isolated as its location might suggest. An advertisement in the *Ashland Press* announced that "every train brings the latest styles and novelties in boots and shoes for the Boston Boot and Shoe House." In April and May, grocers advertised lettuce, radishes, onions, pie plant (rhubarb), bananas, oranges, pineapples, lemons, apples, strawberries, asparagus, spinach, and fresh oysters. Lake Superior whitefish was a staple. The first trial of the Ashland Lighting Company electric plant was a success. Meanwhile, Bayfield enjoyed "three trains each way daily," and although the *Bayfield Press* published a list of wants longer than its town directory in July, the village could already boast of a roller-skating rink and fresh roast peanuts at the newsstand on Dalrymple's dock. Even when Chequamegon Bay froze shut on November 30, 1886, people could easily board a train and head elsewhere if they became claustrophobic.

The most important function of bird's-eye views may have been to help residents of countless towns across the United States come to terms with the fact that their communities were not going to be the next great metropolises of the Western world. Indeed, they would probably remain fairly small. But to see those communities as they were portrayed in the bird's-eye views, such a fate might not have looked too bad; in fact, it looked pastoral. It did not matter so much that the views were not quite accurate. What mattered most was what people believed.

Epilogue

PAGEANTRY, MEMORY, AND PLACE

On July 30, 1924, the *Bayfield County Press* announced that the First Annual Apostle Islands Indian Pageant would begin on schedule two days later, on a Friday. The production, advertised as "authentic history," was also portrayed as the initiation ceremony dream visions of an Ojibwa brave, Mo-kad-ji-wens, concerning the future of his Ojibwa nation. The pageant showcased the key events of a three-hundred-year period that "effected the destinies of the Apostle Islands country" in a total of thirty-five scenes meant to be experienced over three days. The full performance lasted six and a half hours. A front-page story in the *Press* began by describing a tongue-in-cheek scene from day two of the three-day pageant:

> The first prohibition raid in the great northwest was made by the Sieur DuLuth as of 1680, when the debonair soldier of fortune confiscated a jug of hard liquor at the first complete rehearsal . . . of the Apostle Islands Indian Pageant. . . . Instead of being jailed, the "bootlegging" voyageur was

> struck flat by DuLuth's sword. Even in those days prohibition gave promise of being popular, for the Indians, encouraged by the fact that DuLuth's first act on reaching Chequamegon Bay, was made in defense of their interests, invite him to a general council.[1]

What are we to make of this passage and of the historical pageant it was describing? In the first line of the paragraph above, the reality of Prohibition at that time was anachronistically associated with a documented historical event: the arrival of Daniel Greysolon Dulhut (Duluth) at Chequamegon Bay. Duluth did spend the 1679–80 winter in the vicinity of the bay, but if he was welcomed by the Native American residents, it would have been because he was a trader, not because he was a Prohibitionist. Indeed, he more likely would have provided the Indians with alcohol, as was the widespread practice of the time. The last sentence in the above quotation projects a presentist Anglo-American Protestant sentiment onto the indigenous local population.

Whether the Indians as a group felt that a violently enforced Prohibition would have been in their interest is difficult to determine, but at least one Indian who attended the pageant clearly did not believe that it was in *his* best interest. A few days after the pageant opened, the *Bayfield Press* reported that "Indian Moonshiner" Charlie Cloud was arrested at Pageant Park on an outstanding warrant for a liquor charge on the Bad River Indian Reservation. According to the *Press,* Cloud had disappeared when the warrant was issued in 1919. Authorities hypothesized that he could not resist turning up at the pageant to cater to the "thirsty ones who might desire refreshment."[2] Undoubtedly, a high percentage of the thirsty ones were white tourists.

The Apostle Islands Indian Pageant was full of ironies, and although it was touted as portraying "authentic" history, it actually revealed far more about the current ideas of the place than it did about the past. There was a glaring gap in the pageant's chronology: the narrative jumped abruptly from 1854 and the signing of an important treaty between the Indians and the U.S. government to 1918 and the battle trenches of World War I. Looking back at the history of the area from the vantage point of 1924, why did the pageanteers neglect the period that witnessed the most dramatic social and environmental change ever experienced in the region? Furthermore, why was the event called an Indian pageant when, as will be shown, the Indians merely served as ahistorical backdrops to the historical white characters? Finally, what did the pageant reveal about the uses of history and the construction and maintenance of place images?

The popularity of historical pageants in the United States peaked in the early twentieth century. After World War I, according to David Glassberg, historical pageants were increasingly associated with "anti-modernism and the use of tradition as a bulwark against modernity."[3] This fact may partially explain why the local pageant neglected the period of rapid industrialization between 1877 and the war and ignored the heroic attempt to farm the cutover landscape left behind by the lumberjacks. But the production was largely controlled by outsiders and certainly reflected what the pageanteers thought would draw the largest audience from the greatest distance. Although their event was tied to a particular place—the Apostle Islands and Chequamegon Bay—the pageant producers apparently had no special affinity for that locale, beyond the profit that might be made there. In fact, they had no qualms about relocating the pageant if the audience at Bayfield was not large enough to make the project profitable. At the same time, Bayfield offered several advantages, including the fact that some of the events depicted in the pageant really did occur there and—as the audience was frequently reminded—at sites that were visible from the pageant grounds. Furthermore, there was a large local Ojibwa population to draw on for cast members.

It would be easy to dismiss the Apostle Islands Indian Pageant as a glitzy tourist spectacle, but it seems clear that the pageanteers' aims were higher than that. The foreword to the pageant program claimed that the grounds themselves were essential to the aesthetic experience. Unlike a drama or a spectacle, the program explained, a pageant was designed to include the audience member as a participant in the event. One brochure described the site as "the most beautiful pageant ground in America"—a location that could be "reached by the finest automobile highways, an easy two day jaunt from the heart of Chicago, Detroit, or Cincinnati" and was "accessible in a single day from Milwaukee, Minneapolis, or St. Paul." Most "participants" were expected to arrive by automobile, and their experience would begin as they drove "through the last of the great giant pines of the Great West" on Highway 47, through Drummond, or along Highways 13 and 70.[4] A map published the year before by the Wisconsin Motorists Association shows how extensive the road network had become and how dramatically the transportation geography had changed in just a few decades (fig. 7.1).[5] It also reveals that the roadways in the area were still quite rugged. According to the map legend, most stretches of the road were composed of light gravel (described as "good in summer despite rain") and clay ("slippery and heavy going after rains"). Part of Highway 70, between Siren and Spooner, was made of sand ("heavy going at all times"), which must have enhanced the rustic experience of getting to the pageant grounds.

From the parking lot to the pageant grounds, one passed through a "stretch of woodland" that was a "symbol of the thousands of miles of woodlands through which the voyageurs and explorers of the great north west pursued their way so many hundreds of years ago." Even the lack of grandstands or bleachers to accommodate the several thousand expected visitors was promised to enhance the experience by keeping "the spirit of the woods a thing apart." The *real* Indians were also a vital part of the experience: "You are presumed to feel as the hordes of red-skinned warriors descend from the hillside upon which you stand and sit, something of the surprised terror which in the early days filled the breasts of the pioneers as the war cry smote their ears." But the setting itself often took center stage: "By placing yourselves in the atmosphere of the pageant its beauties will become a sentient reality and you will feel to some extent the throb of the romance with which the hills and valleys which surround Chequamegon Bay are filled."[6]

As described by contemporary newspaper accounts, programs, and brochures, the pageant was a lavish production. The script was written by Chicagoan Kenneth Ellis, who claimed that he had based the pageant on sixty-four volumes of "authentic history." The newspaper described the pageant as an accurate portrayal, right down to the buttons on the costumes. As if to bolster the authenticity of the production, "research experts" from the Public Museum of Milwaukee were in the area to attend the event while at the same time conducting research. According to the *Bayfield County Press,* the experts stated that the pageant was "very true to life."[7] But as the Prohibition scene illustrated, it was less concerned with facts than with entertainment.

As noted earlier, the pageant was presented as the vision of the Ojibwa brave Mo-kad-ji-wens regarding the future history of his Ojibwa nation. But

FIGURE 7.1 Section of "Our Own Map," Wisconsin Motorists Association, 1923. Courtesy of the Geography Map Library, University of Wisconsin–Madison.

except in scenes such as the "Dance of the Indian Maidens" (which was "staged by Lucille Stodart, of Milwaukee and New York"[8]) and battle scenes between Ojibwa and Iroquois or Ojibwa and Sioux, the Indians were almost passive witnesses to "their" history and a procession of recognizable and predominantly French historical characters—explorers, priests, fur traders—as well as a supporting cast of mostly nameless Indians and voyageurs. All the actual historical characters were European. Although the white characters were described as "dignified" and "heroic," the Indian characters beat the war drum, whooped, and yelled. According to the *Press*, there were "over 250 complete outfits in the property room for the white actors, in addition to the hundreds of bows, arrows, guns, breech cloths, feathers and the like, for the Indians."[9] As a consequence, the Indians were little more than props in a dramatization of white event history. Most of the scenes occurred in the seventeenth century, a few in the eighteenth, and two in the nineteenth; the sole twentieth-century scene took place on a World War I battlefield "when a company of Indian braves, with Old Glory flying in the breeze" came to the rescue of a reconnaissance party of Yanks in No-Man's Land. It was noted in the program that, as an added touch of authenticity reminiscent of Buffalo Bill's Wild West show, "many of the men playing the part of Indian Yanks have seen service with the Thirty-second division overseas, and some of them are veterans of the Battle of Chateau Thierry."[10] The only nod to the sixty-three-year period between 1854 and World War I was in scene 8 on the first day of the event—"The Dance of the Spirits of the Vanished Pines." The program explained that "in the centuries which have passed since Mokadjiwens lay upon the promontory to take his dream medicine sleep, millions of magnificent pines have been cut down to make dwelling houses for the race which has succeeded his own as proprietors, of the beautiful northland. In his dream the medicine man sees the spirits of these as they appear in a dance of vanished memories." That is all. No boosters, surveyors, miners, lumberjacks, fishermen, mill owners, store clerks, railway engineers, or farmers and no Indians outside their expected roles—the men as noble or ignoble savages and sometimes drunkards, the women as saviors or sexual objects—had parts in the pageant. This was a curious omission because the missing years, especially from 1870 until World War I, comprised a period of dramatic changes in the upper Middle West in general and especially in the Chequamegon Bay region. Overlooking, for the moment, the success of the Washburn log-rolling contest, perhaps the more recent industrial history was not far past enough or remote enough to seem romantic. The pageanteers seemed to think that what would draw an audience was escape from modern realities. In this regard, it is interesting to note an Indian-as-savior theme that recurred in the pageant. For example, in the fictional scene in which Chequamegon Bay Indians forced Radisson and the seriously wounded Groseilliers to leave the shore in their canoe and go back out into the freezing bay after stealing their food, it was an "elderly squaw" who took pity on them and gave them her bowl of rice. And as mentioned in a program footnote, it was the more friendly Ojibwa Indians on Madeline Island (which, by the way, could be seen from the pageant grounds) who saved the white mens' lives by sheltering them through the winter. In another scene, a lone, tattered, and oddly misplaced Franciscan friar came to the shore. According to the program, the scene was based on Frederic Remington's painting *The Missionary* and may have been "within the bounds of historic possibility" because, after all, the "Franciscan friars, of the Recollect order, were the first to penetrate the vastness of the New World." Actually, it was members of a competing order, the Jesuits, who were among the first to visit Chequamegon Bay, and they were not likely to have traveled far alone. Nevertheless, this Franciscan friar angered the people very soon after landing by disrespecting their religious symbols (which was probably an accurate statement), and so the Indians (now depicted as savages) reacted by tying him to a stake to burn. Before they were able to light him afire, the village was fortuitously attacked by a band of Iroquois (in reality, the nearest Iroquois battle was close to Sault Ste. Marie). Meanwhile, a squaw (his savior) took advantage of the confusion and released the friar, who then fled even though he was eager to be a martyr; the squaw, proving herself to be the true martyr, was killed. The most dramatic example came in a final scene when the company of "Indian Braves" saved a company of "Yankees" in the "No-Man's-Land" of a World War I battlefield.

Like Longfellow's epic poem *The Song of Hiawatha*, the Indian pageant allowed the author to use Indian myths to tell American stories. Indeed, it was largely because of *Hiawatha*, first published in 1854, that so-called Indianness became one of the commodities most sought after by tourists who visited the area. As the *Superior Telegram* put it:

> The shores of Lake Superior, it should not be forgotten, are the scene of the greater part of the most famous poem yet dealing with Indian legend, namely, Longfellow's "Hiawatha," and everybody who is interested in the development of American poetry and art, everybody who is a lover either of natural beauty or of pageantry, in its original sense, should see this production.[11]

Presumably, the majority of the audience was familiar with *Hiawatha*. In writing his poem, Longfellow drew heavily on assorted stories collected and published by Henry Rowe Schoolcraft.

Although there has been heated controversy over the issue, it seems certain that Longfellow modeled his telling of *Hiawatha* after the Finnish epic the *Kalevala*. This fact is especially interesting because the authors of both works drew on indigenous oral traditions to create nationalistic tales, based directly or indirectly on the ideas of the German intellectual J. G. Herder. Herder had argued that for a nation to exist, it needed to possess a distinct cultural identity derived from the oral tradition of indigenous local people. In part toward this end, the Finnish scholar Elias Lönnrot collected traditional Finnish peasant stories between 1828 and 1844 and recontextualized the different stories into a coherent poetic narrative, the *Kalevala* As dramatic proof of a national identity, this work quickly became known as the national epic of Finland. The definitive edition was published in 1849. Longfellow had a similar aim, but lacking an indigenous peasant population, he instead drew on Native American stories. His model was a German translation of the *Kalevala*.[12] Longfellow's epic was so successful that even after the poem and its dramatic portrayals declined in popularity, the image of Hiawatha was—and still is—invoked in the Lake Superior country.[13] Clearly, without directly citing Longfellow or even mentioning Hiawatha in the pageant literature, Ellis, by packaging his regional story as an "Indian Pageant," was attempting to capitalize on the success of *Hiawatha* and perhaps even the *Kalevala*. For example, in the detailed description of the pageant in the program where he references a scene entitled "The Victory Dance of the Ojibway Women," Ellis claimed that the women warriors of the Ojibwa culture assumed "something of the position of the Valkyrie of the Norse countries"; similarly, in regard to the seventh act, he asserted that in addition to the sacred songs of the Indian people, "there were many personal songs corresponding to our poetry."[14] But even to the extent that he used local events to tell a regional tale, Ellis aimed his pageant not at the local audience but at a distant audience whose members would take advantage of the new highway system to attend the show.

The pageant, its programs, and newspaper accounts of the event hinted at tensions between local and outside ideas of the place and its relevant history. The chairman of the pageant's Duluth Committee summed it up in this fashion:

> The large summer influx of tourists generally associate Indians, wild life, natural beauty and kindred objects with this part of the country. While we of this section feel as tho' we are as near the center of the most modern civilization and as far from the savages as we possibly could be, still the eastern visitors are bound to associate the historic, the Indian fights, the early trading posts and the like with Duluth, but we should not resent this. This is

> the attraction that brings them out here and instead of resenting it, we should capitalize on it. After all, it is something to be proud of, for people coming from the cut and dried east find a refreshing interest when they visit our part of the country.[15]

He could have been speaking of nearby Bayfield, or Ashland, or any of the other Chequamegon Bay area communities. Despite a long string of local difficulties in attempting to achieve an industrial-based prosperity, many residents still clung to earlier hopes of becoming the Great Metropolis of the Inland Seas, yet by 1924, tourism was one of the few industries left open to further exploitation to boost a sagging economy.

In 1870, Bayfield boosters had confidently predicted that the next great American metropolis would emerge in their vicinity. Merely looking at a map of North America, they argued, showed that Chequamegon Bay was the best port on the west end of the Great Lakes. One only had to enumerate local resources (abundant fisheries, interminable forests that would reveal rich soil once they were cleared, iron ore, and brownstone) to see the inevitability of their prediction. But the fisheries declined, cutover farms did not flourish, the popularity of brownstone was short-lived, and the iron ore was shipped elsewhere—through Ashland's port—to be processed. A few days after the pageant ended, the *Bayfield County Press* announced that the lumber industry was through in Bayfield. The last lumber mill in town had cut all of its holdings and would close its doors.[16]

A basic conflict between local and distant perceptions of the place persisted. Tourists wanted Indians, wildlife (or wild life), and natural beauty, and the pageant committees were determined to give all of that to them; ironically, many locals apparently did not share the same romantic notions of Indians and nature or the same enthusiasm for the pageant. At the close of the second annual Indian pageant in 1925, manager Victor Fay complained that ten thousand of the twelve thousand who saw the show were tourists. He blamed lack of local support for the fact that the Indian Pageant Corporation was in debt to the tune of $60,000. Furthermore, he accused nearby Washburn of nabbing tourists off the highway with their log-rolling contest, scheduled to coincide with the pageant. The last day of the pageant was attended by only one thousand people, whereas the log-rolling contest drew three thousand. He declared that he and his committeee would take the pageant to the audience. The next Indian pageant would be staged at Superior, Duluth, or Chicago.[17]

By the 1920s, the Chequamegon Bay region was fundamentally a different place than it had been in the 1880s. The period after 1900 effectively marked the end of the booster era in the region. Since the population—even of Ashland—never again reached the modest peak of the boom year, 1886, it became increasingly difficult to seriously argue that Ashland or any of the other "future metropolises" on Chequamegon Bay would ever become a big city. Even later resource booms, such as the increased iron ore production for the war effort in both world wars, only seemed to reinforce the fact that the area was a point of extraction to support factories in distant ports. It requires no more than a cursory review of local newspapers to see that the first decades of the twentieth century were difficult for the region, marked by general decline and adjustment.

Gradually, the residents of the Chequamegon Bay area and the larger cutover region adjusted their expectations and adapted to the realities of their place. Today, the cities in the region are modest, and many people find them quite livable. Although the hinterland is largely restored forest, the former cutover has developed productive agriculture. Pulp paper production is significant. The larger region is the top cranberry-producing area in the country, and respectable crops of potatoes, wild rice, ginseng, and Christmas trees are also grown. Taking advantage of the warmer climate near Lake Superior, as well as the frost-resistant higher elevation, Bayfield Peninsula is covered with fertile apple orchards. These agricultural activities coexist well with tourism.

Like countless other "future cities" of the nineteenth century, today's Bayfield and Ashland and the other Chequamegon Bay area communities are typical small towns in many ways, not so different from the images captured in the bird's-eye views of the late 1800s. Over the last century, as highways, radios, television, and the Internet have made places all over the country seem more and more alike, the Chequamegon Bay region retains a distinct identity. More than any other feature, what makes this place unique is its proximity to Lake Superior. Even today, the big lake dominates the scene. As cars pass by, vestiges of the romantic past are still visible. In the layers of imagery that have accumulated about the place, there was plenty of material to envision a very livable place. To the degree that he portrayed idyllic small towns, Wellge was not far off the mark with his bird's-eye views. Many people have been quite happy to live in Ashland or Bayfield or even Hurley. Almost 340 years after Father Claude Allouez climbed ashore from his birchbark canoe, many neoromantics would still agree with his first impression of the place: "It is a beautiful Bay."

Notes

Prologue

1. Father Claude Allouez, "Relation of What Occurred Most Remarkable in the Missions of the Fathers of the Society of Jesus in New France, for the Years 1666–1667, Sent to the Rev. Father Jaques Bordier, Provincial of the Province of France," in *The Jesuit Relations and Allied Documents: Travels and Explorations of the Jesuit Missionaries in New France, 1610–1791*, ed. Reuben Gold Thwaites, 248–311 (Cleveland, OH: Burrows Brothers, 1899).

2. See, for example, William H. McNeill, *Plagues and People* (Garden City, NY: Anchor Press, 1976), and Alfred W. Crosby, *Ecological Imperialism: The Biological Expansion of Europe, 900–1900* (Cambridge: Cambridge University Press, 1986).

3. On the wilderness as demonic haunt, see Roderick Nash, *Wilderness and the American Mind*, 3rd ed. (1967; repr., New Haven, CT: Yale University Press, 1982); Hans Huth, *Nature and the American: Three Centuries of Changing Attitudes* (Berkeley and Los Angeles: University of California Press, 1957); Max Oelschlaeger, *The Idea of Wilderness: From Prehistory to the Age of Ecology* (New Haven, CT: Yale University Press, 1991); and Clarence J. Glacken, *Traces on the Rhodian Shore: Nature and Culture in Western Thought from Ancient Times to the End of the Eighteenth Century* (Berkeley and Los Angeles: University of California Press, 1967).

4. Allouez, "Relation," 251.

5. Ibid., 255–57.

6. Ibid., 263.

7. Allouez and other Jesuits preserved careful ethnological observations in letters that they sent to their Québec superior, who edited them and sent them to France. Between 1896 and 1901, these were compiled, translated, and published in seventy-three volumes as *The Jesuit Relations and Allied Documents* under the direction of Reuben Gold Thwaites, secretary of the State Historical Society of Wisconsin. These documents continue to be a valuable resource for scholars.

8. Allouez, "Relation," 267.

9. Ibid., 265.

10. Ibid., 273.

11. Richard White, *The Middle Ground: Indians, Empires, and Republics in the Great Lakes Region, 1650–1815* (Cambridge: Cambridge University Press, 1991), x.

12. Eugen Weber, *Peasants into Frenchmen: The Modernization of Rural France, 1870–1914* (Stanford, CA: Stanford University Press, 1976), 3.

13. See the works of Grace Lee Nute, especially *The Voyageur* (1931; repr., St. Paul: Minnesota Historical Society, 1955), as well as the works of Sigurd F. Olson, whose many essays and books have inspired generations of canoeists to think of themselves as modern-day voyageurs.

Introduction: Imaginative Geographies

1. See Martyn J. Bowden, "The Great American Desert in the American Mind: The Historiography of a Geographical Notion," in *Geographies of the Mind: Essays in Historical Geosophy in Honor of John Kirtland Wright*, ed. David Lowenthal and Martyn Bowden, 119–47 (New York: Oxford University Press, 1976), and Donald Worster, *Dust Bowl: The Southern Plains in the 1930s* (Oxford: Oxford University Press, 1982).

2. William A. Henry, *Northern Wisconsin: A Handbook for the Homeseeker* (Madison, WI: Democrat Printing, State Printer, 1896), 6.

3. Vernon Carstensen, *Farms or Forests: Evolution of a State Land Policy for Northern Wisconsin* (Madison: University of Wisconsin College of Agriculture, 1958); Arlan Helgeson, *Farms in the Cutover: Agricultural Settlement in Northern Wisconsin* (Madison: State Historical Society of Wisconsin, for Department of History, University of Wisconsin, 1962). It is interesting to compare Carstensen's *Farms or Forests* with Donald Worster's *Dust Bowl*. More recent works include John Vogel, *Great Lakes Lumber on the Great Plains: The Laird, Norton Lumber Company in South Dakota*, ed. Wayne Franklin, *The American Land and Life Series* (Iowa City: University of Iowa Press, 1992), which traces the movements of trees, ironically, from the cutover region to the Great Plains. For a succinct analysis of the morphology and ecological effects of lumber boomtowns, see Randall Rohe, "Lumbering Wisconsin's Northern Urban Frontier," in *Wisconsin Land and Life*, ed. Robert Ostergren and Thomas Vale, 221–40 (Madison: University of Wisconsin Press, 1997). The most recent in a long list of dissertations and theses on the region include Timothy Bawden, "Reinventing the Frontier: Tourism, Nature, and Environmental Change in Northern Wisconsin, 1880–1930" (PhD diss., University of Wisconsin—Madison, 2001), and Mark Davis, "An Empire in Waiting: Northern Wisconsin's Lake Country, 1880–1940" (PhD diss., University of Wisconsin—Madison, 1997). Also of special note is Charles G. Mahaffey, "Changing Images of the Cutover: A Historical Geography of Resource Utilization in the Lake Superior Region, 1840–1930" (PhD diss., University of Wisconsin, 1978). In addition, there are several useful articles in the *Wisconsin Magazine of History*.

4. Robert Gough, *Farming the Cutover: A Social History of Northern Wisconsin, 1900–1940* (Lawrence: University Press of Kansas, 1997).

5. See Timothy Bawden, "The Northwoods: Back to Nature?" in *Wisconsin Land and Life,* ed. Robert C. Ostergren and Thomas R. Vale, 450–69 (Madison: University of Wisconsin Press, 1997), and Bawden, "Reinventing the Frontier."

6. William Cronon, "A Place for Stories: Nature, History, and Narrative," *Journal of American History* 78, no. 4 (March 1992): 1347–76; Worster, *Dust Bowl;* and Paul Bonnifield, *The Dust Bowl: Men, Dirt, and Depression* (Albuquerque: University of New Mexico Press, 1979).

7. Yi-Fu Tuan, "Language and the Making of Place: A Narrative-Descriptive Approach," *Annals of the Association of American Geographers* 81, no. 4 (1991): 684–96.

8. Ibid., 684, 694.

9. Cronon, "A Place for Stories"; Michael Williams, "The Relations of Environmental History and Historical Geography," *Journal of Historical Geography* 20 (1994): 3–21.

10. Ralph Hall Brown, *Historical Geography of the United States,* ed. J. Russell Whitaker (New York: Harcourt, Brace and World, 1948), 3.

11. Within geography, there is a large body of work that explores environmental cognition and behavior. See, for example, H. C. Brookfield, "On the Environment as Perceived," *Progress in Geography* 1 (1969): 51–80; the papers in David Lowenthal, ed., *Environmental Perception and Behavior* (Chicago: Department of Geography, University of Chicago, 1967); and John R. Gold, *An Introduction to the Behavioral Environment* (Oxford: Oxford University Press, 1980). A good overview is Douglas M. Amedeo and Reginald G. Golledge, "Environmental Perception and Behavioral Geography," in *Geography in America at the Dawn of the 21st Century,* ed. Gary L. Gaile and Cort J. Willmott (Oxford: Oxford University Press, 2003), 133–48. In the same volume, see Garth A. Myers, Patrick McGreevy, George O. Carney, and Judith Kenny, "Cultural Geography," 81–96; and Craig E. Colten, Peter J. Hugill, Terrence Young, and Karen Morin, "Historical Geography," 149–63.

12. Seminal works on place include Yi-Fu Tuan, *Topophilia: A Study of Environmental Perception, Attitudes, and Values* (New York: Columbia University Press, 1990); Tuan, *Space and Place: The Perspective of Experience* (Minneapolis: University of Minnesota Press, 1977); E. Relph, *Place and Placelessness,* ed. Allen J. Scott, Research in Planning and Design (London: Pion, 1976); and J. Nicholas Entrikin, *The Betweenness of Place: Towards a Geography of Modernity* (Baltimore, MD: Johns Hopkins University Press, 1991).

13. Carl Ortwin Sauer, "The Morphology of Landscape," *University of California Publications in Geography* 2, no. 2 (1925): 19–53.

14. John Brinckerhoff Jackson, *Discovering the Vernacular Landscape* (New Haven, CT: Yale University Press, 1984), 8.

15. See the journal *Landscape,* the writings of J. B. Jackson, and the influential essays collected in D. W. Meinig, ed., *The Interpretation of Ordinary Landscapes* (New York: Oxford University Press, 1979).

16. Some of the best work is in Denis Cosgrove, ed., *Social Formation and Symbolic Landscape* (1984; repr., Madison: University of Wisconsin Press, 1998), and Trevor J.

Barnes and James S. Duncan, eds., *Writing Worlds: Discourse, Text & Metaphor in the Representation of Landscape* (London: Routledge, 1992).

17. Donald Worster, "Transformations of the Earth: Toward an Agroecological Perspective in History," In A Round Table: Environmental History, *Journal of American History* 76 (1990): 1087–1106.

18. Craig Colten and Lary Dilsaver, "Historical Geography and the Environment: A Preliminary Literature Review," in *The American Environment: Interpretations of Past Geographies,* ed. Craig Colten and Lary Dilsaver (Boston: Rowman and Littlefield, 1992), 1–18.

19. William Cronon, "Modes of Prophesy and Production: Placing Nature in History," in A Round Table: Environmental History, *Journal of American History* 76 (1990): 1122–31, and Cronon, "Kennecott Journey: The Paths out of Town," *Under an Open Sky: Rethinking America's Western Past,* ed. William Cronon, George Miles, and Jay Gitlin, 28–51 (New York: W. W. Norton, 1992). "Kennecott Journey" is especially suggestive on how scholars can integrate the three elements.

20. Arthur McEvoy, *The Fisherman's Problem: Ecology and Law in the California Fisheries, 1850–1980* (Cambridge: Cambridge University Press, 1986). In the following discussion, I have relied on McEvoy, "Toward an Interactive Theory of Nature and Culture: Ecology, Production, and Cognition in the California Fishing Industry," in *The Ends of the Earth: Perspectives on Modern Environmental History,* ed. Donald Worster, 211–29 (Cambridge: Cambridge University Press, 1988), which offers a synopsis of his main argument.

21. McEvoy, "Toward an Interactive Theory of Nature and Culture," 229.

Chapter One: Reconnaissance

1. On Schoolcraft and his role in the 1820 Cass Expedition, I have relied most heavily on Mentor L. Williams, "Editor's Introduction," in Henry R. Schoolcraft, *Narrative Journal of Travels: Through Northwestern Regions of the United States Extending from Detroit through the Great Chain of American Lakes to the Sources of the Mississippi River in the Year 1820,* ed. Mentor L. Williams, 1–24 (East Lansing: Michigan State College Press, 1953), and Richard G. Bremer, *Indian Agent and Wilderness Scholar: The Life of Henry Rowe Schoolcraft* (Mount Pleasant: Clark Historical Library, Central Michigan University, 1987). Roy Harvey Pearce, *Savagism and Civilization: A Study of the Indian and the American Mind* (Berkeley: University of California Press, 1988), especially 120–28, contains a useful section on Schoolcraft's interest in Native Americans and his role in shaping popular images of Indians in the United States.

2. The best single source on McKenney is Herman J. Viola, *Thomas L. McKenney: Architect of America's Early Indian Policy, 1816–1830* (Chicago: Swallow Press, 1974). See also Michael Paul Rogin, *Fathers and Children: Andrew Jackson and the Subjugation of the American Indian* (New York: Alfred A. Knopf, 1975), especially 114–24.

3. Henry R. Schoolcraft, *A View of the Lead Mines of Missouri; Including Some Observations on the Mineralogy, Geology, Geography, Antiquities, and Soil, Climate, Population, and Productions of Missouri and Arkansaw, and Other Sections of the Western Country* (New York: Charles Wiley, 1819).

4. Lewis Cass was an important figure in old Northwest history. Recent works on Cass include Willard Carl Klunder, *Lewis Cass and the Politics of Moderation* (Kent, OH: Kent State University Press, 1996), and Steven Wolenec, "The 'Nerve of the Northwest': Lewis Cass as Michigan Territorial Governor, 1813–1831" (master's thesis, University of Wisconsin–Eau Claire, 2000).

5. Schoolcraft would be credited with discovering the source of the Mississippi River but on a later journey. For background on the expedition, as well as other useful information regarding Schoolcraft, see Williams, "Editor's Introduction," and Bremer, *Indian Agent*. I draw heavily on both of these works. Duane Paul Mosser, "Henry Rowe Schoolcraft: Eyewitness to a Changing Frontier" (PhD diss., University of California–Santa Barbara, 1991), is also useful.

6. Henry R. Schoolcraft, *Narrative Journal of Travels: Through Northwestern Regions of the United States Extending from Detroit through the Great Chain of American Lakes to the Sources of the Mississippi River in the Year 1820*, ed. Mentor L. Williams (East Lansing: Michigan State College Press, 1953). Among other documents, this volume includes the journals of James Doty, secretary to the expedition, and Charles Trowbridge, the assistant topographer. Although my main focus here is Schoolcraft, it is interesting to compare his account with that of other members of the expedition.

7. For a detailed account of the trip, see Viola, *Thomas L. McKenney*, 135–67, and also Viola's introduction to Thomas L. McKenney, *Sketches of a Tour to the Lakes, of the Character and Customs of the Chippeway Indians, and of Incidents Connected with the Treaty of Fond du Lac* (Barre, MA: Imprint Society, 1972), ix–xx.

8. See James A. Clifton, "Wisconsin Death March: Explaining the Extremes in Old Northwest Indian Removal," *Transactions of the Wisconsin Academy of Sciences, Arts and Letters* 75 (1987): 1–39, and Ronald N. Satz, *Chippewa Treaty Rights: The Reserved Rights of Wisconsin's Chippewa Indians in Historical Perspective*, ed. Carl N. Haywood, vol. 79, no. 1 *Transactions* (Madison: Wisconsin Academy of Sciences, Arts and Letters, 1991), 51–59. Also see Lewis Cass, "Removal of the Indians: Documents and Proceedings Relating to the Formation and Progress of a Board in the City of New York, for the Emigration, Preservation, and Improvement of the Aborigines of America." *North American Review* 30 (1830): 62–121.

9. James Monroe to Thomas Jefferson, January 19, 1786, in *The Writings of James Monroe: Including a Collection of His Public and Private Papers and Correspondence, Now for the First Time Printed*, ed. Stanislaus Murray Hamilton (New York: G. P. Putnam's Sons, 1898–1903), 1:117.

10. Quoted in Wolenec, "The 'Nerve of the Northwest,'" 41.

11. See Frank B. Woodford, *Lewis Cass: The Last Jeffersonian* (New Brunswick, NJ: Rutgers University Press, 1950), 109, and Williams, "Editor's Introduction," 11.

12. For an insightful analysis of the process by which traditional stories have been acquired, decontextualized, contextualized, recontextualized, and packaged for a mass audience, using Schoolcraft as an example, see Richard Bauman, "The Nationalization and Internationalization of Folklore: The Case of Schoolcraft's 'Gitshe Gauzinee,'" *Western Folklore* 52 (April 1993): 247–69.

13. For an analysis of Cooper's novels and their contributions to American myth-making, see Richard Slotkin, *The Fatal Environment: The Myth of the Frontier in the Age of Industrialization, 1800–1890* (New York: Atheneum, 1985), 81–106.

14. On Schoolcraft's evolving ideas about American Indians, see Mosser, "Henry Rowe Schoolcraft."

15. Thomas L. McKenney, *Sketches of a Tour to the Lakes, of the Character and Customs of the Chippeway Indians, and of Incidents Connected with the Treaty of Fond du Lac,* facsimile of the first edition published at Baltimore, MD (1827; repr., Minneapolos, MN: Ross and Haines, 1959), 198.

16. Viola, *Thomas L. McKenney,* 153.

17. Margaret Fuller, *Summer on the Lakes, in 1843* (1844; repr., Urbana: University of Illinois Press, 1991), 21.

18. McKenney, *Sketches of a Tour,* 206, 237–38.

19. McKenney's book has a crude illustration of a canoe with canopy. The illustrations in both books vary in quality. Schoolcraft made sketches in the field and later commissioned Henry Inman to redraw some of them. Inman studied with John Wesley Jarvis and became a well-known portrait painter. Most of the illustrations in McKenney's book were done by James Otto Lewis, from Detroit. Lewis was paid to accompany the 1826 expedition and two other expeditions with Cass between 1825 and 1827. He is best known for about 250 Indian portraits from these expeditions. See Viola, "Introduction," xvi–xvii, and Henry Schoolcraft, *Personal Memoirs of a Residence of Thirty Years with the Indian Tribes on the American Frontiers* (Philadelphia: Lippincott, Grambo, 1851), chap. 6.

20. On the various types of birchbark canoes and their use and construction, see Grace Lee Nute, *The Voyageur* (1931; repr., St. Paul: Minnesota Historical Society, 1955), 23–32. One of the best contemporary sources is McKenney, *Sketches of a Tour,* especially 199–200. McKenney made frequent comments on the skill of the voyageurs in handling their canoes and provided detailed descriptions on their technique.

21. Jedidiah Morse, *The American Universal Geography; or, A View of the Present State of All the Kingdoms, States, and Colonies in the Known World,* 7th ed., 2 vols. (Charlestown [Boston, MA]: G. Clarke, 1819), 1:634.

22. Schoolcraft, *Narrative Journal,* 79.

23. McKenney, *Sketches of a Tour,* 165.

24. Schoolcraft, *Narrative Journal,* 95.

25. Ibid., 96. Contrast Schoolcraft's observation with Allouez's stated belief that Lake Superior had been designed to concentrate Indians in one place so that their souls could be more easily saved by Jesuits.

26. For the details of the treaty and its wider implications for the Indians and fur traders of the middle ground, see Richard White, *The Middle Ground: Indians, Empires, and Republics in the Great Lakes Region, 1650–1815* (Cambridge: Cambridge University Press, 1991), 472–73, 476, and 494.

27. Details of this episode vary widely. The preceding is based on the account in Schoolcraft, *Narrative Journey*, 97–100.

28. Philip P. Mason, ed., *Schoolcraft: The Literary Voyageur, or Muzzeniegun* (East Lansing: Michigan University Press, 1962), xxi–xxii.

29. White, *The Middle Ground*, 470n.

30. Mason, *Schoolcraft*, xxii–xxiii.

31. McKenney, *Sketches of a Tour*, 192.

32. Ibid., 194.

33. Schoolcraft, *Narrative Journal*, 102.

34. Charles C. Trowbridge, "Appendix G: The Journal and Letters of Charles Christopher Trowbridge, Expedition of 1820," in Henry R. Schoolcraft, *Narrative Journal of Travels: Through Northwestern Regions of the United States Extending from Detroit through the Great Chain of American Lakes to the Sources of the Mississippi River in the Year 1820*, ed. Mentor L. Williams, (East Lansing: Michigan State College Press, 1953), 470.

35. McKenney, *Sketches of a Tour*, 211.

36. The classic work on engendered landscapes is Annette Kolodny, *The Lay of the Land: Metaphors as Experience and History in American Life and Letters* (Chapel Hill: University of North Carolina Press, 1975).

37. Jedidiah Morse, *American Gazetteer* (Boston: Thomas and Andrews, 1810).

38. Morse, *American Universal Geography*, 1:631.

39. Trowbridge, "Appendix G," 471.

40. Schoolcraft, *Narrative Journal*, 116–17.

41. The copy of Morse's *American Geography* (1794) that I examined is held in the rare books section at the Wisconsin State Historical Society. Unfortunately, the map is too fragile to copy.

42. Morse, *American Universal Geography*, vol. 1.

43. Nute, *The Voyageur*, 46, 50, 58, and 61. See Frances Densmore, *Chippewa Customs* (1929; repr., Minneapolis, MN: Ross and Haines, 1970), 18–19 and 137, for details on how Chippewa measured time and distance, reflecting the cross-cultural exchanges of the fur trade era.

44. Schoolcraft, *Narrative Journal*, 118 and 140.

45. For the "official" distances, I refer to the chart on the recent navigation map "Great Lakes: Lake Champlain to Lake of the Woods" (Washington, DC: U.S. Department of Commerce, National Oceanic and Atmospheric Administration, National Ocean Service, Coast and Geodetic Survey, 1995).

46. See the numerous editorial comments by Mentor Williams regarding discrepancies with other records of the expedition and outright erroneous statements by Schoolcraft in Schoolcraft, *Narrative Journal*.

47. Nute, *The Voyageur*, 258–61.

48. Edmund Jefferson Danziger, *The Chippewas of Lake Superior* (1979; repr., Norman: University of Oklahoma Press, 1990), 39, 40.

49. In part because of the clout of the trader Jean Baptiste Cadotte, the Lake Superior bands did not participate in the general uprising against the British. As their traditional Sioux enemies knew, the Chippewa were fierce warriors, but Chippewa violence toward whites was extremely rare. See ibid., 55.

50. Morse, *American Universal Geography*, 1:634.

51. Schoolcraft, *Narrative Journal*, 103.

52. Ibid., 102.

53. James D. Doty, "Appendix F: The Official Journal of James D. Doty," in Henry R. Schoolcraft, *Narrative Journal of Travels: Through Northwestern Regions of the United States Extending from Detroit through the Great Chain of American Lakes to the Sources of the Mississippi River in the Year 1820*, ed. Mentor L. Williams (East Lansing: Michigan State College Press, 1953), 423.

Chapter Two: Through the Poets' Eyes

1. There is an enormous literature on the sublime, romanticism, and changing attitudes toward nature. For Europe, the classic works include Samuel Monk, *The Sublime: A Study of Critical Theories in XVIII-Century England* (1935; repr., Ann Arbor: University of Michigan Press, 1960), and Marjorie Hope Nicolson, *Mountain Gloom and Mountain Glory: The Development of the Aesthetics of the Infinite* (1959; repr., New York: W. W. Norton, 1963). For the United States, see Roderick Nash, *Wilderness and the American Mind*, 3rd ed. (1967; repr., New Haven, CT, and London: Yale University Press, 1982); Peter J. Schmitt, *Back to Nature: The Arcadian Myth in Urban America* (1969; repr., Baltimore, MD, and London: Johns Hopkins University Press, 1990); and Barbara Novak, *Nature and Culture: American Landscape and Painting, 1825–1875* (New York: Oxford University Press, 1980). More recent works include Andrew Wilton and Tim Barringer, *American Sublime: Landscape Painting in the United States, 1820–1880* (London: Tate Publishing, 2002). For a useful essay that examines romantic landscape descriptions of Lake Superior by Henry Rowe Schoolcraft and David Bates Douglas on the 1820 Lewis Cass Expedition, Schoolcraft on his 1831 expedition, and Bela Hubbard on the 1840 Douglas Houghton Expedition, see Bernard C. Peters, "Revolt from the Wilderness: Romantic Travellers on Lake Superior." *Michigan Academician* 13, no. 4 (Spring 1981), 491–501.

2. Edmund Burke, *A Philosophical Enquiry into the Origin of Our Ideas of the Sublime and Beautiful*, ed. J. T. Boulton (1759; repr., London and New York: Routledge and Kegan Paul, and Columbia University Press, 1958), 39–40; italics in original.

3. Elizabeth McKinsey made the interesting claim that "the most important work in transmitting ideas of the sublime to America was Hugh Blair, *Lectures on Rhetoric and*

Belles Lettres (1783 and numerous subsequent editions), which was the standard rhetoric text in American colleges well into the nineteenth century"; see McKinsey, *Niagara Falls: Icon of the American Sublime* (Cambridge: Cambridge University Press, 1985), 288n49. Indeed, rhetoric was considered a vital part of a person's education until the twentieth century, and even those trained in science would undoubtedly be well versed in rhetoric until the late decades of the nineteenth century.

4. John F. Sears, *Sacred Places: American Tourist Attractions in the Nineteenth Century* (Amherst: University of Massachusetts Press, 1998), 13–14.

5. Quote from McKinsey, *Niagara Falls,* 3. Other key works on Niagara Falls include Patrick V. McGreevy, *Imagining Niagara: The Meaning and Making of Niagara Falls* (Amherst: University of Massachusetts Press, 1994); Sears, *Sacred Places;* and Ralph Greenhill and Thomas D. Mahoney, *Niagara* (Toronto, Canada: University of Toronto Press, 1969). The latter is an important exploration of the iconography of Niagara Falls.

6. McGreevy, *Imagining Niagara,* 3, 11–12, 17.

7. McKinsey, *Niagara Falls,* 127.

8. Quoted in Sears, *Sacred Places,* 42.

9. Ibid.

10. This argument is made most forcefully in McKinsey, *Niagara Falls.*

11. Sears, *Sacred Places,* 13–14.

12. Henry R. Schoolcraft, *Narrative Journal of Travels: Through Northwestern Regions of the United States Extending from Detroit through the Great Chain of American Lakes to the Sources of the Mississippi River in the Year 1820,* ed. Mentor L. Williams (East Lansing: Michigan State College Press, 1953), 42–43. According to Ralph Greenhill and Thomas D. Mahoney, the stairs were built by former state militia general Parkhurst Whitney in 1818. The stairs replaced an "Indian ladder," so the chasm was accessible before the stairs were installed. Whitney also repaired the old log tavern that had been torched by the British during the War of 1812 and called it the Eagle Tavern. See Greenhill and Mahoney, *Niagara,* 110.

13. See Mentor Williams's footnote in Schoolcraft, *Narrative Journal,* 48.

14. Schoolcraft, *Narrative Journal,* 112.

15. Two very helpful anthologies on the history of the discipline of geology in the United States are Ellen T. Drake and William M. Jordan, eds., *Geologists and Ideas: A History of North American Geology,* Centennial Special Volume 1 (Boulder: Geological Society of America, 1985), and Cecil J. Schneer, ed., *Two Hundred Years of Geology in America: Proceedings of the New Hampshire Bicentennial Conference on the History of Geology* (Hanover, NH: University Press of New England, 1979).

16. McKenney identified that place only as "Forsyth's," but it seems certain that he referred to the Pavilion Hotel. See Greenhill and Mahoney, *Niagara,* 110. According to Greenhill and Mahoney, Forsyth had operated the ferry before becoming proprietor of the Pavilion. His partner in the ferry was Parkhurst Whitney, a brigadier general in the War of 1812, owner of the Eagle Tavern, and the man who built the stairs down to the falls in 1818.

17. McKenney, *Sketches of a Tour,* 98–99. For *Childe Harold's Pilgrimage,* see Lord Byron, *The Works of Lord Byron—The Wordsworth Poetical Library* (Hertfordshire, UK: Cumberland House, 1994), 229. This volume also contains a short but useful introduction.

18. The sixty-ninth and seventy-second stanzas of the fourth canto, as quoted by McKenney (ibid.), capture the mood of the poem: "The roar of waters! From headlong height / Niag'ra cleaves the wave-worn precipice; / The fall of waters! Rapid as the light / The flashing mass foams shaking the abyss; / The *hell of waters!* Where the howl and hiss, / And boil in endless torture; while the sweat / Of their agony, wrung out from this / Their Phlegethon, curls round the rocks of jet / That gird the gulf around, in pitiless horror set. . . . / "Horribly beautiful! but on the verge, / From side to side, beneath the glitt'ring morn, / An Iris sits, amidst the infernal surge, / Like Hope upon a death-bed, and unworn / Its steady dyes, while all around is torn / By the distracted waters, bears serene / its brilliant hues with all their beams unshorn: / Resembling, 'mid the torture of the scene, / Love watching Madness with unalterable mien!"

19. McKenney, *Sketches of a Tour,* 93.

20. McKinsey, *Niagara Falls,* 31. For a brief mention of McKenney's formal education, see Herman J. Viola, *Thomas L. McKenney: Architect of America's Early Indian Policy, 1816–1830,* 1st ed. (Chicago: Swallow Press, 1974), 3.

21. See David Potter's "Foreword" and Harold Harding's "introduction" to Hugh Blair, *Lectures on Rhetoric and Belles Lettres,* ed. Harold F. Harding (1783; repr., Carbondale: Southern Illinois University Press, 1965). Also see McKinsey, *Niagara Falls,* 288n49.

22. See Blair, *Lectures on Rhetoric,* especially 47–90.

23. Ibid., 71.

24. McKenney, *Sketches of a Tour,* 96.

25. Ibid., 98. I have not found Ben Hanson's last name in McKenney's book. McKenney's biographer, Herman J. Viola, mentioned Hanson several times but did not tell us much about him. It seems clear that Hanson was well educated, and he accompanied McKenney on some dramatic journeys. He would be a promising subject for a biography. See Viola, *Thomas L. McKenney,* 140, 142, 143, 156, 163, 164, 166, and 206.

26. Maurice Cranston, *The Romantic Movement* (Oxford and Cambridge: Basil Blackwell, 1994), 70. Cranston provided a useful overview of the romantic movement and its main characters in Europe.

27. Schoolcraft, *Narrative Journal,* 102.

28. At the risk of ruining the suspense, I will add that no lives were lost on either trip.

29. Schoolcraft, *Narrative Journal,* 104.

30. Ibid., 105. This is not a surprising observation when one considers that Schoolcraft began his career as a glassblower. Like many practicing geologists of his day, he was largely self-taught. As a youth, he worked in the glass industry and there learned some chemistry. In 1814, while working in a lab associated with a Vermont glassworks, he became acquainted with Frederick Hall, professor of natural philosophy at Middlebury

College. Hall encouraged his growing interest in mineralogy. See Richard G. Bremer, *Indian Agent and Wilderness Scholar: The Life of Henry Rowe Schoolcraft* (Mount Pleasant: Clark Historical Library, Central Michigan University, 1987).

31. Charles C. Trowbridge, "Appendix G: The Journal and Letters of Charles Christopher Trowbridge, Expedition of 1820," in Henry R. Schoolcraft, *Narrative Journal of Travels: Through Northwestern Regions of the United States Extending from Detroit through the Great Chain of American Lakes to the Sources of the Mississippi River in the Year 1820*, ed. Mentor L. Williams, (East Lansing: Michigan State College Press, 1953), 471.

32. James D. Doty, "Appendix F: The Official Journal of James D. Doty," in Henry R. Schoolcraft, *Narrative Journal of Travels: Through Northwestern Regions of the United States Extending from Detroit through the Great Chain of American Lakes to the Sources of the Mississippi River in the Year 1820*, ed. Mentor L. Williams (East Lansing: Michigan State College Press, 1953), 414.

33. Schoolcraft, *Narrative Journal*, 106.

34. Ibid., 107–8. The Scott quote follows: "Their rocky summits split and rent, / Form'd turret, dome, or battlement, / Or seemed fantastically set / With cupola or minaret, / Wild crests as pagod ever decked, / Or mosque of eastern architect."

35. Schoolcraft, *Narrative Journal*, 108.

36. Unfortunately, the 1953 edition is not illustrated, so the illustrations used here are from the 1821 edition of the book. I am grateful for a conversation with David Woodward. I dropped by his office, and from a poor photocopy, he quickly identified the print as a copper engraving and not a lithograph as I had at first suspected. David was a kind and brilliant man and a priceless resource for scholars at the University of Wisconsin–Madison. His presence will be missed in Science Hall.

37. Doty, "Appendix F," 415.

38. Ibid.

39. Trowbridge, "Appendix G," 472.

40. Ibid.

41. Schoolcraft, *Narrative Journal*, 115.

42. Trowbridge, "Appendix G," 476.

43. Doty, "Appendix F," 421.

44. Trowbridge, "Appendix G," 475.

45. Schoolcraft, *Narrative Journal*, 125.

46. Ibid., 128. One cannot help but wonder what the Indians thought of Schoolcraft at this point. It is ironic that he would play such an influential role in romanticizing Indian stories.

47. Trowbridge, "Appendix G," 477.

48. Doty, "Appendix F," 422.

49. McKenney, *Sketches of a Tour*, 223–24.

50. Ibid., 224. It seems telling that, although McKenney's servant accompanied them more or less as an equal (at least he did not feel obligated to stay by McKenney's side),

in his "we" at the beginning of the quote McKenney politely lists Schoolcraft before himself but Ben after. Comparing the men in the distance to Lilliputians was, no doubt, a reference to Jonathan Swift's *Gulliver's Travels*.

51. Viola, *Thomas L. McKenney*, 137.

52. Ibid., 224–25.

53. Michael's Island is now known as Madeline Island. Sometimes, it is simply referred to as La Pointe. See John O. Holzhueter, *Madeline Island & the Chequamegon Region* (Madison: State Historical Society of Wisconsin, 1986).

54. McKenney, *Sketches of a Tour*, 262.

55. Ibid., 263–64. The last line is from William Cowper's poem "The Garden."

56. See article 3, in McKenney, *Sketches of a Tour*, 480.

Chapter Three: Ordering the Landscape

1. I found three works to be most useful for contextualizing the arguments that follow: Nathan Reingold, ed., *Science in America since 1820* (New York: Science History Publications, 1976); Cecil J. Schneer, ed., *Two Hundred Years of Geology in America: Proceedings of the New Hampshire Bicentennial Conference on the History of Geology* (Hanover, NH: University Press of New England, 1979); and Carroll Lane Fenton and Mildred Adams Fenton, *The Story of the Great Geologists* (1945; repr., Freeport, NY: Books for Libraries Press, 1969). All help to set geology in the larger historical and scientific context. Ellen T. Drake and William M. Jordan, eds., *Geologists and Ideas: A History of North American Geology, Centennial Special Volume 1* (Boulder, CO: Geological Society of America, 1985), is uneven but contains several useful essays. Susan J. Thompson, *A Chronology of Geological Thinking from Antiquity to 1899* (Metuchen, NJ, and London: Scarecrow Press, 1988), is indispensable for tracing the development of geological theory and is also useful for assessing the influence of individual geologists. Although the USGS was not organized until 1879, the following publication contains a useful overview of the federal surveys conducted before that date under the Department of War and later the Treasury Department: *The U.S. Geological Survey: Its History, Activities and Organization*, reprint of 1918 ed., Brookings Institution, Institute for Government Research, Service Monographs of the United States Government, no. 1 (New York: AMS, 1974). Mary C. Rabbitt, *Minerals, Lands, and Geology for the Common Defense and General Welfare*, vol. 1, *Before 1879: A History of Public Lands, Federal Science and Mapping Policy in the United States* (Washington, DC: U.S. Government Printing Office, 1979), is an impressive and useful work. Two geologists, David Dale Owen and Charles Whittlesey, will figure prominently in this chapter. One or the other or both are mentioned in each of the works listed in this note.

2. Norman J. W. Thrower, *Original Land Survey and Land Subdivision: A Comparative Study of the Form and Effect of Contrasting Cadastral Surveys—The Monograph Series*

of the Association of American Geographers (Chicago: Rand McNally, 1966). The quotation is from Clarence Glacken's "Preface," vi.

3. All quotations are from *The Compact Oxford English Dictionary: New Edition.*

4. For just one instance of an altercation between surveyors and Indians, see Lowell O. Stewart, *Public Land Surveys: History, Instructions, Methods,* reprint of the 1935 edition by Collegiate Press, The Development of Public Land Law in the United States (New York: Arno Press, 1979), 85. McKenney explained in detail the preparations for the show of military force and the not-so-subtle threats used by the 1826 Cass Expedition to get signatures and to coerce compliance with the 1826 treaty. See Thomas L. McKenney, *Sketches of a Tour to the Lakes, of the Character and Customs of the Chippeway Indians, and of Incidents Connected with the Treaty of Fond du Lac,* facsimile of the first edition published at Baltimore, MD (1827; repr., Minneapolis, MN: Ross and Haines, 1959).

5. Two of the best works that study the cultural, political, and ecological implications of the Public Land Survey are Hildegard Binder Johnson, *Order upon the Land: The U.S. Rectangular Land Survey and the Upper Mississippi Country—The Andrew H. Clark Series in the Historical Geography of North America* (New York: Oxford University Press, 1976), and Thrower, *Original Land Survey.* The classic and still indispensable work on the U.S. Public Lands, their survey, and their disposal is Benjamin Horace Hibbard, *A History of the Public Land Policies* (1924; repr., Madison: University of Wisconsin Press, 1965).

6. See "A Memoir of Dr. Douglass Houghton," *American Journal of Science and Arts* 5, no. 14 (1848): 217–27. Houghton was described as a "backwoods geologist" who, though "neat in dress at home, . . . well knew how to throw aside those restraints that were incompatible with the wilderness." Although a seasoned field geologist, "he paid too little heed to the omens that warned his Canadian voyageurs of the storm." When Charles Whittlesey was returning from his 1845 trip on Lake Superior, he witnessed the search for Houghton's body.

7. On Owen, see Walter B. Hendrickson, *David Dale Owen: Pioneer Geologist of the Middle West, Indiana Historical Collections,* vol. 1 (Indianapolis: Indiana Historical Bureau, 1943), and on Whittlesey, see Charles C. Baldwin, "Memorial of Colonel Charles Whittlesey, Late President of the Western Reserve Historical Society," *Western Reserve Historical Society* 2, no. 68 (1888): 405–35.

8. Figure 3.2 shows the establishment of geological survey offices by state. Note the westward trend, which to a large degree mirrored settlement and early industrial development. One can block off a tier of eastern states with a western boundary that includes, from north to south, Michigan, Indiana, Kentucky, Tennessee, and Georgia, which all had state geologists by 1844; a middle tier of states, with outliers on the Pacific coast, which had offices established by 1890; and a C-shaped cluster of states from the Dakotas to Idaho, New Mexico, and Oklahoma, which did not establish offices until after 1890. Data for the map were derived from the individual chapters in Arthur A. Socolow, ed., *The State Geological Surveys: A History* (n.p.: Association of American State Geologists,

1988). Although dated, another useful source is George P. Merrill, *Contributions to a History of American State Geological and Natural History Surveys* (1920; repr., New York: Arno Press, 1978).

9. Baldwin, "Memorial of Colonel Charles Whittlesey," is the most complete biography available; see Charles Whittlesey, "Two Months in the Copper Regions," in *Fugitive Essays,* 282–344 (Hudson, OH: Sawyer, Ingersoll, 1852).

10. Whittlesey, "Two Months in the Copper Regions," 284.

11. According to Edward Hill, Daniel P. Bushnell was the first Indian agent assigned to La Pointe, and he was there from 1836 to 1842. Actually, Henry Schoolcraft's brother-in-law, George Johnston, was stationed at La Pointe as a subagent from 1826 to 1829. See Edward E. Hill, *The Office of Indian Affairs, 1824–1880: Historical Sketches—The Library of American Indian Affairs* (New York: Clearwater Publishing, 1974), 87–88.

12. Quoted in George Cantor, *The Great Lakes Guidebook: Lake Superior and Western Lake Michigan* (Ann Arbor: University of Michigan Press, 1980), 13.

13. Ibid., 13–14. Although the focus is on the Canadian locks, built much later, useful information on U.S. locks is contained in Brian S. Osbourne and Donald Swainson, *The Sault Ste. Marie Canal: A Chapter in the History of Great Lakes Transport* (Ottawa: Parks Canada, 1986).

14. Baldwin, "Memorial of Colonel Charles Whittlesey"; the quotation is from p. 413. This piece is really more of an extended obituary than a biography. Whittlesey would be an excellent subject for a full biography.

15. Although all page numbers in this chapter refer to the version of Whittlesey's essay published in *Fugitive Essays* (Hudson, OH: Sawyer, Ingersoll, 1852), I compared that version to the original published in the *National Magazine and Industrial Record, New York* 2, no. 9 (1846): 814–46, and found that the texts of the two versions seem identical.

16. The designation Ashland, taken from the name of Henry Clay's home, is unintentionally ironic because though Clay famously promoted development of the West, he considered the Lake Superior country as remote as the moon, as mentioned earlier.

17. Whittlesey, "Two Months in the Copper Regions," 284.

18. Ibid., 285. The term *upper country* was originally used to refer to the region upriver from Montreal, basically the Great Lakes watershed.

19. Ibid. To anyone who has spent time in the wilderness far from the beaten path, it will be obvious that Whittlesey spoke from hard experience and from being among men of even harder experience. His words revealed a deep understanding of the environment, how to survive exposure in it, and how to be as comfortable as possible in such circumstances.

20. This is an example of reverse diffusion that bears further exploration. Although Euramerican emulation of Indianness has been explored, most brilliantly by Philip J. Deloria, *Playing Indian* (New Haven, CT: Yale University Press, 1998), the emulation of white and métis laborers by surveyors and adventure seekers seems to have been little noticed.

21. McKenney, *Sketches of a Tour,* 350–51.

22. Grace Lee Nute, *The Voyageur* (1931; repr., St. Paul: Minnesota Historical Society, 1955), vi.

23. It is important to note that during this same period, some women sought this experience, too. Indeed, Margaret Fuller's *Summer on the Lakes, in 1843* (1844; repr., Urbana: University of Illinois Press, 1991), preceded Whittlesey's trip by two years.

24. Roderick Nash, *Wilderness and the American Mind*, 3rd ed. (1967; repr., New Haven, CT: Yale University Press, 1982), 23–43.

25. Whittlesey, "Two Months in the Copper Regions," 292. Apparently, Nick Adams was not the first to cast a dry fly at the "Big Two-Hearted River."

26. Baldwin, "Memorial of Colonel Charles Whittlesey," 413.

27. Useful works on West Point include James L. Morrison, *"The Best School in the World": West Point, the Pre–Civil War Years, 1833–1866* (Kent, OH: Kent State University Press, 1988), and Stephen E. Ambrose, *Duty, Honor, Country: A History of West Point* (Baltimore, MD: Johns Hopkins University Press, 1966). Geology, surveying, and mapping were part of the early curriculum.

28. Stanley M. Totten and George W. White, "Glacial Geology and the North American Craton: Significant Concepts and Contributions of the Nineteenth Century," in *Geologists and Ideas: A History of North American Geology*, ed. Ellen Drake and William Jordan, (Boulder, CO: Geological Society of America, 1985), 127. See also Susan J. Thompson, *A Chronology of Geological Thinking from Antiquity to 1899* (Metuchen, NJ, and London: Scarecrow Press, 1988), 173, 208, and 219. This useful resource should be used with some caution. In at least one instance, Thompson confused different geologists with the same name. For example, the nineteenth-century American geologist James Hall was given credit for discoveries made by the British geologist Sir James Hall in the eighteenth century. The information on Whittlesey is accurate, if incomplete.

29. Whittlesey, "Two Months in the Copper Regions," 294.

30. David Dale Owen, *Report of a Geological Survey of Wisconsin, Iowa, and Minnesota; and Incidentally a Portion of Nebraska Territory, Made under Directions from the United States Treasury Department* (Philadelphia: Lippincott, Grambo, 1852), xxvi. It is interesting to note that Stephen Harriman Long, head of the Long Expedition, was the first one to label the plains from Nebraska to Oklahoma, which he felt were not fit for cultivation, the Great Desert.

31. For a hagiographic but still informative take on Silliman's importance to the development and organization of American science, see the various Mrs. Hepsa Ely Silliman memorial lectures in *A Century of Science in America: With Special Reference to the American Journal of Science, 1818–1918* (New Haven, CT: Yale University Press, 1918).

32. Walter B. Hendrickson, *David Dale Owen: Pioneer Geologist of the Middle West*, *Indiana Historical Collections*, vol. 27 (Indianapolis: Indiana Historical Bureau, 1943), 66–67.

33. "Abstract of the Proceedings of the Fourth Session of the Association of American Geologists and Naturalists," *American Journal of Science and Arts* 45 (October 1843): 316–19.

34. Totten and White, "Glacial Geology," 127.

35. Hendrickson, *David Dale Owen*, vii.

36. Ibid., 111.

37. Ibid., 85.

38. Ibid., 105–6. Hendrickson described how immigrant handbooks and a newspaper in Iowa quoted Owen and reproduced his charts and drawings to lure settlers to the state. As will be discussed, northern Wisconsin boosters also utilized Owen's *Report*.

39. Owen, *Report*, xvii.

40. For a detailed account of Owen's efforts to ensure the publication quality of his 1852 *Report*, see Hendrickson, *David Dale Owen*, 93–106.

41. Born in New Hampshire, Justin Butterfield was an attorney, served as district attorney for Illinois, and was General Land Office commissioner from 1849 to 1852. See Vernon Carstensen, ed., *The Public Lands: Studies in the History of the Public Domain* (Madison: University of Wisconsin Press, 1968), 506.

42. Owen, *Report*, xiii–xiv.

43. William Arnon Henry, *Northern Wisconsin, a Hand-Book for the Homeseeker* (Madison, WI: Democrat Printing, State Printer, 1896).

44. Owen, *Report*, xxii. Compare to Schoolcraft's description of the Ontonagon River near the copper boulder, quoted in the previous chapter.

45. Thomas Cole, "Essay on American Scenery," in *American Art: 1700–1960*, ed. John W. McCoubrey, (Englewood Cliffs, NJ: Prentice Hall, 1965), 103.

46. Owen, *Report*, xxxiv.

47. "Health and pleasure" would become key selling points in tourist pamphlets. See, for example, Chicago, Milwaukee and St. Paul Railway, *Tourist's Manual to the Health and Pleasure Resorts of the Golden Northwest, Embracing Descriptions of the Principal Summer Resorts in Wisconsin, Iowa and Minnesota, Together with Game and Fish Laws, Hotel Guide, Excursion Rates, etc.* (Milwaukee, WI: Sentinel, 1880).

48. Owen, *Report*, xxii–xxiii.

49. Whittlesey's biographer explicitly compared him to Lapham and stated that Whittlesey was the Lapham of Ohio. See Baldwin, "Memorial of Colonel Charles Whittlesey," 424.

50. According to Totten and White, Whittlesey was one of the very first geologists to use well records to trace drift in the subsurface; see Totten and White, "Glacial Geology," 130–31.

51. Charles Whittlesey, "Geological Report on That Portion of Wisconsin Bordering on the South Shore of Lake Superior, Surveyed in the Year 1849, under the Direction of David Dale Owen, United States Geologist," in *Report of a Geological Survey of Wisconsin, Iowa, and Minnesota; and Incidentally a Portion of Nebraska Territory, Made under Directions from the United States Treasury Department*, ed. David Dale Owen (Philadelphia: Lippencott, Grambo, 1852), 426.

52. Comparison to recent geological maps shows a remarkable correspondence between Whittlesey's mid-nineteenth-century cartographic representation of the area and

a presumably accurate 1985 map. Lee Clayton, "Pleistocene Geology of the Superior Region" (Madison: Geological and Natural History Survey, 1985). Whittlesey's and Clayton's maps may differ in detail, but in broad outline the two maps are remarkably similar.

53. Whittlesey, "Geological Report," 426.

54. By the 1870s, the Mashkeg Fork was known as the White River.

55. Close examination of USGS topographical maps suggests that although there is a Long Lake in the area, the lake Whittlesey called Long Lake is now named Lake Owen.

56. Owen, *Report,* 160.

57. Whittlesey, "Geological Report," 431–32. Based on Whittlesey's numbers and given the tools available to them, the local Indians and métis obtained an astonishing amount of sugar from their trees. It seems highly unlikely that Whittlesey's white informants could have achieved higher productivity.

58. H. R. Aldrich, *The Geology of the Gogebic Iron Range of Wisconsin,* Wisconsin Geological and Natural History Survey Bulletin 71, Economic Series no. 24 (Madison, WI: Published by the State, 1929), 21–22.

59. Whittlesey, "Geological Report," 434.

Chapter Four: Cities in the Wilderness

1. Brian S. Osbourne and Donald Swainson, *The Sault Ste. Marie Canal: A Chapter in the History of Great Lakes Transport* (Ottawa: Parks Canada, 1986).

2. Augustus Barber, "Interior Field Notes (September, 1855)," in Commissioner of Public Lands, United States General Land Office, 1830–65, along with maps; bound manuscript available in Archives Reading Room, State Historical Society of Wisconsin. "Wisconsin Public Land Survey Records: Original Field Notes and Plat Maps" are also available online at http://digicoll.library.wisc.edu/SurveyNotes/.

3. Ibid. As will be discussed in the next chapter, although Barber's assessment of local copper formations, or lack thereof, has proven correct, that did not stop later boosters from showing a copper range on their maps.

4. Quoted in Lowell O. Stewart, *Public Land Surveys: History, Instructions, Methods,* reprint of the 1935 edition by Collegiate Press, The Development of Public Land Law in the United States (New York: Arno Press, 1979), 84.

5. Barber, "Interior Field Notes."

6. Hamilton Nelson Ross, *La Pointe: Village Outpost* (St. Paul, MN: North Central Publishing, 1960), 115–16. Ross's book is the most reliable local history of the region. For the ash tree story, see *Wisconsin: A Guide to the Badger State, American Guide Series* (New York: Duell, Sloan and Pearce, 1941), compiled by Wisconsin members of the Writers Program of the Work Projects Administration.

7. Whittlesey's portrait is locally famous, displayed in the county courthouse, in a recent mural, in local histories—such as Jane S. Smith and Michael J. Goc, eds., *Looking*

Backward, Moving Forward: Ashland, the Garland City of the Inland Seas (Friendship, WI: New Past Press, 1987)—the city website, and elsewhere.

8. Laws of Wisconsin (Madison, WI: State Printer, 1850), 73–74.

9. Ashland County's current boundaries were not set until 1893, when Iron County was created out of a portion of it. See J. E. Boell, *Origin and Legislative History of County Boundaries in Wisconsin—The Wisconsin Historical Records Survey* (Madison: University of Wisconsin and the State Historical Society of Wisconsin, 1942), 17–24.

10. Laws of Wisconsin (Madison, WI: State Printer, April 11, 1861), 32.

11. See Meredith E. Ostrom, "Wisconsin," in *The State Geological Surveys: A History*, ed. Arthur A. Socolow, 462–79 (Association of American State Geologists, 1988).

12. Ibid.; E. F. Bean, "State Geological Surveys of Wisconsin," *Transactions of the Wisconsin Academy of Sciences, Arts, and Letters* 30 (1937): 203–20; and James A. Lake, *Law and Mineral Wealth: The Legal Profile of the Wisconsin Mining Industry* (Madison: University of Wisconsin Press, 1962), 135–38.

13. On the boosterish expectation Wisconsin state legislators had of the state surveys they funded, see Lake, *Law and Mineral Wealth*, 137.

14. Charles Whittlesey, "Paleontology and the Moral Sense," in *Fugitive Essays: By Col. Chas. Whittlesey* (Cleveland, OH: n.p., 1873), 5.

15. Ibid., 4.

16. R. D. Irving, Part 1 (Vol. 3), "The Geological Structure of Northern Wisconsin," in Thomas C. Chamberlin, *Geology of Wisconsin: Survey of 1873–1879* (Madison, WI: Commissioners of Public Printing, 1880), 3:58.

17. Dean Connors made this observation in his *Going for the Iron* (Friendship, WI: New Past Press, 1994), 22. Also see H. R. Aldrich, *The Geology of the Gogebic Iron Range of Wisconsin*, Wisconsin Geological and Natural History Survey Bulletin 71, Economic Series no. 24 (Madison, WI: Published by the State, 1929), for an optimistic assessment of the Penokee-Gogebic, more in line with Whittlesey than Irving. Aldrich had the advantage of knowing the figures of more than forty years of production.

18. There is a huge literature on the role of booster media in creating images of regions. William Wyckoff and Lary M. Dilsaver, "Promotional Imagery of Glacier National Park," *Geographical Review* 87, no. 1 (1987): 1–26, is especially useful as a model for analyzing visual images.

19. Recall that this was the waterfall that Schoolcraft felt was so much more impressive than Niagara Falls.

20. Henry Rowe Schoolcraft, *Narrative Journal of Travels: Through Northwestern Regions of the United States Extending from Detroit through the Great Chain of American Lakes to the Sources of the Mississippi River in the Year 1820* (Albany, NY: E. and E. Hosford, 1821); David Dale Owen, *Report of a Geological Survey of Wisconsin, Iowa, and Minnesota; and Incidentally a Portion of Nebraska Territory, Made under Directions from the United States Treasury Department* (Philadelphia: Lippencott, Grambo, 1852); Thomas C. Chamberlin, *Geology of Wisconsin: Survey of 1873–1879*, vol. 3 (Madison, WI: Commissioners of Public Printing, 1880); *Picturesque Wisconsin* 1, no. 1 (June 1899).

21. Actually, determining the age of the earth is a complicated process that continues to this day and early on involved more evidence than suggested by Hutton's uniformitarianism. Paleontologists and evolutionists challenged the lower estimates of rock geologists. Based on radiometric dating, we now estimate that the earth is 4,600 million years old, give or take a few years. For a useful summary of a complex subject, see Don L. Eicher, *Geological Time,* ed. A. Lee McAlester, 2nd ed., *The Prentice Hall Foundations of Earth Science Series* (Englewood Cliffs, NJ: Prentice Hall, 1972).

22. *Picturesque Wisconsin* 1, no. 1 (June 1899).

23. Wisconsin Central Railroad Company, *Summer Resorts on the Wisconsin Central Railroad* (Milwaukee, WI: Cramer, Hikens and Cramer, Printers, 1877).

24. *Picturesque Wisconsin* 1, no. 2 (July 1899).

25. There is a huge literature on boosterism. The best recent work includes: David Hamer, *New Towns in the New World: Images and Perceptions of the Nineteenth-Century Urban Frontier* (New York: Columbia University Press, 1990); William Cronon, *Nature's Metropolis: Chicago and the Great West* (New York: W. W. Norton, 1991); and Steven Ward, *Selling Places: The Marketing and Promotion of Towns and Cities, 1850–2000* (London: E and FN Spon, 1998).

26. Steven Ward, *Selling Places,* 29–82 and 144–85. The best works on selling "natural" places include John Sears, *Sacred Places: American Tourist Attractions in the Nineteenth Century* (1989; repr., Amherst: University of Massachusetts Press, 1998), and Patrick McGreevy, *Imagining Niagra: The Meaning and Making of Niagra Falls* (Amherst: University of Massachusetts Press, 1994).

27. Ross, *La Pointe,* 120–21 and 121n.

28. *Bayfield, Lake Superior: Early History, Situation, Harbor, &c., Ocean Commerce, Mineral & Agricultural Resources, Rail Roads, Stage Roads, &c., Lumber, Fisheries, &c., Climate of Lake Superior, Pre-emption Lands, Invitation to Settlers: An Account of a Pleasure Tour to Lake Superior, Its Climate, Scenery, Pictured Rocks, Sailing Days of the Steamboats, Fare, &c.* . . . (Philadelphia, 1858). [No author or publishers indicated.]

29. *Ashland Press,* June 29, 1872. Note the "copper range" mapped above the iron range.

30. Ibid. This phrase also reflects the cultural nationalism, or "See America First" campaign, that Alfred Runte argued helped build support for establishing national parks. See Runte, *National Parks: The American Experience* (Lincoln and London: University of Nebraska Press, 1979).

31. *Wisconsin State Register,* July 17, 1877.

32. *Bayfield Press,* November 19, 1870.

33. *Wisconsin Register,* August 18, 1877.

34. *Wisconsin Register,* July 28, 1877.

35. See Ross, *La Pointe,* 172.

36. Quoted in D. J. Frederick et al., "The Original Survey Notes of the Pictured Rocks and Apostle Islands National Lakeshores and Their Use in Reconstructing Original Forests," in *Proceedings of the First Conference on Scientific Research in the National*

Parks, ed. Robert M. Linn, 107–14 (New Orleans: U.S. Department of the Interior, 1976).

37. Sam Fifield, "Among the Historic Apostle Isles," *National Magazine*, 1898.

38. John Sears, *Sacred Places*, 189.

Chapter Five: The Frontier, the Future City, and the Wild West

1. Robert Park offered an early statement, "The Natural History of the Newspaper." In *The City*, ed. Robert E. Park, Ernest W. Burgess, and Roderick D. McKenzie (Chicago: University of Chicago Press, 1925), 80–98. Sydney Kobre, "The Sociological Approach in Research in Newspaper History," *Journalism Quarterly* 22 (1945): 12–22. Donald Oehlerts's "Preface" to *Guide to Wisconsin Newspapers, 1833–1957* (Madison: State Historical Society of Wisconsin, 1958), v–xii, is suggestive. The April 1980 edition (vol. 19, no. 2) of *Journal of the West* is devoted to journalism in the West and contains two articles of special interest to this study: William Lyon's historiographical essay, "The Significance of Newspapers on the American Frontier," 3–13, and B. H. Baltensperger, "Newspaper Images of the Central Great Plains in the Late Nineteenth Century," 64–70. Sally Foreman Griffith's first-rate biography, *Home Town News: William Allen White and the "Emporia Gazette"* (New York: Oxford University Press, 1989), explores the community roles played by small-town newspaper editors. Jack Lule, *Daily News, Eternal Stories: The Mythological Role of Journalism* (New York: Guilford Press, 2001), argues that newspaper stories fit mythological archetypes.

2. G. Malcolm Lewis, "Rhetoric of the Western Interior: Modes of Environmental Description in American Promotional Literature of the Nineteenth Century," in *The Iconography of Landscape: Essays on the Symbolic Representation, Design, and Use of Past Environments*, ed. Denis Cosgrove and Stephen Daniels, 179–93 (Cambridge: Cambridge University Press, 1988). Also see John Allen, "The Garden-Desert Continuum: Competing Views of the Great Plains in the Nineteenth Century," *Great Plains Quarterly* 5 (1985): 207–20. Most of this work focuses on the Great Plains or regions farther west. A notable exception is Ralph Brown, "Fact and Fancy in Early Accounts of Minnesota's Climate," *Minnesota History* 17, no. 3 (1936): 243–61.

3. For a description of the community roles of the archetypal small-town editor and newspaper, see the "Introduction" in Griffith, *Home Town News*, 3–9. I draw heavily on Griffith's interpretation.

4. Thomas Leonard, "Magazines and Newspapers," in *The Reader's Companion to American History*, ed. Eric Foner and John Garraty (Boston: Houghton Mifflin, 1991), 689.

5. Frank Luther Mott, *American Journalism: A History, 1690–1960* (New York: Macmillian, 1962).

6. Ibid.

7. The high point for newspapers peaked in Virginia in 1896 with 180 weeklies and 37 dailies, in Wisconsin in 1905 with 591 weeklies and 61 dailies, and in Colorado in 1913

with 330 weeklies and 50 dailies. The especially high numbers for Wisconsin probably reflected ethnic diversity and the many literate foreign immigrants. Newspaper data for Wisconsin are from Oehlerts, *Guide to Wisconsin Newspapers,* and Ada Tyng Griswold, *Annotated Catalogue of Newspaper Files in the Library of the State Historical Society of Wisconsin* (Madison: State Historical Society of Wisconsin, 1911); data for Colorado are from Donald Oehlerts, *Guide to Colorado Newspapers, 1859–1963* (Denver, CO: Bibliographic Center for Research Rocky Mountain Region, 1964); and data for Virginia are from Lester Cappon, *Virginia Newspapers, 1821–1935* (New York: D. Appleton-Century, 1937).

8. A good overview of the subject is Sally Miller, ed., *The Ethnic Press in America: A Historical Analysis and Handbook* (New York: Greenwood Press, 1987).

9. Oehlerts, *Guide to Wisconsin Newspapers.* Ashland's population boom occurred between the 1885 state census and the 1890 federal census, so precise figures are unavailable.

10. Oehlerts, *Guide to Colorado Newspapers,* and Cappon, *Virginia Newspapers.*

11. *Ashland Press,* June 22, 1872.

12. Ibid.

13. From Fifield's will, printed in the *Ashland Daily Press,* February 23, 1915.

14. *Ashland Press,* December 26, 1885.

15. *Ashland Press,* December 24, 1887.

16. *Ashland Press,* December 28, 1889.

17. Ingolf Vogeler, *Wisconsin: A Geography* (Boulder, CO: Westview Press, 1986), 97.

18. *Ashland Press,* December 31, 1887.

19. The methodology was simply to read the first and last newspaper of every year between 1870 and 1940. In sampling several other possible recurring dates, such as July 4th and Labor Day, I found that the turning of the year was the most likely time for the newspaper editor to reflect on the recent past and the future and to express a vision of the place. Other revealing "moments" were the first issue of a new paper, the completion of a railway to Ashland in 1877, the iron boom years of 1886 and 1887, and the arrival of Buffalo Bill's Wild West show in 1896. By "popular narrative models," I mean similar story lines that tie into larger mythologies such as frontier progression, the westward march of civilization, and the Wild West. They are similar to Lure's "archetypal myths," which he identified in contemporary newspapers. In identifying and interpreting the narrative models, two sources were especially useful: Richard Slotkin, *The Fatal Environment: The Myth of the Frontier in the Age of Industrialization, 1800–1890* (New York: Atheneum, 1985), and Richard White, "Frederick Jackson Turner and Buffalo Bill," in *The Frontier in American Culture: Essays by Richard White and Patricia Nelson Limerick,* ed. James R. Grossman (Berkeley and Los Angeles: University of California Press, 1994), 7–65. Older works that are still useful include Henry Nash Smith, *Virgin Land: The American West as Symbol and Myth* (Cambridge, MA: Harvard University Press, 1950), and Leo Marx, *The Machine in the Garden: Technology and the Pastoral Ideal in America* (New York: Oxford University Press, 1964). I also draw on Roland Barthes—see especially *Mythologies,* trans. Annette Lavers (New York: Hill and Wang, 1972).

20. Frederick Jackson Turner, "The Significance of the Frontier in American History," in *Frederick Jackson Turner: Wisconsin's Historian of the Frontier*, ed. Martin Ridge, 26–47, 68–71 (Madison: State Historical Society of Wisconsin, 1986). The earliest version of the paper appeared in the November 8, 1892, edition of the *Aegis*, but it was first presented in its current form at the American Historical Association meeting in Chicago, July 12, 1893.

21. William Cronon, *Nature's Metropolis: Chicago and the Great West* (New York: W. W. Norton, 1992), 34–35, and Cronon, "Revisiting the Vanishing Frontier: The Legacy of Frederick Jackson Turner," *Western Historical Quarterly* 18 (April 1987): 157–76.

22. Turner, "The Significance of the Frontier," 36–37.

23. White, "Frederick Jackson Turner," 11.

24. Ibid.

25. R. Brian Ferguson and Neil L. Whitehead, "The Violent Edge of Empire," in *War in the Tribal Zone: Expanding States and Indigenous Warfare*, ed. R. Brian Ferguson and Neil L. Whitehead, 1–30 (Santa Fe, NM: School of American Research Press, 1992). See also D. W. Meinig, *The Shaping of America: A Geographical Perspective on 500 Years of History*, vol. 2, *Continental America, 1800–1867* (New Haven, CT: Yale University Press, 1993), especially 78–103.

26. Richard Slotkin, *Gunfighter Nation: The Myth of the Frontier in Twentieth-Century America* (New York: HarperCollins, 1992), 63–87. Like most of the rest of the country, Ashland, too, was at the fair. According to the official catalog, three Chequamegon Bay building-stone companies exhibited at the fair, and according to the *Ashland Weekly Press*, a large delegation of Ashlanders attended the event. Nevertheless, Chequamegon Bay's presence at the fair marked a huge disappointment for Wisconsin. With much hype, the papers announced in April that the "Giant Ashland Monolith" was lying at Prentice's brownstone quarry and ready to be shipped to the fair. At 115 feet, it was 6 feet taller than Cleopatra's Needle and said to be the largest monolith in the world. Unfortunately, the shipping season began too late, and the monolith never made it. See *Ashland Weekly Press*, May 6 and 27, 1893.

27. Ronald Satz, *Chippewa Treaty Rights: The Reserved Rights of Wisconsin's Chippewa Indians in Historical Perspective*, Transactions vol. 79, no. 1 (Madison: Wisconsin Academy of Sciences, Arts and Letters, 1991), 57 and 62.

28. The December 31, 1887, edition of the *Ashland Press* referred to a theft problem, a killing, a shooting, prostitution, labor unrest resulting in a recent "riot," and worries about an overflowing jail. Ashland's population at the time was around ten thousand.

29. William Whipple Warren, *History of the Ojibway Nation* (1885; repr., Minneapolis, MN: Ross and Haines, 1970). "Menabosho" may be a regional variation of "Nanabozho"—see Christopher Vecsey, *Imagine Ourselves Richly: Mythic Narratives of North American Indians* (New York: HarperCollins, 1988), 64–93.

30. Warren, *History of the Ojibway Nation*, 78–84.

31. As Reuben Gold Thwaites wrote, "It became the center of a considerable Indian population, residents of several tribes being drawn thither: first, by the fisheries; second,

by a fancied security in so isolated a region, against the Iroquois of the East and the Wild Sioux of the West. When Allouez arrived in this polyglot village, October 1 [1665], he found here Chippewas, Pottawamies, Kickapoos, Sauks, and Foxes, all of them Wisconsin tribes; besides these were Hurons, Ottawas, Miamis, and Illinois, victims of Iroquois hate who had fled in droves before the westward advances of their merciless tormentors"; see Thwaites, "The Story of Chequamegon Bay," *Wisconsin Historical Collections* 13 (1885): 4056. In *The Middle Ground: Indians, Empires, and Republics in the Great Lakes Region, 1650–1815* (Cambridge: Cambridge University Press, 1991), Richard White suggested that these Indian groups should be thought of as ethnic and that their multiethnic settlements should be seen as foreshadowing the multiethnic white settlements that would follow.

32. Joe Rose, director and professor of Native American studies at Northland College, Ashland, Wisconsin, personal communication, October 13, 1993.

33. On the significance of the different stories people can tell about the same place and on the role of narrative in environmental history, see William Cronon, "A Place for Stories: Nature, History, and Narrative," *Journal of American History* 78, no. 4 (March 1992): 1347–76. For a discussion of the different stories Indians and whites tell reflecting different worldviews, see Cronon, "Kennecott Journey: The Paths out of Town," in *Under an Open Sky: Rethinking America's Western Past*, ed. William Cronon, George Miles, and Jay Gitlin, 28–51 (New York: W. W. Norton, 1992). Works that attempt to evoke or analyze indigenous worldviews include G. Reichell-Dolmatoff, "Cosmology as Ecological Analysis," *MAN* (1976): 307–18; Richard Nelson, *Make Prayers to Raven: A Koyukon View of the Northern Forest* (Chicago: University of Chicago Press, 1983); and, most relevant to the Chequamegon Bay region, Calvin Martin, *Keepers of the Game: Indian-Animal Relationships in the Fur Trade* (Berkeley: University of California Press, 1978).

34. Hamilton Nelson Ross, *La Pointe: Village Outpost* (St. Paul, MN: North Central Publishing, 1960), discussed the early trials of Bayfield and Ashland. The "Great Metropolis" story is repeated in many forms in the pages of the *Bayfield Press* and the *Ashland Press* between 1870 and 1896.

35. Oehlerts, *Guide to Wisconsin Newspapers*, and Griswold, *Annotated Catalogue of Newspaper Files*.

36. At one time or another, each of these nicknames was used to boost Ashland or Bayfield. For an insightful discussion of nicknames and American cities, see Yi-Fu Tuan, *Topophilia: A Study of Environmental Perception, Attitudes, and Values* (1974; repr., New York: Columbia University Press, 1990), 201–4.

37. Cronon, *Nature's Metropolis*, 34–41.

38. *Bayfield Press*, November 26, 1870.

39. Ibid.

40. Exactly which sources influenced Fifield is a mystery. He could have gotten his ideas from other newspapers. During the nineteenth century, some profound thinking was expressed in newsprint. Indeed, William Gilpin worked for a while as a newspaper editor, and Karl Marx earned money as the European correspondent of Horace Greeley's *New York Tribune*.

41. The first issue of the *Bayfield Press* (October 13, 1870) displayed a chart comparing the opening and closing dates of Bayfield's and Superior's harbors. On November 19, 1870, the *Bayfield Press* reported on complaints raised in the Superior newspaper over some inaccuracy in the *Press*'s chart. The *Press* happily corrected the error—in Bayfield's favor.

42. Cronon, *Nature's Metropolis*, 36.

43. Ibid.; Thomas Karnes, *William Gilpin: Western Nationalist* (Austin: University of Texas Press, 1970); William Gilpin, *Mission of the North American People* (Philadelphia: J. B. Lippincott, 1873); Gilpin, *The Cosmopolitan Railway* (San Francisco: History Company, Publishers, 1890); and especially Charles Glaab, "Visions of Metropolis: William Gilpin and Theories of City Growth in the American West," *Wisconsin Magazine of History* 45, no. 1 (1961): 21–31.

44. See, for example, *Bayfield Press*, July 4, 1877.

45. *Ashland Press*, June 2, 1877.

46. *Ashland Press*, December 31, 1887.

47. Richard Canuteson, "The Railway Development of Northern Wisconsin" (master's thesis, University of Wisconsin—Madison, 1930), offers a good overview and an extraordinary collection of maps detailing eighty years of railroad building in Wisconsin year by year.

48. Note how this map, unlike that in figure 4.24, shows Portage as the railway nexus of the state.

49. *Wisconsin State Register*, July 28, 1877. Turner had such flattering things to say about Bayfield that the *Bayfield Press* excerpted a large portion of his account of the excursion. As will be shown, the original article as it appeared in the Portage newspaper is most revealing.

50. *Wisconsin State Register*, July 28, 1877.

51. Ibid.

52. See *Ashland Press*, August 4, 1877, and *Wisconsin State Register*, August 18, 1877.

53. A. J. Turner, "History of Wisconsin Railroads," in *Fifth Annual Report of the Railroad Commissioner of the State of Wisconsin, 1878* (Madison, WI: State Printer, 1879), 379–84.

54. *Ashland Press*, August 4, 1877.

55. Turner, "The Significance of the Frontier," 26.

56. *Wisconsin State Register*, September 18, 1877.

57. *Ashland Press*, August 8, 1877.

58. *Ashland Press*, June 2, 1877.

59. Even though most sources encouraged settlement by families and even colonies and though settlement by single men was frequently discouraged, the sales pitches were usually aimed at men and tended to emphasize "manliness." Women were all but absent from the rhetoric.

60. *Ashland Press*, June 2, 1877.

61. Ibid.

62. Turner, "The Significance of the Frontier," 27.

63. Edmund Jefferson Danziger, *The Chippewas of Lake Superior* (1979; repr., Norman: University of Oklahoma Press, 1990), 77.

64. Slotkin, *Gunfighter Nation,* 21.

65. Don Russell, *The Lives and Legends of Buffalo Bill* (Norman: University of Oklahoma Press, 1960).

66. The original Chequamegon Hotel was built by the Wisconsin Central Railroad Company to attract and house tourists and was completed in 1877. In its heyday, it hosted many prestigious guests, but it was later declared by a fire marshal to be "the finest and most perfectly designed firetrap this side of Hades." See Roy L. Martin, *History of the Wisconsin Central,* Bulletin no. 54 (Boston: Railroad and Locomotive Historical Society, 1941), 25.

67. *Ashland Daily Press,* September 11, 1896.

68. *Ashland News,* September 11, 1896.

69. Russell, *Lives and Legends;* John Burke, *Buffalo Bill: The Noblest Whiteskin* (New York: G. P. Putnam's Sons, 1973); and especially Slotkin, *Gunfighter Nation.*

70. *Ashland News,* September 11, 1896.

71. *Ashland Press,* September 11, 1896.

72. *Ashland Press,* September 12, 1896.

73. See, for example, Russell, *Lives and Legends,* for the publicity argument, and Burke, *Buffalo Bill,* for the altruism argument.

74. *Ashland Press,* September 12, 1896.

75. Gilpin, *The Cosmopolitain Railway.* For an interpretation of Cody's "Congress of Rough Riders" as symbolizing the United States leading the imperial powers into the future, see Slotkin, *Gunfighter Nation.*

76. White, "Frederick Jackson Turner," 12.

77. *Ashland Press,* June 6, 1872.

78. William Whipple Warren, in *History of the Ojibway Nation,* was probably the first to publish this story, but it was recorded long before in the sacred birch scrolls of the Chippewa. Visitors to Madeline Island can hear the story in the museum and also read it in brochures and on historical plaques. The megis was a cowrie shell that appeared to the Chippewa and led them west from the Atlantic Ocean—or so the story goes.

79. Turner, "The Significance of the Frontier," 42–43.

Chapter Six: Northern Exposures

1. According to Ingolf Vogeler, the Montreal and Cary Mines near Hurley produced 94 percent of all the ore from Wisconsin's Gogebic range. Michigan mines produced about four times as much as those in Wisconsin. See Vogeler, *Wisconsin: A Geography* (Boulder, CO: Westview Press, 1986), 97.

2. See, for example, *Bayfield County Press,* August 21, 1886.

3. *Ashland Press,* June 5, 1886. Emphasis on the word *correct* is added.

4. John W. Reps, "The Making and Selling of Urban Views," in *Views and Viewmakers of America: Lithographs of Towns and Cities in the United States and Canada, Notes on the Artists and Publishers, and Union Catalogue of Their Work, 1825–1925,* ed. John W. Reps, (Columbia: University of Missouri Press, 1984), 70. For a similar statement, see Gerald A. Danzer, "Bird's-Eye Views of Towns and Cities," in *From Sea Charts to Satellite Images: Interpreting North American History through Maps,* ed. David Buisseret, 143–63 (Chicago: University of Chicago Press, 1990).

5. Reps, "The Making and Selling of Urban Views," 19.

6. Peter C. Marzio, *The Democratic Art: Pictures for a Nineteenth-Century America: Chromolithography, 1840–1900* (Boston: D. R. Godine, 1979).

7. The *Bayfield County Press* of October 2, 1886, declared of the Bayfield bird's-eye view that "a copy ought to be found in every home in town."

8. Reps, *Views and Viewmakers of Urban America,* 209.

9. Thomas Beckman, *Milwaukee Illustrated: Panoramic and Bird's-Eye Views of a Midwestern Metropolis, 1844–1908—Exhibition and Catalog* (Milwaukee, WI: Milwaukee Art Center, 1978), 2–3. For another argument for the centrality of Wisconsin in the bird's-eye view business, see Elizabeth Singer Maule, *Bird's Eye Views of Wisconsin Communities* (Madison: State Historical Society of Wisconsin Archives, 1977).

10. *Bayfield County Press,* August 28, 1886.

11. *Bayfield, Lake Superior: Early History, Situation, Harbor &C.* (Philadelphia, 1858).

12. *Bayfield Press,* July 3, 1886.

13. *Bayfield Press,* July 10, 1886.

14. *Wisconsin State Register,* July 28, 1877.

15. *Ashland Daily Press Annual Edition,* 1892, 33.

16. *Ashland Press,* December 25, 1886. The information about the ore boats is from J. M. Dodd, "Ashland Then and Now," *Wisconsin Magazine of History* 28, no. 2 (December 1944): 189–96.

17. "Hurley, the 'new town on the range' is long on iron but short on good building stone," *Bayfield Press,* May 22, 1886.

18. Vogeler, *Wisconsin.*

19. The Marr and Richards view is a bit of a mystery. Both John Reps and Elizabeth Maule restricted their lists to bird's-eye views that were produced to be sold separately. Yet both also included this view in their lists, even though it does not seem to have been sold separately. It is certain, though, that the view does appear in the June 6, 1885, edition of the *Ashland Press.* The copy cited by both Reps and Maule is held by the State Historical Society of Wisconsin. This copy lacks a town directory and other features typically found on commercial bird's-eyes. Furthermore, the print was not a lithograph but rather a woodblock print that was widely used by newspapers and magazines.

20. "The Pinery Minautaurs," *Cincinnati Enquirer,* November 6, 1887.

21. See *Encyclopedia of Wisconsin,* Encyclopedia of the United States (New York: Somerset Publishers, 1990), 234.

22. *Bayfield Press,* May 29, 1886.

23. *Montreal River Miner,* July 1, 1886.

24. See, for example, John Bartlow Martin, *Call It Northcountry: The Story of Upper Michigan* (New York: Alfred A. Knopf, 1944).

25. *Bayfield Press,* May 29, 1886.

26. *Ashland Press,* December 31, 1887.

27. Lewis Reimann, *Hurley—Still No Angel* (Ann Arbor, MI: Northwoods Publishers, 1954), 111.

28. See, for example, David Hamer, *New Towns in the New World: Images and Perceptions of the Nineteenth-Century Urban Frontier,* ed. Kenneth T. Jackson, *The Columbia History of Urban Life* (New York: Columbia University Press, 1990), and William Cronon, *Nature's Metropolis: Chicago and the Great West* (New York: W. W. Norton, 1991).

29. *Bayfield County Press,* November 18, 1899.

30. *Bayfield County Press,* December 16, 1899.

31. *Ashland Daily Press,* September 3, 1894.

32. *Bayfield County Press,* December 9, 1899.

33. Larry Lankton, *Cradle to Grave: Life, Work, and Death at the Lake Superior Copper Mines* (New York: Oxford University Press, 1991).

34. *Ashland Weekly News,* September 6, 1899.

35. *Bayfield County Press,* December 16, 1899.

36. Michael Kazin and Steven J. Ross, "America's Labor Day: The Dilemma of a Workers' Celebration," *Journal of American History* 78, no. 4 (March 1992): 1294–1323.

37. Ibid.

38. *Montreal River Miner,* September 1, 1894.

39. *Ashland Daily Press,* September 3, 1894.

40. Ibid.

41. Ibid.

42. Robert W. Ozanne, *The Labor Movement in Wisconsin: A History* (Madison: State Historical Society of Wisconsin, 1984), 16–17.

43. *Ashland Daily Press,* September 4, 1894.

44. *Ashland Daily Press,* September 3, 1894.

45. *Washburn News,* August 31, 1894.

46. *Washburn News,* September 7, 1894.

47. Ibid.

48. *Ashland Weekly News,* September 6, 1899.

Epilogue

1. *Bayfield County Press,* July 30, 1924. According to the program, the voyageurs secretly traded a jug of alcohol with a couple of young men, who get drunk on the liquor. Duluth strikes the voyageur with his sword, then confiscates the jug from one of the

youth, hurling it into the lake. "The Indians follow the action of the first prohibition in the Chequamegon district, and greet his action with vociferous shouts of approval." Kenneth M. Ellis, "Ke-wa-de-no-kwa: First Annual Apostle Islands Indian Pageant," 1924. Probably artistic license rather than historical fact, this scene made the past seem to resonate with the current experience of the audience, and it may also have been a political plug for Prohibition.

2. *Bayfield County Press,* August 6, 1924.

3. David Glassberg, *American Historical Pageantry: The Uses of Tradition in the Early Twentieth Century* (Chapel Hill and London: University of North Carolina Press, 1990), 5. This is probably the best current work on historical pageants in the United States. A key work on public spectacle is Susan G. Davis, *Parades and Power: Street Theater in Nineteenth-Century Philadelphia* (Philadelphia: Temple University Press, 1986). An important recent work on a similar theme by a geographer is Steven D. Hoelscher, *Heritage on Stage: The Invention of Ethnic Place in America's Little Switzerland* (Madison: University of Wisconsin Press, 1998).

4. This is quoted from a pamphlet titled "First Annual Apostle Islands Indian Pageant: 'Ke-wa-de-no-kwa,' Girl of the North," Bayfield, Wisconsin, August 1–21 [1924], L. E. McKenzie, secretary-manager.

5. "Our Own Map: Never Sold, Always Free" (Milwaukee: Wisconsin Motorists Association, 1923).

6. Foreword to Kenneth M. Ellis, "Ke-wa-de-no-kwa: First Annual Apostle Islands Indian Pageant," pamphlet, 1924.

7. *Bayfield County Press,* August 6, 1924.

8. Ellis, "Ke-wa-de-no-kwa."

9. *Bayfield County Press,* July 30, 1924.

10. The Thirty-second was also known as the Red Arrow Division.

11. Quoted in the *Bayfield County Press,* August 6, 1924, 1.

12. For a useful analysis of the process by which traditional stories are decontextualized, contextualized, and recontextualized for a larger national and international audience, see Richard Bauman, "The Nationalization and Internationalization of Folklore: The Case of Schoolcraft's 'Gitshe Gauzinee,'" *Western Folklore* 52 (April 1993): 247–69. For the context of the dramatization of Longfellow's *Hiawatha,* see Michael V. Pisani, "Longfellow, Robert Stoepel, and an Early Musical Setting of Hiawatha (1859)," *American Music* 16, no. 1 (1998): 45–85. For an early analysis of the "authenticity" of Longfellow's *Hiawatha,* see Stith Thompson, "The Indian Legend of Hiawatha," *Publications of the Modern Language Association of America* 37 (1922): 128–40. For a full but provincial account of the Schoolcraft connection to *Hiawatha,* which tries (too hard) to downplay the *Kalevala* connection, see Chase Osborn and Stellanova Obsborn, *Schoolcraft, Longfellow, Hiawatha* (Lancaster, PA: Jaques Cattell Press, 1942). For a thorough, if equally provincial, documentation of the influence of the *Kalevala* on Longfellow's *Song of Hiawatha,* see Ernest J. Moyne, *Hiawatha and Kalevala, FC Communications for the Folklore Fellows*

(Helsinki: Suomalainen Tiedeakatemia, 1963). There is a large literature on the history of the *Kalevala* and its significance to Finnish nationalism. I found the following works especially useful: Michael Branch, "Kalevala: From Myth to Symbol," in *Kalevala: 1835–1985, the National Epic of Finland* (Helsinki: Helsinki University Library, 1985), 1–11; M. A. Branch, "Introduction," in *Kalevala: The Land of the Heroes,* xi–xxxiv (London: Athlone Press, 1985; Helsinki: Helsinki University Library, 1985); and Eino Friberg, "Translator's Preface: The Significance of the Kalevala to the Finns," in *The Kalevala: Epic of the Finnish People,* ed. George C. Schoolfield, 11–19 (Helsinki: Otava Publishing, 1988). Also of interest is Leonard Cline's novel *God Head* (New York: Viking Press, 1925), which begins in a Finnish labor hall not far from Hurley and climaxes just east of Chequamegon Bay, near the mouth of the Black River on Lake Superior. Cline structured his ultimately tragic story around stories from the *Kalevala,* taking on the persona of various characters from the epic with increasingly disturbing consequences. The novel can be read as pathologically individualistic modernity literally slaying romanticized communal traditionalism.

13. For a rich analysis of the decline of Longfellow's "sentimental masculinity," see Eric L. Haralson, "Mars in Petticoats: Longfellow and Sentimental Masculinity," *Nineteenth-Century Literature* 51, no. 3 (1996): 327–55.

14. Ellis, "Ke-wa-de-no-kwa."

15. *Bayfield County Press,* August 20, 1924. Note that in the first sentence, the author may have meant "wildlife" but could just as easily have meant "wild life."

16. "The Lumber Industry through in Bayfield," *Bayfield County Press,* August 27, 1924; see also "The Last Log Cut at the Wacshmuth Mill," *Bayfield County Press,* September 10, 1924.

17. *Bayfield County Press,* August 27, 1925. Actually, there would be one more Indian pageant at Bayfield, completely rewritten and apparently consisting of more Indians—although not in elevated roles. It was written and directed by Theodore H. Steinmetz, "former bandmaster of the Red Arrow Division during World War I." According to the newspaper, all of the roles except the dancing girls and the two principal characters were taken by Indians, "descendants of Hiawatha." See *Bayfield County Press,* August 29, 1926.

Selected Bibliography

Newspapers

Ashland Daily Press
Ashland Press
Ashland Weekly News
Ashland Weekly Press
Bayfield County Press
Bayfield Press
Bayfield Progress
Capital Times
Cincinnati Enquirer
Milwaukee Sentinel
Montreal River Miner
Wisconsin State Journal
Wisconsin State Register

Books, Articles, Pamphlets, Theses, Dissertations, and Other Publications

"Abstract of the Proceedings of the Fourth Session of the Association of American Geologists and Naturalists." *American Journal of Science and Arts* 45 (October 1843): 135–65; 310–52.

Adamson, Jeremy Elwell. "Nature's Grandest Scene in Art." In *Niagara: Two Centuries of Changing Attitudes, 1697–1901*, edited by Jeremy Elwell Adamson, 11–81. Washington, DC: Corcoran Gallery of Art, 1985.

Aldrich, H. R. *The Geology of the Gogebic Iron Range of Wisconsin*. Vol. Bulletin 71, Economic Series No. 24., *Wisconsin Geological and Natural History Survey*. Madison, WI: Published by the State, 1929.

Allen, John L. "An Analysis of the Exploratory Process: The Lewis and Clark Expedition of 1804–1806." *Geographical Review* 62 (1972): 13–39.

———. "The Garden-Desert Continuum: Competing Views of the Great Plains in the Nineteenth Century." *Great Plains Quarterly* 5 (1985): 207–20.

Allouez, Father Claude. "Relation of What Occurred Most Remarkable in the Missions of the Fathers of the Society of Jesus in New France, for the Years 1666–1667, Sent to the Rev. Father Jaques Bordier, Provincial of the Province of France." In *The Jesuit Relations and Allied Documents: Travels and Explorations of the Jesuit Missionaries in New France, 1610–1791*, edited by Reuben Gold Thwaites, 248–311. Cleveland, OH: Burrows Brothers, 1899.

Ambrose, Stephen E. *Duty, Honor, Country: A History of West Point*. Baltimore, MD: Johns Hopkins University Press, 1966.

Amedeo, Douglas M. and Reginald G. Golledge, "Environmental Perception and Behavioral Geography." In *Geography in America at the Dawn of the 21st Century*, edited by Gary L. Gaile and Cort J. Willmott, 133–48. Oxford: Oxford University Press, 2003.

Baldwin, Charles C. "'Memorial of Colonel Charles Whittlesey, Late President of the Western Reserve Historical Society.'" *Western Reserve Historical Society* 2, no. 68 (1888): 405–35.

Baltensperger, B. H. "Newspaper Images of the Central Great Plains in the Late Nineteenth Century." *Journal of the West* 19, no. 2 (1980): 64–70.

Barber, Augustus. "Interior Field Notes (September, 1855)." In *Interior West, Vol. 38:* Commissioner of Public Lands, United States General Land Office, 1830–65.

Barnes, Trevor J., and James S. Duncan, eds. *Writing Worlds: Discourse, Text and Metaphor in the Representation of Landscape*. 1st ed. London: Routledge, 1992.

Barthes, Roland. *Mythologies*. Translated by Annette Lavers. New York: Hill and Wang, 1972.

Bauman, Richard. "The Nationalization and Internationalization of Folklore: The Case of Schoolcraft's 'Gitshe Gauzinee.'" *Western Folklore* 52, (April 1993): 247–69.

Bawden, Timothy. "The Northwoods: Back to Nature?" In *Wisconsin Land and Life*, edited by Robert C. Ostergren and Thomas R. Vale, 450–69. Madison: University of Wisconsin Press, 1997.

———. "Reinventing the Frontier: Tourism, Nature, and Environmental Change in Northern Wisconsin, 1880–1930." PhD diss., University of Wisconsin–Madison, 2001.

Bayfield, Lake Superior—Early History, Situation, Harbor, &c., Ocean Commerce, Mineral & Agricultural Resources, Rail Roads, Stage Roads, &c., Lumber, Fisheries, &c., Climate of Lake Superior, Pre-emption Lands, Invitation to Settlers: An Account of a Pleasure Tour to Lake Superior, Its Climate, Scenery, Pictured Rocks, Sailing Days of the Steamboats, Fare, &c. . . . Philadelphia, 1858.

Bean, E. F. "State Geological Surveys of Wisconsin." *Transactions of the Wisconsin Academy of Sciences, Arts, and Letters* 30 (1937): 203–20.

Beckman, Thomas. *Milwaukee Illustrated: Panoramic and Bird's-Eye Views of a Midwestern Metropolis, 1844–1908: Exhibition and Catalog*. Milwaukee, WI: Milwaukee Art Center, 1978.

Berry, Brian J. L. *America's Utopian Experiments: Communal Havens from Long-Wave Crises.* Hanover, NH: University Press of New England, 1992.

Blair, Hugh. *Lectures on Rhetoric and Belles Lettres.* Edited by Harold F. Harding. 1783. Reprint, Carbondale: Southern Illinois University Press, 1965.

Boell, J. E. *Origin and Legislative History of County Boundaries in Wisconsin—The Wisconsin Historical Records Survey.* Madison: University of Wisconsin and State Historical Society of Wisconsin, 1942.

Bonnifield, Paul. *The Dust Bowl: Men, Dirt, and Depression.* Albuquerque: University of New Mexico Press, 1979.

Bowden, Martyn J. "The Great American Desert in the American Mind: The Historiography of a Geographical Notion." In *Geographies of the Mind: Essays in Historical Geosophy in Honor of John Kirtland Wright,* edited by David Lowenthal and Martyn Bowden, 119–47. New York: Oxford University Press, 1976.

Branch, Michael. "Introduction." In *Kalevala: The Land of the Heroes,* trans. W. F. Kirby, xi–xxxiv. London: Athlone Press, 1985.

———. "Kalevala: From Myth to Symbol." In *Kalevala: 1835–1985, the National Epic of Finland,* 1–11. Helsinki: Helsinki University Library, 1985.

Bremer, Richard G. *Indian Agent and Wilderness Scholar: The Life of Henry Rowe Schoolcraft* Mount Pleasant: Clark Historical Library, Central Michigan University, 1987.

Broek, J. O. M. "The Concept of Landscape in Human Geography." *Comptes Rendus du Congres International Geographique* 2 (1938): 103–9.

Brookfield, H. C. "On the Environment as Perceived." *Progress in Geography* 1 (1969): 51–80.

Brown, Ralph Hall. "Fact and Fancy in Early Accounts of Minnesota's Climate." *Minnesota History* 17, no. 3 (1936): 243–61.

———. *Historical Geography of the United States.* Edited by J. Russel Whitaker. New York: Harcourt, Brace and World, 1948.

Burke, Edmund. *A Philosophical Enquiry into the Origin of Our Ideas of the Sublime and Beautiful.* Edited by J. T. Boulton. 1759. Reprint, London: Routledge and Kegan Paul, and New York: Columbia University Press, 1958.

Burke, John. *Buffalo Bill: The Noblest Whiteskin.* New York: G. P. Putnam's Sons, 1973.

Buttimer, Anne. *Society and Milieu in the French Geographical Tradition.* Chicago: Published for the Association of American Geographers by Rand McNally, 1971.

Byron, George Gordon. *The Complete Poetical Works of Byron.* Edited by Paul E. More. 1905. Reprint, Cambridge: Riverside Press, 1933.

Byron, Lord. *The Works of Lord Byron—The Wordsworth Poetical Library.* Hertfordshire, UK: Cumberland House, 1994.

Cantor, George. *The Great Lakes Guidebook: Lake Superior and Western Lake Michigan.* Ann Arbor: University of Michigan Press, 1980.

Canuteson, Richard. "The Railway Development of Northern Wisconsin." Master's thesis, University of Wisconsin, 1930.

Cappon, Lester. *Virginia Newspapers, 1821–1935*. New York: D. Appleton-Century, 1937.

Carstensen, Vernon. *Farms or Forests: Evolution of a State Land Policy for Northern Wisconsin*. Madison: University of Wisconsin College of Agriculture, 1958.

———, ed. *The Public Lands: Studies in the History of the Public Domain*. Madison: University of Wisconsin Press, 1968.

Cass, Lewis. "Removal of the Indians: Documents and Proceedings Relating to the Formation and Progress of a Board in the City of New York, for the Emigration, Preservation, and Improvement of the Aborigines of America." *North American Review* 30 (1830): 62–121.

Chamberlin, Thomas C. *Geology of Wisconsin: Survey of 1873–1879*. Vol. 3. Madison, WI: Commissioners of Public Printing, 1880.

Chicago, Milwaukee and St. Paul Railway. *Tourist's Manual to the Health and Pleasure Resorts of the Golden Northwest, Embracing Descriptions of the Principal Summer Resorts in Wisconsin, Iowa and Minnesota, Together with Game and Fish Laws, Hotel Guide, Excursion Rates, etc.* Milwaukee, WI: Sentinel, 1880.

Clasby, Nancy Tenfelde. "'Maabozho': A Native American Resurrection Myth." *Studies in Short Fiction* 30, no. 4 (1993): 583–94.

Clayton, Lee. "Pleistocene Geology of the Superior Region." Madison, WI: Geological and Natural History Survey, 1985.

Clifton, James A. "Wisconsin Death March: Explaining the Extremes in Old Northwest Indian Removal." *Transactions of the Wisconsin Academy of Sciences, Arts and Letters* 75 (1987): 1–39.

Cline, Leonard. *God Head*. New York: Viking Press, 1925.

Cole, G. D. H. *The Life of Robert Owen*. 3rd ed. Hamden, CT: Archon Books, Shoestring Press, 1966.

Cole, Thomas. "Essay on American Scenery." In *American Art: 1700–1960*, edited by John W. McCoubrey, 98–110. Englewood Cliffs, NJ: Prentice Hall, 1965.

Colten, Craig, and Lary Dilsaver, eds. *The American Environment: Interpretations of Past Geographies*. Boston: Rowman and Littlefield, 1992.

Colten, Craig E., Peter J. Hugill, Terrence Young, and Karen Morin, "Historical Geography," *Geography in America at the Dawn of the 21st Century*, edited by Gary L. Gaile and Cort J. Willmott, 149–163. Oxford: Oxford University Press, 2003.

Connors, Dean. *Going for the Iron*. Friendship, WI: New Past Press, 1994.

Cranston, Maurice. *The Romantic Movement*. Oxford: Basil Blackwell, 1994.

Cronon, William. *Changes in the Land: Indians, Colonists, and the Ecology of New England*. New York: Hill and Wang, 1983.

———. "Kennecott Journey: The Paths out of Town." In *Under an Open Sky: Rethinking America's Western Past*, edited by William Cronon, George Miles, and Jay Gitlin, 28–51. New York: W. W. Norton, 1992.

———. "Modes of Prophesy and Production: Placing Nature in History." *Journal of American History* 76 (1990): 1122–31.

———. *Nature's Metropolis: Chicago and the Great West*. New York: W. W. Norton, 1991.

———. "A Place for Stories: Nature, History, and Narrative." *Journal of American History* 78, no. 4 (March 1992): 1347–76.

———. "Revisiting the Vanishing Frontier: The Legacy of Frederick Jackson Turner." *Western Historical Quarterly* 18 (1987): 157–76.

Crosby, Alfred W. *Ecological Imperialism: The Biological Expansion of Europe, 900–1900*. Cambridge: Cambridge University Press, 1986.

———. "Virgin Soil Epidemics as a Factor in the Aboriginal Depopulation in America." *William and Mary Quarterly* 33 (1976): 293–94.

Cullon, Joseph F. "Landscapes of Labor and Leisure: Common Rights, Private Property, and Class Relations along the Bois Brule River, 1870–1940." Master's thesis, University of Wisconsin–Madison, 1995.

Dana, Edward Salisbury, Charles Schuchert, H. E. Gregory, J. Barrell, G. O. Smith, R. S. Lull, L. V. Pirsson, W. E. Ford, R. B. Sosman, H. L. Wells, H. W. Foote, L. Page, W. R. Coe, and G. L. Goodale. *A Century of Science in America, with Special Reference to the "American Journal of Science," 1818–1918*. New Haven, CT: Yale University Press, 1918.

Daniel, Glenda, and Jerry Sullivan. *A Sierra Club Naturalist's Guide to the North Woods of Michigan, Wisconsin, Minnesota and Southern Ontario—The Sierra Club Naturalist's Guides*. San Francisco: Sierra Club Books, 1981.

Danzer, Gerald A. "Bird's-Eye Views of Towns and Cities." In *From Sea Charts to Satellite Images: Interpreting North American History through Maps*, edited by David Buisseret, 143–63. Chicago: University of Chicago Press, 1990.

Danziger, Edmund Jefferson. *The Chippewas of Lake Superior*. 1979. Reprint, Norman: University of Oklahoma Press, 1990.

Davies, Charles. *Elements of Surveying, and Navigation: With Descriptions of the Instruments and the Necessary Tables*. Rev. ed. New York: A. S. Barnes, 1856.

Davis, Mark. "An Empire in Waiting: Northern Wisconsin's Lake Country, 1880–1940." PhD diss., University of Wisconsin, 1997.

Davis, Susan G. *Parades and Power: Street Theater in Nineteenth-Century Philadelphia*. Philadelphia: Temple University Press, 1986.

Deloria, Philip J. *Playing Indian*. New Haven, CT: Yale University Press, 1998.

Densmore, Frances. *Chippewa Customs*. 1929. Reprint, Minneapolis, MN: Ross and Haines, 1970.

Doty, James D. "Appendix F: The Official Journal of James D. Doty." In Henry R. Schoolcraft, *Narrative Journal of Travels: Through Northwestern Regions of the United States Extending from Detroit through the Great Chain of American Lakes to the Sources of the Mississippi River in the Year 1820*, edited by Mentor L. Williams, 403–60. East Lansing: Michigan State College Press, 1953.

Drake, Ellen T., and William M. Jordan, eds. *Geologists and Ideas: A History of North American Geology, Centennial Special Volume 1*. Boulder, CO: Geological Society of America, 1985.

Eicher, Don L. *Geological Time*. Edited by A. Lee McAlester. 2nd ed. The Prentice Hall Foundations of Earth Science Series. Englewood Cliffs, NJ: Prentice Hall, 1972.

Ellis, Kenneth M. *Ke-wa-de-no-kwa: First Annual Apostle Islands Indian Pageant: Bayfield, Wisconsin*. N.p., 1924.

Encyclopedia of Wisconsin, Encyclopedia of the United States. New York: Somerset Publishers, 1990.

Entrikin, J. Nicholas. *The Betweenness of Place: Towards a Geography of Modernity*. Baltimore, MD: Johns Hopkins University Press, 1991.

Fenton, Carroll Lane, and Mildred Adams Fenton. *The Story of the Great Geologists*. 1945. Reprint, Freeport, NY: Books for Libraries Press, 1969.

Ferguson, R. Brian, and Neil L. Whitehead. "The Violent Edge of Empire." In *War in the Tribal Zone: Expanding States and Indigenous Warfare*, edited by R. Brian Ferguson and Neil L. Whitehead, 1–30. Sante Fe, NM: School of American Research Press, 1992.

Fifield, Sam. "Among the Historic Apostle Isles." *National Magazine*, 1898.

Finch, Vernor C. "Montfort: A Study in Landscape Types in Southwestern Wisconsin." *Geographic Society of Chicago Bulletin* 9 (1933): 3–44.

Frederick, D. J., L. Rakestraw, C. R. Eder, R. A. Van Dyke, B. J. Griewe, and M. A. Anderson. "The Original Survey Notes of the Pictured Rocks and Apostle Islands National Lakeshores and Their Use in Reconstructing Original Forests." In *Proceedings of the First Conference on Scientific Research in the National Parks*, edited by Robert M. Linn, 107–14. New Orleans: U.S. Department of the Interior, 1976.

Friberg, Eino. "Translator's Preface: The Significance of the Kalevala to the Finns." In *The Kalevala: Epic of the Finnish People*, edited by George C. Schoolfield, 11–19. Helsinki: Otava Publishing, 1988.

Friis, Herman R. "The David Dale Owen Map of Southwestern Wisconsin." *Prologue: The Journal of the National Archives* 1 (1969): 9–28.

Fuller, Margaret. *Summer on the Lakes, in 1843*. 1844. Reprint, Urbana: University of Illinois Press, 1991.

Gaile, Gary L., and Cort J. Willmott, eds. *Geography in America*. Columbus, OH: Merrill Publishing, 1989.

Gilpin, William. *The Cosmopolitan Railway*. San Francisco: History Company, Publishers, 1890.

———. *Mission of the North American People*. Philadelphia: J. B. Lippincott, 1873.

Glaab, Charles. "Visions of Metropolis: William Gilpin and Theories of City Growth in the American West." *Wisconsin Magazine of History* 45, no. 1 (1961): 21–31.

Glacken, Clarence J. *Traces on the Rhodian Shore: Nature and Culture in Western Thought from Ancient Times to the End of the Eighteenth Century*. Berkeley and Los Angeles: University of California Press, 1967.

Glassberg, David. *American Historical Pageantry: The Uses of Tradition in the Early Twentieth Century*. Chapel Hill: University of North Carolina Press, 1990.

Gold, John R. *An Introduction to the Behavioral Environment*. Oxford: Oxford University Press, 1980.

Goodrum, Charles, and Helen Dalrymple. *Advertising in America: The First 200 Years*. New York: Harry N. Abrams, 1990.

Gough, Robert. *Farming the Cutover: A Social History of Northern Wisconsin, 1900–1940*. Lawrence: University Press of Kansas, 1997.

Granö, Johannes Gabriel. *Pure Geography*. Translated by Malcolm Hicks, edited by Olavi Granö and Anssi Paasi. Baltimore, MD: Johns Hopkins University Press, 1997.

"Great Lakes: Lake Champlain to Lake of the Woods" (map). Washington, DC: U.S. Department of Commerce, National Oceanic and Atmospheric Administration, National Ocean Service, Coast and Geodetic Survey, 1995.

Greenhill, Ralph, and Thomas D. Mahoney. *Niagara*. Toronto: University of Toronto Press, 1969.

Griffith, Sally Foreman. *Home Town News: William Allen White and the "Emporia Gazette."* New York: Oxford University Press, 1989.

Griswold, Ada Tyng. *Annotated Catalogue of Newspaper Files in the Library of the State Historical Society of Wisconsin*. Madison: State Historical Society of Wisconsin, 1911.

Hamer, David. *New Towns in the New World: Images and Perceptions of the Nineteenth-Century Urban Frontier*. The Columbia History of Urban Life, edited by Kenneth T. Jackson. New York: Columbia Univerity Press, 1990.

Haralson, Eric L. "Mars in Petticoats: Longfellow and Sentimental Masculinity." *Nineteenth-Century Literature* 51, no. 3 (1996): 327–55.

Harris, Walt. *The Chequamegon Country: 1659–1976*. Fayetteville, AR: Walt Harris, 1976.

Hartshorne, Richard. *The Nature of Geography: A Critical Survey of Current Thought in Light of the Past*. Lancaster, PA: Association of American Geographers, 1976.

Helgeson, Arlan. *Farms in the Cutover: Agricultural Settlement in Northern Wisconsin*. Madison: State Historical Society of Wisconsin, for Department of History, University of Wisconsin, 1962.

Hendrickson, Walter B. *David Dale Owen: Pioneer Geologist of the Middle West*. Vol. 27, *Indiana Historical Collections*. Indianapolis: Indiana Historical Bureau, 1943.

———. "Documents: David Dale Owen and the Chippewa Land Survey." *Wisconsin Magazine of History* 28 (1944): 210–24.

Henry, William Arnon. *Northern Wisconsin, a Hand-Book for the Homeseeker*. Madison, WI: Democrat Printing, State Printer, 1896.

Hibbard, Bejamin Horace. *A History of the Public Land Policies*. 1924. Reprint, Madison: University of Wisconsin Press, 1965.

Hill, Edward E. *The Office of Indian Affairs, 1824–1880: Historical Sketches—The Library of American Indian Affairs*. New York: Clearwater Publishing, 1974.

Hise, Charles Richard Van, and Charles Kenneth Leith. *The Geology of the Lake Superior Region*. Vol. 52, Monographs of the United States Geological Survey, Department of the Interior. Washington, DC: Government Printing Office, 1911.

Hoelscher, Steven D. *Heritage on Stage: The Invention of Ethnic Place in America's Little Switzerland*. Madison: University of Wisconsin Press, 1998.

Holzhueter, John O. *Madeline Island & the Chequamegon Region*. Madison: State Historical Society of Wisconsin, 1986.

Hubbard, Bela. *Lake Superior Journal: Bela Hubard's Account of the 1840 Houghton Expedition*. Edited by Bernard C. Peters. Marquette: Northern Michigan Press, 1983.

Huth, Hans. *Nature and the American: Three Centuries of Changing Attitudes*. Berkeley and Los Angeles: University of California Press, 1957.

Jackson, John Brinckerhoff. *Discovering the Vernacular Landscape*. New Haven, CT: Yale University Press, 1984.

Johnson, Hildegard Binder. *Order upon the Land: The U.S. Rectangular Land Survey and the Upper Mississippi Country—The Andrew H. Clark Series in the Historical Geography of North America*. New York: Oxford University Press, 1976.

Jordon, William. "Application as Stimulous in Geology: Some Examples from the Early Years of the Geological Society of America." In *Geologists and Ideas: A History of North American Geology*, edited by Ellen Drake and William Jordan, 443–52. Boulder, CO: Geological Society of America, 1985.

Kalevala: 1835–1985, the National Epic of Finland. Helsinki: Helsinki University Library, 1985.

Karnes, Thomas. *William Gilpin: Western Nationalist*. Austin: University of Texas Press, 1970.

Kazin, Michael, and Steven J. Ross. "America's Labor Day: The Dilemma of a Workers' Celebration." *Journal of American History* 78, no. 4 (March 1992): 1294–1323.

Klunder, Willard Carl. *Lewis Cass and the Politics of Moderation*. Kent, OH: Kent State University Press, 1996.

Kobre, Sydney. "The Sociological Approach in Research in Newspaper History." *Journalism Quarterly* 22 (1945): 12–22.

Kolodny, Annette. *The Lay of the Land: Metaphors as Experience and History in American Life and Letters*. Chapel Hill: University of North Carolina Press, 1975.

Kuhn, Thomas S. *The Structure of Scientific Revolutions*. 2nd ed. Chicago: University of Chicago Press, 1970.

Lake, James A. *Law and Mineral Wealth: The Legal Profile of the Wisconsin Mining Industry*. Madison: University of Wisconsin Press, 1962.

Lane, N. Gary. "New Harmony and Pioneer Geology." *Geotimes* 11, no. 9 (1966): 18–22.

Lankton, Larry. *Beyond the Boundaries: Life and Landscape at the Lake Superior Copper Mines, 1840–1875*. Oxford: Oxford University Press, 1997.

———. *Cradle to Grave: Life, Work, and Death at the Lake Superior Copper Mines*. New York: Oxford University Press, 1991.

Lapham, Increase Allen, J. G. Knapp, and H. Crocker. *Report on the Disasterous Effects of the Destruction of Forest Trees Now Going on So Rapidly in the State of Wisconsin*. Madison, WI: Atwood and Rublee, State Printers, 1867.

Laws of Wisconsin. Madison, WI: State Printer, 1850–61.

Lears, Jackson. *Fables of Abundance: A Cultural History of Advertising in America*. New York: Basic Books, 1994.

Leonard, Thomas. "Magazines and Newspapers." In *The Reader's Companion to American History*, edited by Eric Foner and John Garraty, 689–92. Boston: Houghton Mifflin, 1991.

Levine, Lawrence W. *Highbrow/Lowbrow: The Emergence of Cultural Hierarchy in America*. Cambridge, MA: Harvard University Press, 1988.

Lewis, G. Malcolm. "Rhetoric of the Western Interior: Modes of Environmental Description in American Promotional Literature of the Nineteenth Century." In *The Iconography of Landscape: Essays on the Symbolic Representation, Design, and Use of Past Environments*, edited by Denis Cosgrove and Stephen Daniels. Cambridge: Cambridge University Press, 1988.

Lowenthal, David, ed. *Environmental Perception and Behavior*. Chicago: Department of Geography, University of Chicago, 1967.

———. *The Past Is a Foreign Country*. Cambridge: Cambridge University Press, 1985.

Lowenthal, David, and Martyn Bowden, eds. *Geographies of the Mind: Essays in Historical Geosophy in Honor of John Kirtland Wright*. New York: Oxford University Press, 1976.

Lule, Jack. *Daily News, Eternal Stories: The Mythological Role of Journalism*. New York: Guilford Press, 2001.

Lyon, William. "The Significance of Newspapers on the American Frontier." *Journal of the West* 19, no. 2 (1980): 3–13.

Mahaffey, Charles G. "Changing Images of the Cutover: A Historical Geography of Resource Utilization in the Lake Superior Region, 1840–1930." PhD diss., University of Wisconsin, 1978.

Martin, Calvin. *Keepers of the Game: Indian-Animal Relationships in the Fur Trade*. Berkeley: University of California Press, 1978.

Martin, John Bartlow. *Call It Northcountry: The Story of Upper Michigan*. New York: Alfred A. Knopf, 1944.

Martin, Roy L. *History of the Wisconsin Central*. Bulletin no. 54. Boston: Railroad and Locomotive Historical Society, 1941.

Marx, Leo. *The Machine in the Garden: Technology and the Pastoral Ideal in America*. New York: Oxford University Press, 1964.

Marzio, Peter C. *The Democratic Art: Pictures for a Nineteenth-Century America: Chromolithography, 1840–1900*. Boston: D. R. Godine, 1979.

Mason, Philip P., ed. *Schoolcraft: The Literary Voyageur, or Muzzeniegun*. East Lansing: Michigan University Press, 1962.

McEvoy, Arthur. "Toward an Interactive Theory of Nature and Culture: Ecology, Production, and Cognition in the California Fishing Industry." In *The Ends of the Earth: Perspectives on Modern Environmental History*, edited by Donald Worster, 211–29. Cambridge: Cambridge University Press, 1988.

McGreevy, Patrick V. *Imagining Niagara: The Meaning and Making of Niagara Falls.* Amherst: University of Massachusetts Press, 1994.

McKenney, Thomas L. *Sketches of a Tour to the Lakes, of the Character and Customs of the Chippeway Indians, and of Incidents Connected with the Treaty of Fond du Lac.* Facsimile of the first edition pubished at Baltimore, MD, in 1827. Minneapolis, MN: Ross and Haines, 1959.

McKinsey, Elizabeth. *Niagara Falls: Icon of the American Sublime.* Cambridge: Cambridge University Press, 1985.

McNeill, William H. *Plagues and People.* Garden City, NY: Anchor Press, 1976.

Meinig, D. W., ed. *Continental America, 1800–1867.* Vol. 2, *The Shaping of America: A Geographical Perspective on 500 Years of History.* New Haven, CT: Yale University Press, 1993.

———. *The Interpretation of Ordinary Landscapes.* New York and Oxford: Oxford University Press, 1979.

Meisel, Max. *A Bibliography of American Natural History: The Pioneer Century, 1769–1865.* Vol. 3. New York: Premier Publishing, 1929.

"A Memoir of Dr. Douglass Houghton." *American Journal of Science and Arts* 5, no. 14 (1848): 217–27.

Merrill, George P. *Contributions to a History of American State Geological and Natural History Surveys.* 1920 reprint. History of Geology. New York: Arno Press, 1978.

Mikesell, Marvin. "The Rise and Decline of 'Sequent Occupance': A Chapter in the History of American Geography." In *Geographies of the Mind: Essays in Historical Geosophy in Honor of John Kirtland Wright,* edited by David Lowenthal and Martyn Bowden, 149–67. New York: Oxford University Press, 1976.

Miller, Sally. *The Ethnic Press in America: A Historical Analysis and Handbook.* New York: Greenwood Press, 1987.

Monk, Samuel H. *The Sublime: A Study of Critical Theories in XVIII-Century England.* 1935. Reprint, Ann Arbor: University of Michigan Press, 1960.

Monroe, James. *The Writings of James Monroe: Including a Collection of His Public and Private Papers and Correspondence, Now for the First Time Printed.* Edited by Stanislaus Murray Hamilton. New York : G. P. Putnam's Sons, 1898–1903, vol. 1.

Morrison, James L. *"The Best School in the World": West Point, the Pre–Civil War Years, 1833–1866.* Kent, OH: Kent State University Press, 1988.

Morse, Jedidiah. *American Gazetteer.* Boston: Thomas and Andrews, 1810.

———. *The American Geography.* London: John Stockdale, 1794.

———. *The American Universal Geography; or, A View of the Present State of All the Kingdoms, States, and Colonies in the Known World.* 7th ed., vol. 1. Charleston: G. Clarke, 1819.

Mosser, Duane Paul, "Henry Rowe Schoolcraft: Eyewitness to a Changing Frontier." PhD diss., University of California Santa Barbara, 1991.

Mott, Frank Luther. *American Journalism: A History, 1690–1960.* New York: Macmillan, 1962.

Moyne, Ernest J. *Hiawatha and Kalevala, FC Communications for the Folklore Fellows.* Helsinki: Suomalainen Tiedeakatemia, 1963.

Myers, Garth A., Patrick McGreevy, George O. Carney, and Judith Kenny. "Cultural Geography." In *Geography in America at the Dawn of the 21st Century*, edited by Gary L. Gaile and Cort J. Willmott, 81–96. Oxford: Oxford University Press, 2003.

Nash, Roderick. *Wilderness and the American Mind.* 3rd ed. 1967. Reprint, New Haven, CT: Yale University Press, 1982.

Nelson, Richard K. *Make Prayers to Raven: A Koyukon View of the Northern Forest.* Chicago: University of Chicago Press, 1983.

Nicolson, Marjorie Hope. *Mountain Gloom and Mountain Glory: The Development of the Aesthetics of the Infinite.* 1959. Reprint, New York: W. W. Norton, 1963.

Novak, Barbara. *Nature and Culture: American Landscape and Painting, 1825–1875.* New York: Oxford University Press, 1980.

Nute, Grace Lee. "The American Fur Company's Fishing Enterprises on Lake Superior." *Mississippi Valley Historical Review* 12, no. 4 (1926): 483–503.

———. *Lake Superior.* 1944. Reprint, Minneapolis: University of Minnesota Press, 2000.

———. *The Voyageur.* 1931. Reprint, St. Paul: Minnesota Historical Society, 1955.

Oehlerts, Donald E. *Guide to Colorado Newspapers, 1859–1963.* Denver, CO: Bibliographic Center for Research Rocky Mountain Region, 1964.

———. *Guide to Wisconsin Newspapers, 1833–1957.* Madison: State Historical Society of Wisconsin, 1958.

Oelschlaeger, Max. *The Idea of Wilderness: From Prehistory to the Age of Ecology.* New Haven, CT: Yale University Press, 1991.

Olmanson, Eric D. "Northern Exposures: Bird's-Eye Views of Nature and Place on Wisconsin's Lake Superior Coast during the Summer of 1886." In *Wisconsin Land and Life,* edited by Robert C. Ostergren and Thomas R. Vale, 470–88. Madison: University of Wisconsin Press, 1997.

Osborn, Chase, and Stellanova Obsborn. *Schoolcraft, Longfellow, Hiawatha.* Lancaster, PA: Jaques Cattell Press, 1942.

Osbourne, Brian S., and Donald Swainson. *The Sault Ste. Marie Canal: A Chapter in the History of Great Lakes Transport.* Ottawa: Parks Canada, 1986.

Ostergren, Robert C., and Thomas R. Vale, eds. *Wisconsin Land and Life.* Madison: University of Wisconsin Press, 1997.

Ostrom, Meredith E. "Wisconsin." In *The State Geological Surveys: A History,* edited by Arthur A. Socolow, 462–79. Association of American State Geologists, 1988.

"Our Own Map: Never Sold, Always Free." Milwaukee: Wisconsin Motorists Association, 1923.

Owen, David Dale. "Introduction." In David Dale Owen, *Report of a Geological Survey of Wisconsin, Iowa, and Minnesota; and Incidentally a Portion of Nebraska Territory, Made under Directions from the United States Treasury Department,* xvii–xxxviii. Philadelphia: Lippincott, Grambo, 1852.

———. "Introductory Letter." In David Dale Owen, *Report of a Geological Survey of Wisconsin, Iowa, and Minnesota; and Incidentally a Portion of Nebraska Territory, Made under Directions from the United States Treasury Department*, xiii–xv. Philadelphia: Lippincott, Grambo, 1852.

———. *Report of a Geological Survey of Wisconsin, Iowa, and Minnesota; and Incidentally a Portion of Nebraska Territory, Made under Directions from the United States Treasury Department*. Philadelphia: Lippencott, Grambo, 1852.

Ozanne, Robert W. *The Labor Movement in Wisconsin: A History.* Madison: State Historical Society of Wisconsin, 1984.

Park, Robert E. "The Natural History of the Newspaper." In *The City*, edited by Robert E. Park, Ernest W. Burgess, and Roderick D. McKenzie, 80–98. Chicago: University of Chicago Press, 1925.

Pearce, Roy Harvey. *Savagism and Civilization: A Study of the Indian and the American Mind*. Rev. ed. of *The Savages of America*, 1953 ed. Berkeley: University of California Press, 1988.

Peters, Bernard C. "Introduction." In Bela Hubbard, *Lake Superior Journal: Bela Hubbard's Account of the 1840 Houghton Expedition*, edited by Bernard C. Peters, 1–13. Marquette: Northern Michigan University Press, 1983.

———. "Revolt from the Wilderness: Romantic Travellers on Lake Superior." *Michigan Academician* 13, no. 4 (Spring 1981), 491–501.

Picturesque Wisconsin: Legends and History. Journal edited by Harry E. Thomas. Two issues: vol. 1, nos. 1 (June 1899) and 2 (July 1899). Milwaukee, WI: Thomas Publishing, 1899.

Pisani, Michael V. "Longfellow, Robert Stoepel, and an Early Musical Setting of Hiawatha (1859)." *American Music* 16, no. 1 (1998): 45–85.

Rabbitt, Mary C. *Minerals, Lands, and Geology for the Common Defence and General Welfare.* Vol. 1, *Before 1879: A History of Public Lands, Federal Science and Mapping Policy in the United States.* Washington, DC: U.S. Government Printing Office, 1979.

Reichell-Dolmatoff, G. "Cosmology as Ecological Analysis: The View from the Rain Forest." *MAN: The Journal of the Royal Anthropological Institute* 2 n.s., no. 3 (1976): 307–18.

Reimann, Lewis. *Hurley—Still No Angel.* Ann Arbor, MI: Northwoods Publishers, 1954.

Reingold, Nathan, ed. *Science in America since 1820.* New York: Science History Publications, 1976.

Relph, E. *Place and Placelessness.* Edited by Allen J. Scott. Research in Planning and Design 1. London: Pion, 1976.

Reps, John W. "The Making and Selling of Urban Views." In *Views and Viewmakers of America: Lithographs of Towns and Cities in the United States and Canada, Notes on the Artists and Publishers, and Union Catalogue of Their Work, 1825–1925*, edited by John W. Reps, 3–94. Columbia: University of Missouri Press, 1984.

Rogin, Michael Paul. *Fathers and Children: Andrew Jackson and the Subjugation of the American Indian*. New York: Alfred A. Knopf, 1975.

Rohe, Randall. "Lumbering Wisconsin's Northern Urban Frontier." In *Wisconsin Land and Life,* edited by Robert Ostergren and Thomas Vale, 221–40. Madison: University of Wisconsin Press, 1997.

Ross, Hamilton Nelson. *La Pointe: Village Outpost*. St. Paul, MN: North Central Publishing, 1960.

Runte, Alfred. *National Parks: The American Experience*. Lincoln: University of Nebraska Press, 1979.

Russell, Don. *The Lives and Legends of Buffalo Bill*. Norman: University of Oklahoma Press, 1960.

Sack, Robert David. *Homo Geographicus: A Framework for Action, Awareness, and Moral Concern*. Baltimore, MD: Johns Hopkins University Press, 1997.

———. *Human Territoriality: Its Theory and History*. Edited by Alan R. Baker, J. B. Harley, and David Ward. Cambridge Studies in Historical Geography 7. Cambridge: Cambridge University Press, 1986.

Satz, Ronald N. *Chippewa Treaty Rights: The Reserved Rights of Wisconsin's Chippewa Indians in Historical Perspective*. Edited by Carl N. Haywood. *Transactions* 79, no. 1. Madison: Wisconsin Academy of Sciences, Arts and Letters, 1991.

Sauer, Carl Ortwin. *Land & Life*. Edited by John Leighly. Berkeley: University of California Press, 1963.

———. *Selected Essays, 1963–1975*. Edited by Bob Callahan. Berkeley, CA: Turtle Island Foundation, 1981.

Schick, Irvin C. *The Erotic Margin: Sexuality and Spatiality in Alterist Discourse*. London: Verso, 1999.

Schmitt, Peter J. *Back to Nature: The Arcadian Myth in Urban America*. 1969. Reprint, Baltimore, MD: Johns Hopkins University Press, 1990.

Schneer, Cecil J., ed. *Two Hundred Years of Geology in America: Proceedings of the New Hampshire Bicentennial Conference on the History of Geology*. Hanover, NH: University Press of New England, 1979.

Schoolcraft, Henry R. *Narrative Journal of Travels: Through Northwestern Regions of the United States Extending from Detroit through the Great Chain of American Lakes to the Sources of the Mississippi River in the Year 1820*. Albany, NY: E. and E. Hosford, 1821.

———. *Narrative Journal of Travels: Through Northwestern Regions of the United States Extending from Detroit through the Great Chain of American Lakes to the Sources of the Mississippi River in the Year 1820*. Edited by Mentor L. Williams. East Lansing: Michigan State College Press, 1953. Reprint of Schoolcraft's 1821 edition, with related documents.

———. *Personal Memoirs of a Residence of Thirty Years with the Indian Tribes on the American Frontiers: With Brief Notices of Passing Events, Facts, and Opinions, A.D. 1812 to A.D. 1842*. Philadelphia: Lippincott, Grambo, 1851.

———. *A View of the Lead Mines of Missouri; Including Some Observations on the Mineralogy, Geology, Geography, Antiquities, and Soil, Climate, Population, and Productions of Missouri and Arkansaw, and Other Sections of the Western Country.* New York: Charles Wiley, 1819.

Sears, John F. *Sacred Places: American Tourist Attractions in the Nineteenth Century.* 1989. Reprint, Amherst: University of Massachusettes Press, 1998.

Semple, Ellen Churchill. *Influences of Geographical Environment: On the Basis of Ratzel's System of Anthropo-geography.* New York: Henry Holt, 1911.

Skinner, Brian J., and Barbara L. Narendra. "Rumaging through the Attic; or, A Brief History of the Geological Sciences at Yale." In *Geologists and Ideas: A History of North American Geology,* edited by Ellen Drake and William Jordan, 355–76. Boulder, CO: Geological Society of America, 1985.

Slotkin, Richard. *The Fatal Environment: The Myth of the Frontier in the Age of Industrialization, 1800–1890.* New York: Atheneum, 1985.

———. *Gunfighter Nation: The Myth of the Frontier in Twentieth-Century America.* New York: HarperCollins, 1992.

Smith, Henry Nash. *Virgin Land: The American West as Symbol and Myth.* Cambridge, MA: Harvard University Press, 1950.

Smith, Jane S., and Michael J. Goc, eds. *Looking Backward, Moving Forward: Ashland, the Garland City of the Inland Seas.* Friendship, WI: New Past Press, 1987.

Socolow, Arthur A., ed. *The State Geological Surveys: A History.* N.p.: Association of American State Geologists, 1988.

St. John, John R. *A True Description of the Lake Superior Country; Its Rivers, Coasts, Bays, Harbours, Islands, and Commerce, with Bayfield's Chart; Showing the Boundary Line as Established by Joint Commission; Also a Minute Account of the Copper Mines and Working Companies, Accompanied by a Map of the Mineral Regions; Showing, by Their No. and Place, All the Different Locations; and Containing a Concise Mode of Assaying, Treating, Smelting, and Refining Copper Ores.* 1846. Reprint, Grand Rapids, MI: Black Letter Press, 1976.

Stewart, Lowell O. *Public Land Surveys: History, Instructions, Methods.* Reprint of the original 1935 edition by Collegiate Press, The Development of Public Land Law in the United States. New York: Arno Press, 1979.

Summer Resorts on the Wisconsin Central Railroad. Milwaukee, WI: Cramer, Hikens and Cramer, Printers, 1877.

Thompson, Stith. "The Indian Legend of Hiawatha." *Publications of the Modern Language Association of America* 37 (1922): 128–40.

Thompson, Susan J. *A Chronology of Geological Thinking from Antiquity to 1899.* Metuchen, NJ: Scarecrow Press, 1988.

Thrower, Norman J. W. *Original Land Survey and Land Subdivision: A Comparative Study of the Form and Effect of Contrasting Cadastral Surveys—The Monograph Series of the Association of American Geographers.* Chicago: Rand McNally, 1966.

Thwaites, Reuben Gold. "The Story of Chequamegon Bay." *Wisconsin Historical Collections* 13 (1885), 397–425.

Torgovnick, Marianna. *Gone Primitive: Savage Intellects, Modern Lives.* Chicago: University of Chicago Press, 1990.

Tortora, Phyllis G., and Keith Eubank. *Survey of Historic Costume.* 2nd ed. New York: Fairchild Publications, 1994.

Totten, Stanley M., and George W. White. "Glacial Geology and the North American Craton: Significant Concepts and Contributions of the Nineteenth Century." In *Geologists and Ideas: A History of North American Geology,* edited by Ellen Drake and William Jordan, 125–41. Boulder, CO: Geological Society of America, 1985.

Trowbridge, Charles C. "Appendix G: The Journal and Letters of Charles Christopher Trowbridge, Expedition of 1820." In Henry R. Schoolcraft, *Narrative Journal of Travels: Through Northwestern Regions of the United States Extending from Detroit through the Great Chain of American Lakes to the Sources of the Mississippi River in the Year 1820,* edited by Mentor L. Williams, 461–500. East Lansing: Michigan State College Press, 1953.

Tuan, Yi-Fu. "The City: Its Distance from Nature." *Geographical Review* 68, no. 1 (1978): 1–12.

———. "The City and Human Speech." *Geographical Review* 84, no. 2 (1994): 144–51.

———. *Escapism.* Baltimore, MD: Johns Hopkins University Press, 1998.

———. "Images and Mental Maps." *Annals of the Association of American Geographers* 65, no. 2 (1975): 205–13.

———. *Landscapes of Fear.* Minneapolis: University of Minnesota Press, 1979.

———. "Language and the Making of Place: A Narrative-Descriptive Approach." *Annals of the Association of American Geographers* 81, no. 4 (1991): 684–96.

———. *Space and Place: The Perspective of Experience.* Minneapolis: University of Minnesota Press, 1977.

———. "Thought and Landscape: The Eye and the Mind's Eye." In *The Interpretation of Ordinary Landscapes,* edited by D. W. Meinig, 89–102. Oxford: Oxford University Press, 1979.

———. *Topophilia: A Study of Environmental Perception, Attitudes, and Values.* 1974. Reprint, New York: Columbia University Press, 1990.

———. "A View of Geography." *Geographical Review* 81 (1991): 99–107.

Turner, Andrew Jackson. "History of Wisconsin Railroads." In *Fifth Annual Report of the Railroad Commissioner of the State of Wisconsin, 1878,* 313–87. Madison, WI: David Atwood, State Printer, 1879.

Turner, Frederick Jackson. "The Significance of the Frontier in American History." In *Frederick Jackson Turner: Wisconsin's Historian of the Frontier,* edited by Martin Ridge, 26–47. Madison: State Historical Society of Wisconsin, 1986.

The U.S. Geological Survey: Its History, Activities and Organization. Reprint of 1918 edition. Vol. 1. Institute for Government Research: Service Monographs of the United States Government. New York: AMS, 1974.

Vale, Thomas R., and Geraldine R. Vale. "Reflections on Landscape Change." *Midwest Quarterly* 27, no. 3 (1986): 316–26.

Viola, Herman J. "Introduction." In *Sketches of a Tour to the Lakes, of the Character, and Customs of the Chippewa Indians, and of Incidents Connected with the Treaty of Fond du Lac*, ix–xx. Barre, MA: Imprint Society, 1972.

———. *Thomas L. McKenney: Architect of America's Early Indian Policy, 1816–1830*. 1st ed. Chicago: Swallow Press, 1974.

Vogel, John N. *Great Lakes Lumber on the Great Plains: The Laird, Norton Lumber Company in South Dakota*. Edited by Wayne Franklin. *The American Land and Life Series*. Iowa City: University of Iowa Press, 1992.

Vogeler, Ingolf. *Wisconsin: A Geography*. Boulder, CO: Westview Press, 1986.

Ward, Steven. *Selling Places: The Marketing and Promotion of Towns and Cites, 1850–2000*. London: E and FN Spon, 1998.

Warren, William Whipple. *History of the Ojibway Nation*. 1885. Reprint, Minneapolis, MN: Ross and Haines, 1970.

Warren, Louis S. *Buffalo Bill's America: William Cody and the Wild West Show*. New York: Alfred A. Knopf, 2005.

Weber, Eugen. *Peasants into Frenchmen: The Modernization of Rural France, 1870–1914*. Stanford, CA: Stanford University Press, 1976.

Weiskel, Thomas. *The Romantic Sublime: Studies in the Structure and Psychology of Transcendence*. Baltimore, MD: Johns Hopkins University Press, 1976.

White, Richard. "Frederick Jackson Turner and Buffalo Bill." In *The Frontier in American Culture:Essays by Richard White and Patricia Nelson Limerick*, edited by James R. Grossman, 7–65. Berkeley and Los Angeles: University of California Press, 1994.

———. *The Middle Ground: Indians, Empires, and Republics in the Great Lakes Region, 1650–1815*. Cambridge: Cambridge University Press, 1991.

———. *The Roots of Dependency: Subsistence, Environment, and Social Change among the Choctaws, Pawnees, and Navajos*. Lincoln: University of Nebraska Press, 1980.

Whittlesey, Charles. "Geological Report on That Portion of Wisconsin Bordering on the South Shore of Lake Superior, Surveyed in the Year 1849, under the Direction of David Dale Owen, United States Geologist." In *Report of a Geological Survey of Wisconsin, Iowa, and Minnesota; and Incidentally a Portion of Nebraska Territory, Made under Directions from the United States Treasury Department*, edited by David Dale Owen, 423–47. Philadelphia: Lippencott, Grambo, 1852.

———. "On the Fresh-Water Glacial Drift of the Northwestern States." *Smithsonian Contributions to Knowledge* 197 (1866): 1–34.

———. "Paleontology and the Moral Sense." In *Fugitive Essays: By Col. Chas. Whittlesey*. Cleveland OH, 1873.

———. "Two Months in the Copper Regions." In *Fugitive Essays*, 282–344. Hudson, OH: Sawyer, Ingersoll, 1852.

Whittlesey, Derwent. "Sequent Occupance." *Annals of the Association of American Geographers* 19 (1929): 162–65.

Williams, Michael. *Amercians and Their Forests: A Historical Geography.* Cambridge: Cambridge University Press, 1992.

———. "The Relations of Environmental History and Historical Geography." *Journal of Historical Geography* 20 (1994): 3–21.

Williams, Mentor L. "Editor's Introduction." In Henry R. Schoolcraft, *Narrative Journal of Travels: Through Northwestern Regions of the United States Extending from Detroit through the Great Chain of American Lakes to the Sources of the Mississippi River in the Year 1820*, edited by Mentor L. Williams, 1–24. East Lansing: Michigan State College Press, 1953.

Wisconsin: A Guide to the Badger State, American Guide Series. New York: Duell, Sloan and Pearce, 1941.

Wolenec, Steven. "The 'Nerve of the Northwest': Lewis Cass as Michigan Territorial Governor, 1813–1831." Master's thesis, University of Wisconsin–Eau Claire, 2000.

Woodford, Frank B. *Lewis Cass: The Last Jeffersonian.* New Brunswick, NJ: Rutgers University Press, 1950.

Worster, Donald. *Dust Bowl: The Southern Plains in the 1930s.* Oxford: Oxford University Press, 1982.

———. "Transformations of the Earth: Toward an Agroecological Perspective in History." *Journal of American History* 76 (1990): 1087–1106.

Wright, John K. "Terrae Incognitae: The Place of the Imagination in Geography." *Annals of the Association of American Geographers* 37 (1947): 1–15.

Wyckoff, William, and Lary M. Dilsaver. "Promotional Imagery of Glacier National Park." *Geographical Review* 87, no. 1 (1987): 1–26.

Index